ASSAULT FROM THE SEA 1939-45

From Memorandum to Chiefs of Staff, 22 March 1943

The preparation for, and mounting of, a combined operation is far more complex than that of a land battle, and requires considerably greater time. This time cannot be reduced, if serious opposition is to be encountered, without accepting grave risks of failure.

HQ Combined Commanders Planning Staff.

Public Records Office file Wo 106 4221: Selection of Assault Areas in NW Europe

Extract from Crown Copyright record, by permission of the Controller of HM Stationery Office

ASSAULT
FROM THE SEA 1939-45

The Craft, The Landings, The Men

J. D. LADD

DAVID & CHARLES
NEWTON ABBOT   LONDON   VANCOUVER

ISBN 0 7153 6937 7

Set in 11/13pt Imprint
and printed in Great Britain
by Biddles Limited Guildford
for David & Charles (Publishers) Limited
Brunel House Newton Abbot Devon

Published in Canada
by Douglas David & Charles Limited
1875 Welch Street North Vancouver BC

CONTENTS

Tonnages are given in UK (long)
tons unless otherwise stated
1 UK (long) ton = 2,240lb = 1,016kg
1 US (short) ton = 2,000lb = 907kg
1 tonne $\qquad$ = 2,205lb = 1,000kg

PREFACE

The greatest armadas of history, and perhaps of all time, carried Allied assaults in World War II. At Normandy on the French coast, 132,715 troops were landed in sixteen hours on 6 June 1944 against some of the most sophisticated shore defences then known. At Okinawa, an island about 600 miles south of Japan, over 183,000 men in 1,300 vessels made the last in a succession of major landings by United States amphibious forces against determined Japanese defenders in April 1945.

This book tells how the assault forces were created, the techniques they used, and something of the men who made the landings, a story which centres on the landing craft and assault ships which were the backbone of combined operations. The landings called for intricate planning, daring seamanship and great determination by soldiers and marines fighting their way ashore, supported by airmen flying sometimes at wavetop height.

Final victory and demobilisation, and the slow return to normal civilian life, could not banish the unique personal recollections of the soldiers, sailors, aircrews and marines who took part in the landings. It is hoped that the book may reflect these memories, and that readers who did not participate will have a better understanding of a bold and complex aspect of World War II.

To the memory of all those who did not return from amphibious assaults and the defence of the beaches, the book is offered as a tribute.

J. D. Ladd
London, January 1975

7

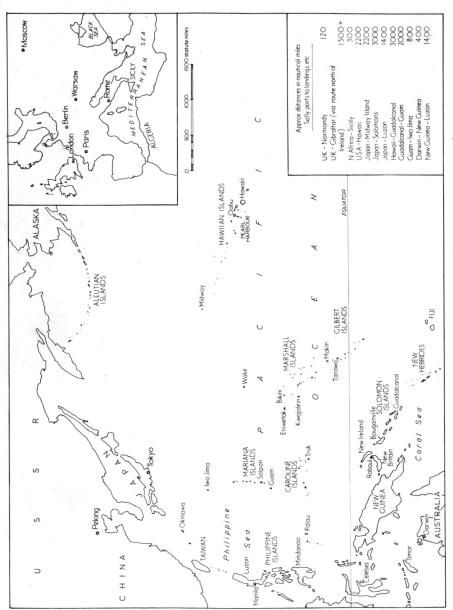

Fig 1 Comparison of European and Pacific theatres, World War II amphibious operations

1 THE PURPOSE OF LANDING CRAFT

Early developments

When the war began in Europe, few commanders or troops – except the Japanese – had experience of amphibious assaults. Yet the Allied invasion landings around the world (*Fig 1*) would require daring seamanship from butchers' boys, bakers' roundsmen and garage mechanics. No doubt there were also a few candlestick-makers among the ordinary Jacks and Joes who manned landing craft. Certainly they came from all walks of life, and were at sea – if not in action – after little more than six weeks' training. In all, some 62,000 Royal Marine and Royal Navy crews were trained between 1942 and 1945, over 400,000 British army and air force personnel took part in landings, and 3,000,000 Americans were trained for amphibious operations; this had to be done at a time when there was not even a wide experience of ordinary vehicles, for the motor car was not the universal transport it is today in Europe. The crews for landing craft had therefore to be trained in basic mechanical engineering as well as in seamanship, gunnery and signals.

The craft and ships they manned can be divided into basic types. First chronologically were designs for minor craft (*Pl 1*), open boats used to ferry men or vehicles from transports six or more miles off a beach. Then in 1940, with the increase in numbers and sizes of tanks, major landing craft were built for 1-day or 2-day passages from a sally port to a beach. There, these craft could land in shallow water and offload men or vehicles over ramps. In parallel with the development of craft, landing ships were built or merchantmen

9

converted as carriers for minor craft, and other ships were designed to beach – like major landing craft – for offloading. After these early craft and ships (*Pl 2*), amphibious wheeled and tracked vehicles were introduced to carry men, guns and stores from transports to the perimeter of a beachhead. The generally accepted distinction of a minor craft was that its crew did not live aboard; the crew of a major craft lived aboard in harbour as well as on passage.

Landing ships were larger than landing craft.

Initials do not always accord with the words they stand for; for example, the Tank Landing Craft is abbreviated LCT and has been designated Landing Craft, Tank since 1942, but references may contain both the earlier description and the later initials.

The tactics of beach assaults

The following is an oversimplification and omits many aspects of landings which will become apparent as the features of different craft and operations are explained.

Before all landings there were a number of questions to be answered besides the usual military intelligence on enemy dispositions and terrain. How steep was the slope of the beach? Were there any false beaches on which craft would ground, leaving troops to wade through a deep channel to the shore? How strong were the inshore currents? What routes were possible for tanks going inland from the shore? Answers were provided by beach survey teams, landing weeks if not months before an assault. In 1940, the small boat section attached to 8 Commando made the first of these reconnaissances on the French beaches. Aerial photographs, holiday snapshots and local underground forces also provided information from which the planners chose the landing points, perhaps on rocky but sparsely defended beaches where the elements and not the enemy were the greater danger, or across open beaches reached more easily though usually heavily defended. Here, the attackers relied on heavy naval and air bombardment to soften the defences over days or even weeks before the landings. Whatever the beach, the time of the assault – H-hour – was chosen

Plate 1 Major landing craft LCT No 766 follows LCA minor craft towards beaches, May 1944

for full daylight and thus easier control of craft, or pre-dawn half-light when defenders could not see targets clearly though landing craft had to be marshalled in the dark. Occasionally, night landings were made when surprise without prior bombardment helped in overcoming relatively few defenders.

In tidal waters craft might beach below the tide-line with its anti-boat obstacles and mines, though troops then had to cross open beaches under fire, or the craft might come in on the full tide through cleared lanes to reach only a short width of beach under fire. Before sufficient numbers of craft were built, many army commanders were also faced with a Hobson's choice in the composition of their assault wave: adequately equipped but with too few men to guarantee success, or with sufficient men but reduced equipment, putting the beachhead at risk until craft returned with reserves of ammunition and weapons. When all relevant decisions had been made the troops could be assembled at the sally ports and convoys arranged. The slow Landing Craft, Tank (LCT) sailed before the transports with Landing Craft, Assault (LCA) or other minor craft on the davits.

Plate 2 LST launching amphibious tractor LVTs during Iwo Jima landings, February 1945

When the transports reached the dropping zone, maybe six miles offshore, the minor craft were launched and formed up in waves perhaps twenty LCAs abreast. Each wave had a timed start, so at the end of their 2-hour run-in the craft reached the beach in a sequence that brought army formations ashore in the correct order of battle. Co-ordinated with the waves of minor craft might be LCTs, six or more to a wave and moving at different speeds to the minor craft. Figure 2 shows a sequence of waves forming part of the assault force in a Pacific landing. The flotillas formed up beyond the range of coastal batteries, which might be knocked out in airborne and commando raids before the main landings. At the same time, underwater clearance divers came inshore to defuse mines on beach obstacles and destroy these defences in the immediate area of the landing. In a different but co-ordinated part of the operation, midget submarines and/or scout boats took station to mark the limits of the landing areas by light signals to incoming craft. When the assault was underway the whole area was isolated under an umbrella of naval and air cover, preventing enemy naval attacks and land reinforcements reaching their defences.

The exact pattern and composition of landing waves changed with the nature of the assault, but for this simplified example the following illustrates a possible sequence of events:

H minus 3 hours   Naval big ship bombardment begins and only stops at H − 35 minutes for long enough to allow a low-level air strike against beach strong points.

H − 25 minutes   The leading wave of landing craft – specially armoured gun 'ships' with army and/or naval heavy calibre weapons, the fire support craft – join the bombardment, engaging individual strong points as they protect the 'soft' waves of wooden personnel-carrying craft behind them.

H − 10   The fire support craft move to the flanks of the assault, continuing to engage strong points but now also making smoke to cover the assault waves.

H − 8   The naval bombardment lifts from the shore line to targets 400yd inland.

H − 5   Amphibious DD tanks land to knock out machine gun positions near the shore line.

H − 3   Rocket-firing craft fire over the DD tanks from 1,000yd or more off the beach; salvos of 5in rockets cut lanes through wire and minefields making paths for tanks to drive out of the beach.

H − 1   LCTs land engineers and tanks with flailing chains (Flails) to explode beach mines or with concrete-breaking rams to smash shore obstacles; they also bring in armourplated bull-dozers for this and clearing roadways.

H-hour   The first wave of the assault infantry brigade touch down to follow the engineers up the beach.

H + 15   The army's self-propelled guns land from LCTs to support the infantry, having fired at targets during the run in.

H + X minutes   Reserve infantry companies of the assault brigades follow the assault troops. These follow-up waves might be in troop-carrying major craft (the Landing Craft, Infantry (Large), for example) and be called in as needed or land to a timetable, their troops passing through the assault companies to advance the attack. If things went badly, however, these second-wave troops might have to land among the wreckage of the first wave's craft and tanks, with little room to deploy for action.

13

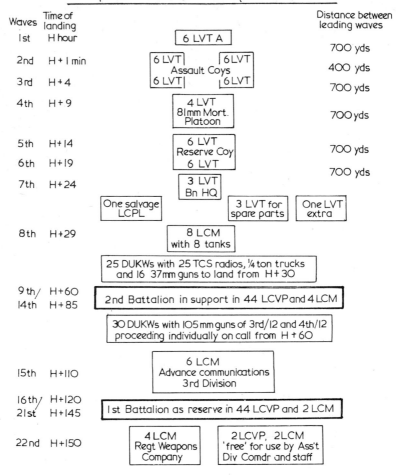

Assault on Green Beach by 3rd Battalion 21st US Marines
part of Third Marine Division (reinforced)

Waves	Time of landing		Distance between leading waves
1st	H hour	6 LVT A	
			700 yds
2nd	H + 1 min	6 LVT | |6 LVT	400 yds
		Assault Coys	
3rd	H + 4	6 LVT| |6LVT	700 yds
4th	H + 9	4 LVT 81mm Mort. Platoon	700 yds
5th	H+14	6 LVT Reserve Coy	700 yds
6th	H+19	6 LVT	700 yds
7th	H+24	3 LVT Bn HQ	
		One salvage LCPL 3 LVT for spare parts One LVT extra	
8th	H+29	8 LCM with 8 tanks	
		25 DUKWs with 25 TCS radios, ¼ ton trucks and 16 37mm guns to land from H+30	
9th/	H+60	2nd Battalion in support in 44 LCVP and 4 LCM	
14th	H+85		
		30 DUKWs with 105mm guns of 3rd/12 and 4th/12 proceeding individually on call from H+60	
15th	H+110	6 LCM Advance communications 3rd Division	
16th/	H+120	1st Battalion as reserve in 44 LCVP and 2 LCM	
21st	H+145		
22nd	H+150	4 LCM Regt Weapons Company	2 LCVP, 2 LCM 'free' for use by Ass't Div Comdr and staff

LVT = Amphib. tractor   LCVP = Wooden personnel-craft   LCM = Steel craft
DUKW = Amphib. truck

Fig 2 Simplified landing plan for part of US Marines' assault on
Guam

14

Despite the difficulties of keeping such a timetable, which looks tight enough in print but in choppy water might be tumbled to confusion, most Allied invasion landings made a successful initial bridgehead and none were repulsed entirely. The second phase, breaking out from the bridgehead, was by far the most difficult part of amphibious operations. To build up forces and supplies for this critical phase depended on getting landing ships to the area and unloading them quickly. They might be beached, at the risk of stranding when bombed or shelled, or they might lie off the beach while their cargoes were ferried ashore in amphibious trucks (DUKWs) and minor landing craft.

Radio communications – the key to flexibility in any battle – were vitally important at all stages in a landing. Comprehensive radio networks were ultimately evolved, but in the early landings the coxswain of a British LCA might get only flag signals from his flotilla leader and information from his 'cargo' platoon's wireless set (by 1944 most craft carried 2-way radios that were reliable by standards of the early 1940s). Messages were winked on the aldis lamps of the craft marshalling these early flotillas and occasionally a loudhailer warning of trouble – for the LCA – came from a destroyer's bridge, but communications were the least of the coxswain's worries. He must keep station in his flotilla despite the wandering LCT with no right to be in this lane. There might be a testy lieutenant aboard, convinced the LCA was taking his platoon to the wrong smoke-shrouded beach. Meanwhile the coxswain steered to avoid other craft and dodge beach obstacles. He must drop his kedge anchor astern at the correct moment to hold the LCA at right angles to the beach while his pongos landed. If the anchor did not bite, his craft would swing parallel to the beach; broached-to in this way, she filled or rolled in heavy seas. The protective doors near the bow were opened seconds before touchdown after the bow ramp had been lowered. Out went the troops. Up ramp and slow astern, the coxswain manoeuvred to pick up the hook and get back out to sea, threading his way through incoming waves of craft. And there were still those beach obstacles to be avoided.

15

The good training and initiative of these crews proved invaluable for the Canadians at Dieppe in August 1942, when LCA No 250 and No 315 and other assault craft ferried 1,000 men back to safety in the transports, and at Bougainville in the North Solomon Islands (1 November 1943) when the boat group commander's craft was shot to pieces the American LCPs carried through the landing successfully though in the wrong sequence.

Techniques in different theatres

Techniques differed between landings for a number of reasons not all of which were technical, as the attitudes of senior commanders understandably influenced events.

Before World War II British and American staffs made some plans for amphibious landings, though never on the scale achieved during the war. Both Allies produced manuals for staff on the coordination of services during landings, and other reports including an American scheme for a possible recapture of the Marshall Islands. This plan, devised in 1921, was one of several that proved a sound basis for operations over twenty years later. The British staffs, conscious of the casualties in the Gallipoli landings of 1915, and the possible devastation of air attack, were less certain of the value of seaborne assaults than their traditions might suggest, but in 1924 they set up the Landing Craft Committee, a large group of representatives from interested authorities, though this body was without detailed guidelines on service needs. Not until 1938 were techniques of landing studied in detail, when the British Chiefs of Staff created the Inter-Services Training and Development Centre (the ISTDC) under the chairmanship of Capt (later Rear-Admiral) L. E. H. Maund. In America the Marine Corps were responsible for amphibious operations, and remained so until parts of these responsibilities were taken over in 1942 by the Amphibious Warfare Section of the Navy Department. There appears to have been little if any formal contact between the future Allies during these pre-war years so far as amphibious warfare was concerned, but after 1940 a steady flow of British information passed to the marines, reciprocated later from the Pacific.

The British pre-war theory of a nearly silent approach by minor craft launched from carriers for a dawn landing was tried out in two exercises during 1938-9. These landings proved how difficult it would be to co-ordinate naval gunfire support with the advance of an assault wave, for there was no radar and few reliable radio sets. The only recorded comment of (then) Brigadier B. L. Montgomery, leading one assault brigade, put the value of the exercise in its physical hardening of the troops. The method relied on wooden personnel-carrying minor craft under ten tons, light enough to be lifted by a ship's davits, or the steel vehicle-carrying Landing Craft, Mechanised (LCM) of less then twenty tons for passage as deck cargo and launching by derrick. When war broke out in September 1939 prototypes of the LCA and the LCM were not fully developed, and the many priorities of a British expeditionary force to France, of civilian defence against air raids and possible gas attacks, of building up convoy defences against U-boats, and of equipping the Royal Air Force came before amphibious operations and craft. Indeed the only possible target beaches for raids were on the North Sea German coast or in the Baltic Sea, the latter being considered for fleet operations though beyond British resources for even a major raid. The few Motor Landing Craft (MLC) available from various craft commissioned by the Landing Craft Committee were not suitable for lifting on the davits of ships earmarked as carriers. The 'ten-year' rule by which successive governments barred the services from planning against the possibility of war during that period ensured the lack of preparation.

The ISTDC worked on integrating army, navy and air force commands in amphibious operations, with a headquarters ship to handle communications, supply by air (the Centre was not concerned with amphibious operations only), and methods of supply and support for landings. Their recommendations were ignored in the Narvik landings in north Norway where, in April and May 1940, ships were loaded economically to make the best use of hold space, and not tactically so that weapons and vehicles were unloaded in an appropriate military order. The navy and army commanders travelled in different ships and apparently had never met, while the various authorities at home did not seem to appreciate that the base port of Harstad, sixty miles from Narvik, was not equipped with harbour installations as comprehensive as Liverpool's or Southampton's. This, among other confusions, contributed to the force's withdrawal early in June after four new LCAs, an LCM and three old MLCs had at least proved in several minor actions that landings were possible.

On 4 June 1940 the Admiralty officially ended the evacuation of Dunkirk at 1423 hours, and on the same day Prime Minister Winston Churchill – later Sir Winston – sent a minute to the Chiefs of Staff: '. . . if it is so easy for the Germans to invade us . . . why should it be thought impossible for us to do anything of the same kind to them?' Churchill became interested in more than the strategy of combined operations; he delighted in its offensive spirit and made a number of proposals for operations and designs of craft. But craft were being built only in very small numbers during 1940 when active invasion preparations were being made in Germany, where the High Command viewed the cross-Channel assault on Britain – operation Sea Lion – as a major river crossing. They had plans at one stage to land 700,000 men and 125,000 *horses* in the first three waves; initial studies began in November 1939, but as no ship larger than a destroyer was to be launched in Germany during the war and their shipyard resources were concentrated on building U-boats, the craft for Sea Lion had to be found from among the barges, tugs and motorboats on European waterways. But collecting these vessels at Channel ports led to congestion and their modification strained resources.

In Britain the real measure of what would be needed to put an invading army ashore was becoming apparent. During 1941 there were conflicts between the needs for short-term training for the 'next operation' and the longer-term build-up of an invasion force, but after October 1941, when Admiral Lord Louis Mountbatten took over Combined Operations Headquarters, the priority was given by the Chiefs of Staff to invasion preparations. Dramatic changes were soon to alter the whole emphasis of amphibious developments, however; early in December the Japanese launched their Pacific offensive.

Relying on surprise, the Japanese army landed comparatively small formations of assault troops from cruisers and destroyers against thinly defended beaches. These units captured airfields and ports through which the main body of invading armies landed. In Malaya they brought in railway engines and trucks, an indication of the speed with which they intended to reach their strategic objective of forming a ring of defended territory around captured sources of oil and other raw materials. Although the Japanese army operated troopships as well as landing craft, or maybe because of this unusual command structure, by 1943 they were forced to operate without naval escorts and to move at night hugging the island coasts.

The most crucial factor in Allied amphibious operations after the summer of 1942 was the size of the armadas built by American mass-production methods. Some 45,000 vessels and 56,000 amphibians were built in the two and a half years to August 1945. In addition, innumerable barges, pontoons and harbour installations were completed in this short time, though the programme was only a part of the total US war effort, which rose from 2% in 1939 to 40% of the 1944 national output. Men had to be trained and yards built to meet these programmes, quite apart from the training of crews to man the craft. The British had many crew and assault troop training centres; Warsash, Hampshire (HMS *Tormentor*) for 6-week courses in landing craft maintenance and handling; Northney holiday (?) camp at Hayling Island, Sussex, where 3,000 men had been trained by December 1940; Inverary, Argyll (HMS *Quebec*) where major landing craft crews worked up; Castle Howard, Yorkshire, used by the Royal Armoured Corps; Troon, Ayrshire, for LCMs; Dundonald, Ayrshire, for signallers; North Wales camps for Royal Marines gunners, and the minor landing craft base at Southend-on-Sea, Essex (HMS *Westcliff*) opened in November 1942. Of the commando training centres, the most remembered is probably Achnacarry a few miles northeast of Fort William, Inverness-shire.

American training was built on pre-war experiences of the Marine Corps and the army's 1 Infantry Division, and after June 1942 it expanded rapidly. In that month 3,000 naval and coast guard personnel were drafted for training in the new major landing craft, and the army formed twelve Engineer Special Brigades to man minor craft and form beach control or working parties. These engineers, based in the Boston (Mass) area, recruited many New England fishermen and small-boat enthusiasts giving the brigades a basis for their well-earned reputation in boat handling. The British drafted Royal Marines in July 1943 to man all minor craft and by 1944 500 officers and 12,500 marines were in landing craft crews, along with 5,500 RNVR and 43,500 hostilities-only ratings. Through all the Allied crews ran a strong streak of individuality; their craft and ships might be standardised but they certainly were not. Crews will remember all manner of personalised accommodation – panelled wardrooms and silvered wall lamps, maybe – as yards provided some comforts at the expense of yacht stores. In armament the ingenuity of crews and yards was even more prolific, increasing ships' fire-power far beyond the designed maxima.

This build-up of craft and crews is reflected in changes in the techniques possible in the Pacific, although these followed a pattern in the capture of islands for airfields to support subsequent landings. The distances between bases and target beaches were another factor, with amphibious forces operating as much as 2,000 miles from base (Fig 1). They had to be entirely self-sufficient and protected by a fleet of warships with its attendant fleet train of supply ships. These enabled assault forces to remain at sea for long periods – they were four weeks aboard the transports before landing at Guam in July 1944, and during this time had only six days ashore in landing exercises. Some 1,800 fever casualties – many with *filaris* – were replaced, yet reasonable fitness was maintained by good food and physical training. Sleep in the transports' stifling lower decks was difficult, however, and the lucky few were on LSTs (Landing Ship, Tank) sleeping under makeshift awnings above the upper decks. This landing delay, caused by a

Japanese fleet moving into the area, was unusual, but long spells aboard transports on passage were frequent.

Guam was typical of a landing in the Marianas and the Philippines during 1944, with conventional battles for limited land areas – Guam is a rice- and copra-growing island of about 200 square miles – and very different from landings in the Solomons and the atoll reefs of the Gilbert and Marshall Islands. These earlier landings began on 7 August 1942 at Guadalcanal in the Central Solomons, some 1,200 land miles from Tokyo. Jungle- and swamp-fringed beaches restricted movement both in the Solomons and New Guinea, making this phase of the war a series of soldiers' battles fought between small units, and at Guadalcanal amphibious tractors (LVTs) were used for the first time. As the Americans advanced into the Gilbert and Marshall Islands late in 1943, each small island needed a sustained action for its capture with amphibians playing an increasing role in landing and the supply of troops. Then came the Mariana and Philippine landings; to describe them as conventional is perhaps an understatement – in Leyte (Philippines) 23½in of rain fell during the November after the island was secured, making amphibious vehicles essential in the swampy ground.

The final phase in the Pacific included assaults against heavily fortified islands. Iwo Jima, lying 600 miles south of Tokyo, and part of the Tokyo prefecture, was invaded on 19 February 1945 after the longest pre-assault bombardment in the amphibious war; and the last major seaborne assault was at Okinawa on 1 April when 50,000 American soldiers and marines were landed by nightfall.

The evolution of techniques during the thirty months between Guadalcanal and Iwo Jima can be seen in comparisons between the assault waves. At Guadalcanal two US Marine Corps battalions landed initially in different areas. A, B and D companies of the 7th Marines were left on Kukum beach when an air raid forced their supporting destroyer, USS *Bullard*, and the landing craft back to sea, and only the actions of Lt Dale M. Leslie, flying an SBD plane, saved the forward companies without radios. He strafed

Japanese positions, passed back target information to the returning support ship and shepherded the landing craft back to the beach. Although these companies were withdrawn the battalions took the island with a slim margin between success and failure, having only 470 landing craft.

At Iwo Jima, in addition to the naval bombardment there were 227 air strikes including a low-level US navy strafe five minutes before the leading sixty-eight amphibians – LVT(A)s (Landing Vehicle, Tracked (Armoured)) with army-type guns or howitzers – hit the beach at 0902 (many, but not all, Pacific landings were made in daylight as the naval staff preferred to marshal the forces when their control craft could see what they were doing). In all there were 482 amphibious tractors of one type or another at Iwo Jima and the complex logistics included landing heavy (by comparison with earlier models) Sherman Mk4(A3) tanks from LSMs, pre-loaded cargo-carrying tracked Weasels, and artillery in DUKW amphibious trucks; and before the landing a daring clearance of beach obstacles by underwater teams working at point blank range in front of the enemy's guns. Particular care was taken to organise medical facilities and evacuation, for despite the previous landing bombardment US marine casualties were heavy. In the thirty-six days before victory, 5,931 marines were killed and 17,292 wounded; and less than 1,000 Japanese survived from the 20,000 defenders of this island fortress.

In looking at the detailed developments of craft and techniques, the importance of the individual – soldier, sailor, airman or marine – can be illustrated only by selected examples, yet every man who took part in these operations had his moments of drama and recalls hours of tension, often in the fatigue of seasickness, with the salt- and diesel-fume-laden atmosphere laced by the sharp whiff of burning cordite just before a landing. And the noises: clattering diesels drowning the pound of surf on shingle; the chatter of the craft's machine guns answering the crump of enemy mortars, while angry wasps of heavier automatic fire passed overhead as ominous thuds shook the boat with near misses.

2 SHIP-TO-SHORE MINOR LANDING CRAFT

The concept

Each minor craft carried a small but complete fighting unit of troops or a tank or other vehicle from the transports to the beach. The design had to meet several basic criteria: the total weight of the craft was limited by the power of the carrier ships' davits, though craft might be lowered when empty, their cargo-personnel boarding from scramble nets down the side of a troop ship; these troops must be offloaded in minutes if not seconds after beaching in shallow water; and speed for the 2-hour run to a beach was judged against an optimum of armour protection for troops and/or armament which could provide them with some covering fire as they landed. The Landing Craft, Personnel(Large) supplied to the Royal Navy had a range and speed for raiding, while these early American craft with their own fleets had some armour and mountings for five ·30in machine guns. Before the war a number of features – low silhouettes, muffled engines and little disturbance of the water – were suggested for surprise landings, but radar and pre-landing bombardments later made such factors of little importance except in small raids.

Royal Navy flotillas of three craft with their crews under the command of a junior naval or Royal Marine officer were usually allocated to specific carrier ships aboard which the landing craft crews lived. Two or more LCA flotillas with perhaps a couple of LCMs, their squadron commander and specialist ratings for maintenance and repair might be aboard one carrier.

Minor craft spread the risk for a force as they landed in a large number of boats. Using larger craft, on the other hand, was thought in 1940 to put too many men in one basket and not give the necessary flexibility in ferrying reinforcements which minor craft also carried.

LANDING CRAFT, PERSONNEL

History

Experiments with new types of craft to land troops began in America in 1936. Some of the prototypes sank in the surf and others did not prove practical, but the craft designed by the Eureka Tug-Boat Company of New Orleans, the 28ft R-boat, was both seaworthy and a good beaching boat; it was based on a 1926 spoonbill-bowed craft used by trappers. The general lines of the boat were accepted by the US Marine Corps and in September 1940 they asked Andrew J. Higgins who ran the tug-boat company if he would build a slightly larger craft to carry twenty-four fully-equipped troops. He produced the 32ft Eureka or Higgins boat. This was the craft first used in American landing exercises in 1941 but before this date the Admiralty's need for a raiding craft brought the first enquiries for an even larger boat, a 36ft 8in craft, originally intended to carry a full British platoon and two or three attached signallers or assault engineers. An initial order for 136 was placed and the first fifty were delivered to the UK in October 1940. Mr Higgins is said to have preferred this larger craft and as the LCP(Large) she was the forerunner of all American LCP types (*Fig 3a*).

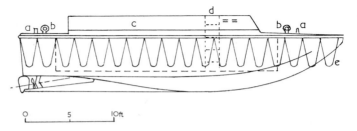

Fig 3a LCP(L) with Royal Navy (a) bollard (b) davit lifting eye (c) canvas awning (d) inboard ladder (e) lifelines

24

Plate 3 Royal Navy LCP(L)s with escort ML; the shape of the LCP(L)'s bows and her cockpit protection made her a good sea-boat

The British LCP(L)s, with identifying numbers under 500, had a forward cockpit, side decking to the well, and a canopy protecting troops from the weather (*Pl 3*) but there was no protection from shell splinters until armour was added later to some craft. The US Navy Department also ordered this basic LCP(L) in a version that had 10lb armoured bulkheads and ·30in machine guns. Two ring mountings for these replaced the cockpit forward in the well, and three transverse mountings were fitted. Armour and armament reduced speed by a knot or so, though the more open well with narrower side decks enabled more troops to be carried – officially thirty to thirty-six to the British LCP(L)'s twenty-five. Cargo-troop numbers varied with the equipment carried, though references here and later in this book relate to fully equipped men for whom the craft were designed.

The Royal Navy LCP(L) had a greater range than the US type;

25

this, and protection from the weather for the troops, made the craft suitable for raids. The US type with greater load capacity was more suitable for mass landings but both designs were based on the same hull, which had a drawback: the high prow meant that troops had a leap of four feet or more on to the shore. This may sound a small drop to the average sportsman, but with a rifle and fighting order (webbing equipment including ammunition pouches and a small pack), carrying perhaps spare ammunition or an awkward load like a 2in mortar, climbing out of an LCP(L) took long enough to expose troops unnecessarily. By the middle of 1942 it was apparent that a ramp was essential, and the Americans built only 2,193 of the original LCP(L)s.

The LCP(Ramped) (*Pl 4*) was introduced with only minor hull differences from the LCP(L) except for the ramp at the bow. All LCPs – both Large and Ramped – were of wood, with conventional planked bottoms and tough plywood sides built up over timber frames, a construction that was durable enough for ordinary small boat work but all too easily holed by obstacles or wrecks on a beach. In 1942 at Guadalcanal and in the North African landings many of these craft were damaged, and half the LCP(L)s landing in the first wave at Casablanca were wrecked. Although this did not prevent 3,500 men being landed here in the first hour, the need for craft to return for reinforcements and stores essential in the build-up against counterattacks in a heavily pressed beachhead made such losses unacceptable for future operations. After 2,631 LCP(R)s were built, therefore, the design was replaced by the Landing Craft, Vehicle Personnel (LCVP), which had a slightly different role because by that time, late 1942, many assault waves were carried in amphibious LVTs.

Handling

The 3-man crew of a British LCP(L) were led by a Leading Seaman or Royal Marine Corporal coxswain who steered the boat and operated engine controls on the port side of the cockpit. Beside him was the Lewis gunner who also acted as bowman handling any ropework forward. The third man was a mechanic who might also handle stern ropes. American craft carried two gunners and the coxswain, one of the gunners also acting as mechanic. The craft's raked bow made beaching comparatively easy, and the craft came off without difficulty when unloaded though she could snag on rocks or poor ground as any other small boat does. She could be loaded before launching 'unless otherwise specified by the warning plate in the boat', for her construction as much as her light weight made this speeding up of the launching-load time possible. Other craft, especially those with a ramp like the LCV, could not be loaded before lowering from davits; cargo-personnel climbed down scramble nets into the boat.

At other times LCP(L)s might be led or towed by coastal forces craft when a raid was within reasonable range of a sally port. A number of these raids were made in 1940 to 1942 by British forces, sometimes using LCP(L)s though more often going ashore by canoe. The first major landing from LCP(L)s in Europe took place in August 1942 when the Canadians with elements of the British army and Royal Marines landed at Dieppe. The fortunes of the

LCP(L) flotillas showed here how units and even individual craft could have very different luck in a landing.

Raids supporting a major landing

On the evening of 18 August 1942 twenty LCP(L)s carrying the British 3 Commando – some 450 men – and twenty-five LCP(L)s carrying men of the Camerons of Canada sailed from Newhaven, Sussex, as part of the Royal Naval groups carrying the assault force. Other groups included troops in carrier transports and a third group of twenty-five LCP(L)s. The commandos were to knock out the Goebbels battery of heavy guns among the outer defences six miles from Dieppe, an action that should have prevented these guns firing on the main force attacking the town's beaches in a landing due half an hour after the commandos' assault. It was a calm night with a southerly breeze and the first part of the 100-mile passage went to time, with steam gun boat No 5 leading the LCP(L)s in four columns followed by Landing Craft, Flak No 1 and Motor Launch No 346.

At 0350, exactly an hour before they were due to land, the LCP(L)s were sighted by a German coastal convoy. In the action that followed, the commando's craft along with others on the eastern flank of the force were dispersed. In the dark, reforming the columns proved difficult and there were breakdowns in radio communication. Only seven LCP(L)s supported by Motor Launch No 346 reached the beach below the batteries. There, the commando managed to subdue the most easterly positions but came under withering fire below the Goebbels battery. Too few men were ashore to launch a proper assault but the LCP(L) crews last saw them attempting to scale the steep slopes behind the beach as Germans, firing down gullies in the approaches to the battery, broke up any concerted attacks.

By now the LCP(L)s were also in trouble, for they had been under fire since they arrived in the half light before dawn and many had holes to plug. Some became stuck on rock outcrops. Tow lines were passed, one by a seaman with complete disregard for the heavy fire around him as he swam inshore with a line. Despite

28

such bravery very few troops were brought off this beach. On the western flank, however, some twelve miles from the Goebbels battery, Lord Lovat's 4 Commando stormed the Hess battery and took it at bayonet point, then made a perfect withdrawal. Other defences on the western flank were not so successfully subdued. Nevertheless, the main force landed at 0520 in front of the town.

Engines

Engines were 80-octane petrol or diesel in most minor craft, but until production could be increased a number of different makes were used in one type of craft; for example, the LCP(L)s had single Hall-Scott 250hp petrol or one of several makes of diesel engine: Kermath 225hp, Gray 165–225hp or Superior 150hp. These were often based on the designs for lorry engines, with water-circulating equipment and filter screens added, among other modifications. Some examples of the characteristics of these engines are given as an Appendix.

Craft identification and numbering

Early types of LCP(L) are known as Y, T and CRC as well as R-craft, and the early Higgins designs are referred to as Higgins Boats. These were not included in the identification number series for LCP(L).

Series numbers were not always used in unbroken sequence; the 001–500 block was used for LCP(L)s on lease-lend to the Royal Navy, though less than 500 were actually built to this specification. British craft carried their LSI number on the bow. American minor craft had a similar identification though they were regarded as equipment and were not therefore on the US Naval Vessel Register. Classes of both minor and major craft might be identified by a particular lead ship's number when this was the first to carry a major modification, although more frequently a new mark number was allocated.

In the outline specifications that follow, tonnages refer to UK long tons of 2,240lb and US short tons of 2,000lb. Draughts refer to fully loaded craft 'at the bow' with troops fully equipped.

Readers will realise that there would be minor variations in performance according to which yard built a craft. The general quality was good and few dud craft of any type were built.

LCP(L) AND LCP(R) OUTLINE SPECIFICATION: *Hull:* wood   Length 36ft 8in, beam 10ft 10in; the LCP(R)'s ramp was 3ft 4in wide and the gun rings moved slightly outboard of their original position to give clear access to the ramp   *Displacement:* 18,000lb   *Mean Draught:* 42in   *Loads carried:* up to 8,100lb depending on fuel load; for troop-cargo loads see text   *Crew:* 3   *Engines:* see page 29 for LCP(L); LCP(R)s had single 225hp Gray diesel, 105hp Buda diesel, 115hp Chrysler Royal petrol or 150hp Palmer petrol engines   *Range:* UK craft, 120 miles on 200 US galls at speeds from 9 to 11 knots; US types had ranges varying from 69 nautical miles in the 225hp LCP(R)s to 145 miles with Buda diesels, and between 50 miles for petrol LCP(L)s and 130 miles for diesel LCP(L)s, all with a fuel capacity of 120 US galls and an optimum speed of 8 knots   *Armour:* 10lb plate usually fitted to bulkheads; when fitted to LCP(L)s in British service, 10lb plate to the forward bulkhead, control position, side decks and sides was carried aft protecting engines and fuel tanks under a plated quarter deck at the stern   *Armament:* UK craft had single Lewis ·303in machine gun, US craft had two ·30in machine guns (use of cargo-troops' weapons on the three transverse mountings might have been an original design intention).

British LCPs and other small types

The British designed and built an LCP(Small) Mk2 (*Fig 3b*) as a personnel carrier for 'second flight' use in landing follow-up waves of troops behind an assault wave. This wooden 25ft 6in craft with a 6ft 3in beam had a fixed bow, some foredecking and narrow side decks to an open well with an engine compartment and steering position amidships but aft of her centre section. The light plywood construction and single Chrysler 60hp petrol engine gave an unloaded weight of 4,000lb, and may have given rise to a rumour that these LCP(S)s were 'American craft for one-time

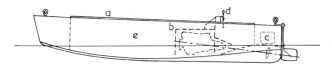

Fig 3b LCP(S) Mk2 (a) side decks (b) engine cover (c) p and s petrol tanks (d) wheel (e) troop well with central bench seat

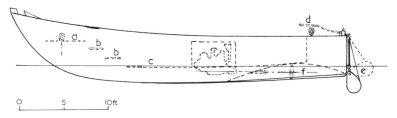

Fig 3c LCP(M); usually painted grey, the LCP(M) – like most craft after 1943 – was not given camouflage colours (a) foredeck (b) thwarts (c) troop area floor (d) tiller (e) lifting rudder (f) prop tunnel

use only'. They certainly would not stand persistent beaching in the role of training craft for which most of the 300 built were used. With a large lifting eye forward and aft these craft could be carried on ships' davits and a few were used from destroyers in the Mediterranean. Their designed cargo is recorded as thirty troops but the author's recollection is that eighteen was nearer the mark. They could make about 10 knots with a range of up to 30 miles on the 30 Imperial gallons of fuel carried. Without armour or armament they were satisfactory sea boats as long as they were not left thumping about on a beach; as there is nearly always some movement at the water's edge this was a serious handicap. A number of these craft and some LCP(L)s were fitted out as water ambulances with four or six positions for stretchers under the side decks. Records of a British LCP(S) Mk1 show the design as a 20ft ×6ft engineless wooden craft for towing by an LCP(S) Mk2, but there is no trace of any number being built in the UK though some Mk2s and Mk1s were built in the Levant as late as the spring of 1944. They may be the 'small LCAs' which Admiral

31

Maund found unsatisfactory because they were built with green timbers. Twelve LCP(S) Mk2s were used from three cruisers in an unopposed landing of 500 Royal Marines (from the fleet detachments) in the Arakan at Cheduba Island on 26 January 1945.

The titles of LCP(S) Mks1 and 2 were originally 'second flight craft', their designation being shown in some records without the suffix 'small'. However, by 1942 the builders' records show LCP(S) as the Admiralty title. There is also a record of a 30ft LCP(S) with an 8¾ft beam which may have been the proposed British version of the LCVP.

The LCP(Medium) (*Fig 3c*) was built on the lines of a northeast coast coble and had a high sharp bow suitable with sea room for work in rough weather. An open clinker-built 38ft 11in heavy boat with a 10ft 1in beam, she was intended for landing in rough waters on rocky coasts and designed accordingly, with a pair of lifting rudders and a propellor protected by the lower edges of twin keels forming part of a simple three-sided tunnel. A single 65hp Scripps Ford V8 petrol engine gave 7½ knots at 2,800rpm over 112 miles on 100 Imperial gallons of fuel carried in two self-sealing linatex tanks as a fire precaution. The single Lewis gun with its metal-protected ammunition box were forward. At least sixty of these craft were built in early 1943 and records show that seventy were ordered. They carried only twenty troops with a crew of three on somewhat wet passages in the rocky inshore waters where they were used for training. They drew more forward (2ft 1in) than they did aft but despite their fixed outboard stern steps and movable bow ladders they were difficult to land from.

A number of other British designs were mooted: the LCP(Utility) on similar lines to an LCP(L) but for landing troops not under fire, and the LCW air-propeller-driven craft of 31ft×9ft for use in the swamps of the Far East. Neither were apparently used operationally, nor was an American LCP(Nested) designed for easy stowage on carriers' decks. Twelve of these 32ft×7ft 10in LCP(N)s were built, with plastic skins on wooden frames, but their 60hp 4-cylinder outboards proved impractical as they were swamped in heavy surf.

The basic LCP(L) hull was also used with special equipment for survey work off beaches before or during a landing. This British LCP(Sy) with echo sounder and 'taut wire' gear had a crew of six including specialist naval commandos, probably. Other LCP(L)s were fitted for in-harbour minesweeping, and a flotilla with Royal Marine crews cleared Cherbourg and other Channel ports in 1944, using mini-paravanes to sweep moored mines.

LANDING CRAFT, ASSAULT

Built for the job

The crisis year of 1938 led to many changes in British military policies, among which was a proposal in the November for a new type of landing craft. Up to this time the Landing Craft Committee had produced some Motor Landing Craft without perhaps adequate study of the assault role of these boats, but now the ISTDC specified what the new craft must be able to do. They must be under ten long tons, enabling lifting by passenger liner davits; apart from crew they should carry the thirty-two men of an army platoon and five assault engineers or signallers, and be able to land them in eighteen inches of water. These criteria made them essentially personnel carriers; a separate set of requirements were laid down for vehicle carriers, although previously the two roles were combined in the Motor Landing Craft. Tests on a model showed that the intended load would not be carried in the proposed boat and other designs were commissioned.

J. S. White of Cowes built a prototype to designs by Mr Fleming, the inventor of the Fleming lifeboat. On her trials on a misty morning, the noise from the two 120hp Chryslers in the Birmabright alloy hull scared some mothers who hurried their children away from the Isle of Wight beaches as she came inshore. A second prototype from J. I. Thornycroft Ltd had a double-diagonal mahogany hull with twin engines and those features – low silhouette, quiet engines, little bow wave – which appealed to the Centre's staff in their search for a craft that could make surprise landings. The craft beached satisfactorily, a quality retained in all LCA designs, but the troops took too long to disembark across this

33

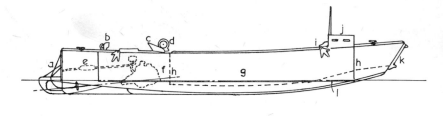

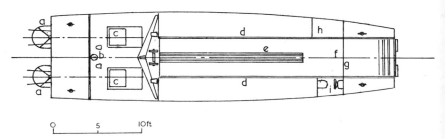

Fig 4 LCA, typical of Nos 142–220 (*Above*) Profile (a) anchor (45lb) stowed (b) p and s vents (c) breakwater (washboard) (d) kedge-rope reel and windlass (e) exhaust (f) eng compt (g) troop well–benches under side decks (h) bp bkhd (i) chainplate with eye for sling wires (j) non-mag bp shelter (k) ramp (l) bottom edge side armour (*Below*) Plan (a) rudder guards (b) davit sling (c) escape hatches (d) side deck, bulletproof (e) portable seat (f) davit sling stowed (g) armoured doors open forward (h) Lewis gun cockpit (i) coxswain

prototype's narrow ramp. A third prototype – ALC No 2 – was therefore built after the Admiralty's Department of Naval Construction had worked with Thornycroft on her design.

This ALC – LCA was not used until later – had Hadfield's Resista ¼in armour protection and two Ford V8 engines in a slightly smaller (38ft 9in × 10ft × 4ft 7¾in) hull than the eventual production design (*Fig 4*). ALC No 2 was also fitted with sufficient Onozote buoyant material to support her when swamped. Her forward steering position (starboard side) and other details were modified in later variants on the LCA but the basic design remained unchanged for the 1,929 craft that were built. By 1944 production from British firms rose to sixty LCAs a month; 371 were lost during the war but many more survived to become houseboats with cabins over the well. The LCA met the more stringent demands of active service; she was a strong little craft, standing up better to the pounding in rough landings than the LCPs, especially on the rocky offshore islands in the south of France landings of 1944 when many LCVPs were lost.

Working the boat

The LCA (*Pl 5*) handled well enough in moderate seas when waves were 3–5ft but could make no speed against rough weather, demonstrated in the number of LCA-hulled support craft that foundered in 6ft waves while on tow to Normandy. Nevertheless the bow lines and small ramp made the LCA a better sea boat than the slab-bowed LCVPs with their large ramp. Figure 4 shows the pair of forward-opening armour-plate doors leading to the ramp, which was lowered and raised by a simple arrangement of pulleys and wire, the two rollers on its outboard end providing some freedom of movement when the ramp was grounded. Over this ramp troops could come ashore in two to three minutes, or less if the soldiers and crews were well trained.

The craft were steered by twin rudders with steering wires that ran aft through an unarmoured section of the stern. On ALC No 2 there was a small telegraph, featherspray control lever, and a tip-up seat in the non-magnetic bulletproof steering shelter with its hinged double-door roof. While no compass is shown in the general arrangement drawing for No 2 she was no doubt later fitted (as were most LCAs) with a compass; in other respects she was lavishly equipped by later standards.

Operations

The first four LCAs in action landed 120 Free French legionnaires near Narvik in the May 1940 Norwegian campaigns. At Dieppe, flotillas landed troops from carrier ships, and here 40 Royal Marine Commando transferred to minor craft when diverted from their intended role of cutting out German barges, being used

Plate 5 Flotilla of Royal Navy LCAs manoeuvring to flag signals from leading craft as they form a line abreast for the run to the beach

instead as reinforcements to the main Canadian assault. The commando's CO, Lt-Col J. P. Phillipps, realised the futility of this tactic as his craft cleared the smoke cover. Putting on white gloves, he stood up at the cost of his life to signal back some 200 of his men. Their craft turned away from the murderous fire back into the smoke.

LCA flotillas served on the Glen ships in the Mediterranean and also in the North African landings, where craft from the *Winchester Castle* landed A Company, 168 US Infantry, near Fort Sidi (Ferruch). The coxswains, forming up in the dark, brought their craft to the wrong beach but fortunately there was no opposition. There were 448 LCAs in the Normandy landings (6 June 1944), including forty with RN crews operating with American forces. It was off the Normandy beaches that a Royal Marine corporal coxswain kept his LCA in action although her steering was shot away. He hung over the stern of the craft and made several trips from the carrier ship to the shore, steering the boat by using his feet to move the rudder. By late 1944 the British were using tracked amphibians for the landing at Walcheren, Holland, which had many features of a medieval assault on a fortified castle, though at Flushing LCAs also were used, and in the spring of 1945 the shallow draught of LCAs enabled them to run up the mangrove swamp channels – the *chaungs* – amongst Japanese defenders during the Arakan (Burma) advances. By then the craft had proved her value as a versatile assault boat.

Development of LCAs

By 1945 the all-up loaded weight of the LCA had reached $13\frac{1}{2}$ tons, the result of adding armour and the armament now carried by assault infantry, so the original idea of using merchant ship davits was abandoned as many carriers had more powerful means of launching craft. The original LCAs weighed less and ALC No 2 was only 9 tons; her forward steering position was modified for the first production orders, which had flush-decked hulls to a low protective bulkhead carrying the doors and projecting some two feet above the deckline, with only side plates adding protection for the coxswain and the gunner. Several variations were built with more armour protection around the forward steering and gun positions, one form of which is shown in Fig 4. These early craft carried scaling ladders on the side decks, had canvas awnings over the well, and several refinements that were dropped when the craft was mass-produced. Later, some craft were fitted with a parapet of armour 18in high along the inboard edges of the side decks, which gave added protection to the four crewmen (coxswain, gunner-bowman, a seaman and a mechanic) and to troops seated on benches under the side decks. Changes were made in the method of slinging the boats and eventually chains were replaced by bars to hold craft stowed on ship's davits.

All minor craft carried the usual small boat's equipment. On an LCA this might include – if some items had not been 'borrowed' by other crews – an anchor and its cable, together weighing 68lb;

lubrication oil – 18lb; a lifebuoy; two coir fenders; a 4ft length of spare packing for the stern glands; 14lb of heavy grease; a beach mooring line; a heaving line; a bucket and mop.

Ford V8 marine conversions by Thornycroft were used in the first LCAs, these water cooled petrol engines developing 65hp each when driving a 19in × 14in 2-bladed propeller through a 41:20 gear reduction. The twin propulsion units gave a speed of 10½ knots at 2,800 revolutions per minute with a load of 8,300lb in the boat. As with all wooden boats, however, weight increased and therefore performance fell off after prolonged immersion. Some craft – Nos 24 to 29 and 51 – were fitted with Parson conversions of the Ford V8, driving propellors similar to the standard type but on a 2:1 gear reduction; these LCAs did 12 knots at 3,300rpm. The standard engine fitted in almost all other craft was the Scripps conversion of the Ford V8. Official trial results for craft built in 1940–1 with this engine show a consistent performance with an unladen speed of 11 knots at 2,800rpm. This may not be surprising as these boats came from established yards, but in circumstances of nightly blackouts, air raids and other wartime restrictions it was a good achievement.

While some LCA-type hulls were used for support craft, others were given an extra 34-Imperial-gallon tank for an extended range to 100 miles at 7 knots when loaded, but the weight of extra fuel naturally reduced their load. LCA bakery barges were used to feed crews and beach personnel after a landing. LCAs fitted for clearing beach obstacles, the LCA(OC), were used at Normandy, and there is a record of LCAs fitted with flame-throwers, the LCA (FT), but no trace of their use in action.

LCA OUTLINE SPECIFICATION: *Hull:* wood   Length 41ft 6in overall including propellor guards, beam 10ft *Displacement:* 10 long tons, 13 long tons loaded *Draught:* 2ft 3in *Load carried:* 35 troops with 800lb of equipment *Crew:* 4 *Engines:* see above – the loaded operational speed was 7 knots but craft could make 2–3 knots on one engine *Range:* 50–80 miles on 64 Imperial gallons; might even be 100 miles when light, but wind and sea conditions seriously affected range of all minor landing craft *Armour:* Basically 10lb D1HT to bulkheads and sides, 7–8lb D1HT on side decking over troop well *Armament:* Bren gun aft and two Lewis guns in port forward position; two 2in mortars were fitted aft on some craft in 1943–4.

LANDING CRAFT, MECHANISED
Landing vehicles
There are obvious difficulties in landing vehicles on a beach and in 1938 the ISTDC considered a separate type of craft for this work. Before then there was in existence a Motor Landing Craft with origins in a dual-purpose personnel and/or vehicle carrier, MLC No 1, built for the Landing Craft Committee in 1926 by J. S. White of Cowes. This vessel, with an all-up weight of 36,000lb, could carry 100 troops from ships to a beach. She had jet propulsion, using hydraulic pump action 'propellers' and tiller steering. The hinged bow ramp on this and other pre-war MLCs was too steep to land many types of contemporary vehicles, which had less ground clearance than World War I veterans, but a further prototype – MLC No 10 with Gill-type jet propulsion – was ordered in 1927 to carry a 12-ton army tank. This 42ft × 12ft steel craft weighed 45,200lb and was completed by Rowhedge Iron Works in September 1929. Three more were ordered. They could make only 5 knots carrying 10 tons of stores and a row of mules. Alternatively each could carry 6in gun without its mounting. The hull, shaped somewhat like half an egg, was unsuitable for loading the MLC as deck cargo. In spite of these drawbacks, a further six were built in 1938 with a bulletproof steering position, and a number of these early MLCs were used at Narvik and got their tanks ashore, although one was lost when trying to load a tank off a pier. Eventually all the minor craft at Narvik were lost, either in the landings or in heavy weather while being towed back.

Thornycroft designed the ISTDC's 1938 craft in steel but weighing less than twenty long tons so she could be hoisted out by ships' heavy derricks and carry a 14-ton tank. This 44ft 8in × 14ft LCM Mk1 had successful trials in February 1940, but before these were complete an initial twenty-four were ordered. They had twin 28in screws with two 6ohp Thornycroft engines – Chryslers were fitted later – giving 7½ knots when loaded over a range of 56 miles. At the time of Dunkirk (May 1940) and until the autumn of 1941 this was the only craft that could land a Valentine tank. The British built some 500 LCM Mk1s, many of them in the workshops of the Great Western Railway at Swindon, Wiltshire, at the Southern Railway shops at Eastleigh, Hampshire and in other metalworking factories.

While the British LCM programme expanded, in America Andrew J. Higgins (who built the first LCPs) was experimenting with modifications to the bows of a tug originally ordered for Peru by one of his customers. By September 1940 the US Marine Corps had formulated their requirements for a craft to land tanks, and a number of prototypes were built. Higgins's tug conversion gave some trouble because it leaked at the hinges of the bow-ramp, which were raised further above the level of her waterline by adding side buoyancy tanks and a double bottom. An LCM – the Mk2 – was evolved from these experiments as a steel 45ft × 14ft 1in craft that could carry a 16-ton army tank (short tons), the craft having an unladen weight of 58,000lb and a mean draught of 3ft. The prototype was accepted by the marines and all work concentrated on these designs, although only 147 Mk2s were built before they were superseded by Higgins's improvement on the early craft with a 50ft Mk3. This became one of the most successful vehicle-landing craft of the war and 8,631 were built. An alternative to the Mk3 of approximately twice its size was considered, the Bureau LCM which was designed by the American Bureau of Ships, but only a very few were built. The later Mk6s, sometimes described as US Mk4s, were virtually Mk3s with an extra 6ft section welded into the hull; 2,718 were built. The British ordered 250 Mk6s as they could carry the 30-ton Sherman tank of that time, although the later Sherman Mk4 (A3) gave these LCMs a dangerously low freeboard and were therefore usually carried on Landing Ships, Medium.

The Mks3 and 6 were fundamentally different from the British Mk1s because the American types carried their cargo on the inner

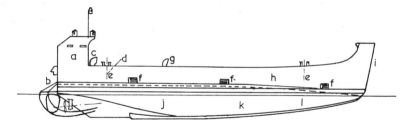

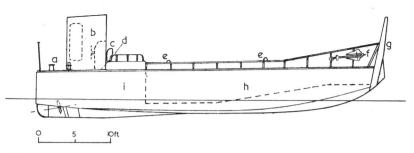

Fig 5 LCM British Mk1 and American Mk3 (*Above*) LCM
Mk1 (a) steering space (b) cqr anchor stowed (c) vents p and s
(d) hand windlass for ramp and anchor cables (e) davit sling (f) drain
port (g) vents p and s (h) vehicle well (i) ramp (j) engines (k) watertight compartment (l) ballast tank (*Below*) LCM Mk3 (a) cavel
capstan (b) steering shelter (c) vent p and s (d) ramp winch on
stbd deck (e) tie rings (f) anchor (g) ramp (h) vehicle well (i) engines

bottom of the craft with a resulting very low centre of gravity and
some residual stability if the cargo well flooded. The Mk1 was
designed more like a 'powered pontoon with bulwarks', to quote
R. Baker, a senior (later chief) constructor of the Admiralty's
Department of Naval Construction. Among Baker's many other
wartime achievements he had a considerable influence on the successful design of British landing craft and assault ships. Despite
the tendency to capsize if her cargo space flooded, and a poorer
cargo-to-craft-weight ratio than the American types, the LCM
Mk1 continued to be built as it could be loaded and hoisted on

carrier ships' davits. The American craft were launched without a cargo by extra-heavy jumbo booms. Alternatively, the LCM could be loaded and then carried on LSDs (Landing Ship, Dock) to be floated off at the dropping zone. Figure 5 shows the general arrangement of the LCM Mk1 (British) and Mk3 (American).

Waterproofing vehicles

The vehicles landing from LCMs were expected to travel through about thirty inches of water, a factor that gave designers many problems not only on LCMs but on larger craft and ships. If a beach had a gentle slope the craft grounded by the stern with her bows still in water too deep to wade. The Mk1 needed a beach with a slope exceeding 1:43 to land waterproofed vehicles. There were limits to the length of the ramp. The angle the ramp made to a beach was another feature affecting LCM designs; too steep a ramp, and the vehicle stuck on the ramp-hinge because the ground clearance was too small. Also, the vehicle had to be able to climb virtually from a standing start up the deck to the ramp. These features were taken into account in LCM designs and a pair of portable extensions were sometimes laid from part-way down the ramp to give a shallower and longer slope to the beach.

Whatever the conditions, however, vehicles had to be water-

Plate 6 Waterproofed Sherman tank with air intake and exhaust trunks welded and wire-braced behind turret; these tanks could wade in up to six feet of water

proofed or they would 'drown' and need towing ashore by recovery tractors. The Royal Electrical and Mechanical Engineers (REME) and US army engineers therefore set up waterproofing units at points of embarkation, where tanks had air breather and exhaust extensions fitted (*Pl 6*) and their hulls were made watertight with a waterproof, heat-resistant and non-conductive mastic material. Lorries were given exhaust pipes extending above the driver's cab and had modifications which enabled their engines to 'breath' although partly submerged. All vehicles, including British 3-ton lorries, American jeeps and 'armoured bulldozers, were water-proofed. Once ashore the engineers de-waterproofed them at special centres in the beach area to restore the full range of per-formance. Waterproofed vehicles were not able to float like the swimming tank but should they become buoyant in deep water they were liable to be swept along the shore until they grounded or sank. They had little difficulty in getting across the ramp and on to the beach, but once there they could bog down easily in soft sand or surfaces like the volcanic ash of Iwo Jima.

Loads and handling

The loads for LCM Mk1s were officially scheduled as a single tank or truck of less than 16 tons; or a 25lb field gun and a DUKW; or a DUKW with kitchen trailer; or two 37mm anti-tank guns and two weapon carriers; or one 37mm anti-tank gun, its carrier and two jeeps; or a staff car; or six jeeps. The loads might be varied within these groupings and some craft could carry 17½ tons but drew an extra inch, though most ships' derricks could only lift a Mk1 with a 10-ton cargo. The Mk3 (*Pl 7*) loads included a 30-ton tank; or 60,000lb of cargo; or 60 troops. In practice loading was not entirely related to weight or deck area in the cargo space for, as the commander of 8 US Amphibious Force reported after the Salerno landings, 'the LCM Mk3's use as a (medium) tank carrier is seriously restricted by practical considerations; the width of the tank is such that there is only eight inches clearance between the sides of the tank and the sides of the LCM Mk3.' He goes on to explain how difficult and sometimes impossible this made the

Plate 7 LCM Mk3 No 46 offloading bulldozer, July 1944; all craft landing vehicles needed beaching firmly

loading of tanks by ships' booms when the landing craft was alongside the transport in anything but a flat calm. But he emphasised the LCM's value as a cargo carrier, one Mk3 being regarded by his transport commanders as 'equivalent to from three to five LCVPs', and recommended that the number with each transport be increased from two to four although this meant adding a second jumbo boom.

LCM designs of 1943–4

British LCMs were originally designed to carry fresh water in the 'pontoon' hull, but later craft carried only ballast in a minor modification of the Mk1 design. Seventy-seven Mk4 LCMs were built in 1943–4 with special bilge pumps and ballast arrangement that enabled them to alter their trim by filling ballast tanks when partly loaded. A Mk5 British type is recorded but none appears to have been built. The only major redesign during the latter part of the war was the British Mk7 – a 60ft 3in × 16ft steel craft (*Pl 8*) – intended for operations in the Far East. This super-Mk3 was even

44

larger than the American Mk6 (the Mk3 plus 6ft referred to earlier) and intended to carry 35-ton British army tanks or bulldozers. She had twin Hudson Invader diesel engines giving a speed of 9·8 knots and greater range than the Mk1; the first Mk7 was completed in October 1944 and the programme for building 250 was in full swing at the end of the war.

There were modifications during the life of all marks of LCM with for example increased armour in the Mk1s from 8lb of 5mm to 10lb of 6·4mm. The lifting chains were also strengthened from 18 through 20 to 30 tons early in the life of the Mk1, indicating the trend for heavier loads and the stresses expected on each of the four chains. A variety of steering position shelters, ramps with extensions, and the fitting of smoke generators were typical modifications to all marks, British and American. The American craft were all-welded, but some British LCMs including a few of the Mk7s were of composite construction, with rivets in parts of the hull as well as welds. This arose because of the limited welding capacity in the UK and was one reason why Mk3s were not built in Europe as their design could not be readily adapted to composite construction.

These strongly built craft (*Pl 9*) were used for many purposes with little or no adaptation, but on the Mindanao River in the Philippines and elsewhere several Mk3s were adapted for use as

Plate 8   British LCM Mk7 with Royal Marine crew preparing to lower ramp; the winchman aft is about to release the winch-brake

Plate 9 The position of cargo in the hold or well was important for the safe trim of all craft; here an LCM carries a light tank to the Sicily beaches in July 1944, with the craft properly trimmed on the water

gunboats. In some a 40mm cannon was mounted forward and several 20mm cannon fitted to fire from the cargo well. Another layout had a 75mm howitzer in the bow and an armoured deck-house with four twin ·50in machine guns in mounting rings set in its roof. Rocket launchers also were fitted to some craft, with 25mm machine guns to give support in landings. Such arsenals of weapons came from army and navy engineers' resources or, more exactly, their resourcefulness, for in all landing craft operations a great deal of what was available in the last resort depended on individual ingenuity in scrounging equipment.

LCM MKI OUTLINE SPECIFICATION: *Hull:* steel Length 44ft 8in, beam 14ft *Displacement:* 36 long tons loaded *Draught:* 30in (less at point below ramp-hinge) *Loads carried:* see page 43; 32,000lb and more could on occasion be landed from MkIs though 22,400lb was considered the maximum load for craft to be hoisted for passage on a carrier *Crew:* 6 *Engines:* Two 60hp petrol Chryslers each driving 28in props *Range:* Early craft, 56 miles at 7½ knots on 100 Imperial gallons   *Armour:* 8–10lb plate on decks, steering house, bulwarks and fuel tanks   *Armament:* Two Lewis guns.

LCM MK3 OUTLINE SPECIFICATION: *Hull:* All-welded steel Length 50ft overall, beam 14ft 1in   *Displacement:* 52 short tons loaded   *Draught:* 36in   *Loads carried:* Up to 60,000lb; see also page 43 (craft usually hoisted without cargo)   *Crew:* 4   *Engines:* two 110–225hp diesels   *Range:* 140 miles at 11 knots, increased at cruising speed of 6¼ knots to 850 miles on about 200 US gallons *Armour:* High tensile steel, ¼in, to sides of control station/steering position; bulletproof mattresses fitted to some Royal Naval Mk3s *Armament:* Two ·50in machine guns.

LANDING CRAFT, VEHICLE AND VEHICLE PERSONNEL

Mass landings
By the summer of 1942 British and American staffs fully realised the extent of troop movements necessary for a successful invasion of Europe and the Pacific islands. They already had amphibious tractors in the final stages of development for landing assault waves but these LVTs were slow and could not manoeuvre safely alongside big ships, so boats were needed to transfer troops from the transports to the LVTs. There was also an increasing number of small vehicles including the Bren gun carrier to be landed with troops in the build-up phase of an invasion bridgehead, so the basic design of the LCP(L), already modified with a ramp – the LCP(R) – was further redesigned with a large armoured ramp. It became the LCV; only 2,366 were built before the craft was improved as the LCVP.

The LCV was similar in appearance to the LCM Mk3, though 15ft shorter, but the wooden construction and much smaller cargo space (17ft 6in × 6ft 4in) made her less versatile in choice of landing sites and load-carrying. She was inclined to take in water when her heavy ramp was lowered unless she was very firmly beached. The British ordered a number of LCVs through the lease-lend programme, President Roosevelt's 'hose-pipe for a neighbour to put out a fire' in Europe. These British LCVs had minor differences from the American standard, in particular a single Lewis gun while American craft had no armament; none had armour. Maybe the designers considered personnel in light fighting vehicles had sufficient protection, but the unprotected and exposed steering position high on the stern was vulnerable to anti-boat fire. The LCV was not designed for launching by davit when loaded; cargo-personnel boarded down nets and vehicles were lowered by derricks into the craft alongside. A number of LCVs with canvas-covered frames over the well were fitted for minesweeping inshore by the Royal Navy. Pictures of these craft indicate they may have carried degaussing gear – fitted to all major ships – as a protection against magnetic mines.

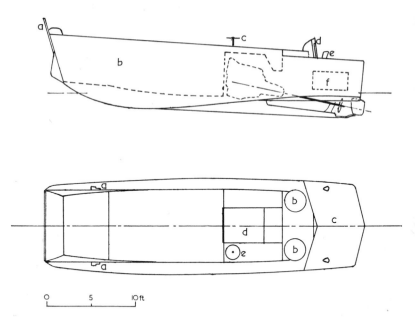

Fig 6 LCVP (*Above*) Profile (a) ramp (b) cargo well (c) wheel (d) washboard (e) Samson post (to keel) (f) p and s fuel tanks (*Below*) Plan (a) ramp winch (b) gunners' cockpits (c) deck (d) engine (e) steering position

The LCVP, a development of the LCV, had armour, two ·30in machine guns in ring mountings aft, and the steering position was moved inside the cargo well to a position by the port forward corner of the engine compartment (*Fig 6*). Carried on deck or in single or three-tier davits of American transports, the LCVP could be launched when loaded, but only from appropriate davits. Loaded craft were launched from LSDs on occasion and in the latter part of the war were carried as workboats by all assault ships. By then the beaching technique for minor craft was simplified: they were driven hard ashore to be nudged off by trucks.

Between 1942 and 1945 23,358 LCVPs were built, some of them being sent as component parts for assembly by US army engineers in plants like the three-production-line unit at Cairns, Australia. There, 1,145 officers and men of 411 Engineer Base Shop Battalion who had been trained in landing craft maintenance quickly adapted their work to this building programme, which later included LCMs.

Traffic density

The numbers of craft used in some 1944–5 operations gave the dropping zones the appearance of city centres at rush hour, without the convenience of traffic lanes. When the LCVP, with its 36ft length and 10ft 10in beam, is compared to a bus, and when it is remembered that landing craft had no brakes, it is possible to gain some idea of the marshalling problems of boat commanders. Nor were these landings a short flurry of activity, for the build-up after an initial assault required days or even weeks of ferrying supplies.

American LCVPs had TCS or TBK radios, essential for communication with the carrier and control ships. In the early stages of a landing, as at Roi and Namur in the Marshall Islands in January 1944, reserve companies might lie off the beach all morning in LCVPs until called in – a practice more common in the Pacific than landing to reserves' timetable – or the amphibians returned from landing assault waves. At other times the LCVPs would take their cargoes of troops to the reef's edge where the men transferred

Plate 10 US Marines land over an LCVP's ramp; the small number-board above the port bow was used for identification

to amphibians. Then, in building up the supplies ashore, bulk cargoes from LCVPs and LCMs would be manhandled on to piers by Construction Battalion engineers; or the CBs might have pontoon cranes 1,000yd from the beach to transfer loads from LCVPs to amphibians. A continuous search for better methods of landing stores went on right up to the end of the war. At Peleliu – one of the steps from New Guinea to the Philippines – on 15 September 1944, some LCVPs were pre-loaded with specific stores so that LVTs might collect whatever was needed, identifying the different items carried by code numbers on the LCVPs. By 1945, LCVPs and LCMs loaded with ammunition, water and the army's radio communications equipment were launched from LSDs to bring in the first supplies for amphibians to tranship and carry inland. However, there were unforeseen problems even at this date and unexpected sandbanks off Alacan caused LCVPs to ground twenty or thirty yards off the beach, with LCTs as much as one hundred yards out, delaying the build-up of supplies and slowing the advance. It was across these beaches, near Lingayen in Northern Luzon, that the Japanese had come ashore in 1941.

LCVPs (*Pl 10*) had many roles: water ambulances for casualties – they could be hoisted aboard in calm weather carrying seven litters; ferries to take the wounded to LSTs fitted as hospital ships; forty-five LCVPs and the same number of LCMs were brought by LSD to Ostend and taken by tank-transporters to help the British Twenty-first Army Group in the Rhine crossing; use with RASC and RE waterborne units for towing heavy bridge sections. There were few amphibious operations in the last two years of the war in which LCVPs did not take a major part.

There were some minor design changes. The engine was either a Hall Scott 250hp petrol or a Gray 225hp diesel. Apart from the extra fire hazard with petrol engines, they generally needed more frequent service than the diesels, which were therefore preferred for ferry work, especially as this helped to reduce the variety of fuels needed in a landing. Petrol engines, however, have a better power-to-weight ratio and give continuous high-speed running, limited in a boat's ordinary diesels to relatively short bursts above their cruising speed. Some references name the LCV as VLC, YR and TR, but the LCVP appears to have had no pseudonyms. Although building LCVPs (which had a better power-to-weight ratio than LCAs) was considered by the Admiralty, the war ended before a decision could be made.

LCV OUTLINE SPECIFICATION: *Hull:* wood Length 36ft 3in, beam 10ft 10in *Displacement:* 22,000lb *Draught:* 26in *Loads carried:* 36 troops, or 10,000lb of cargo, or 1-ton truck or Bren gun carrier (if loaded with care) *Crew:* 3 *Engine:* One 225hp diesel or 250hp petrol, various makes *Range:* 68 miles at 9 knots, 120 miles at 7 knots, varying within these limits according to type of engine; some later craft were given fuel capacity for 200 miles *Armour:* Ramp *Armament:* On craft in British service only, one Lewis gun.

LCVP OUTLINE SPECIFICATION: *Hull:* wood   Length 36ft, beam 10ft 5¼in *Displacement:* Unladen, 18,000lb *Draught:* 26in *Loads carried:* 36 troops, or 3-ton truck, or 8,100lb cargo *Engine:* As LCV *Range:* According to engine type, but officially 102 miles at 9 knots *Armour:* ¼in STS on ramp and sides *Armament:* Two ·30in machine guns.

LANDING CRAFT, RUBBER

Stealth

Inflatables were used by clearance divers (*Pl 11*), beach survey companies and sections from commando troops, a troop being equivalent to the infantry platoon, going ashore for reconnaissance before a landing. Launched from a submarine or coastal forces motorboat, they were paddled inshore and could be hidden while the scouting party tested the sand for firmness and studied the foreshore for suitable landing points. The patrols also examined exit routes from the beach to see how tanks might move out from an initial bridgehead. There were two sizes of LCR in general use: the 16ft ×8ft LCR(Large) and the 12ft 5in × 5ft 11in LCR(Small). A third 2-man inflatable boat was used by the US army. The

Plate 11 Party of Royal Navy Clearance Divers paddles ashore in LCR, August 1945

LCR(L) carried eight men who could paddle a wearying three miles at less than 2mph, though some experienced paddlers achieved 3¼mph over this distance and were still fit to fight on landing. The smaller craft carried fewer men but was lighter – 277·4lb to the 474lb of the LCR(L). Outboards could be fitted but they were noisy and destroyed any possibility of surprise during an approach to the shore.

In the spring of 1943 a number of US Marine Corps patrols of six or so men with a junior officer carried out reconnaissances among the Japanese-held islands of the Central Solomons. Patrols lasted up to three weeks and inflatables were the only means of crossing the many lake-sized lagoons with their islets and coral pillars. The Coast Watching Service, that brave band of individuals who stayed behind during the Japanese advance to radio reports on their activities, worked with these patrols, and both were dependent on support from local people who lived in settlements around the lagoons such as the Roviana Lagoon, 1–3 miles wide and about thirty miles long.

Other uses

A large number of inflatables were manufactured – 10,123 LCR(L)s and 8,150 LCR(S)s – for use as tenders or dinghies for minor craft. Useful for carrying stores over the last few yards from a stranded LCVP or LCM, the LCVPs might carry a couple and the LCMs up to six. These were used to evacuate wounded from assault waves when larger craft were still drawing enemy fire. But they were not made of as tough a fabric as modern leisure inflatables, for twelve out of fifteen were sunk landing US marines at Umtingalu, New Britain, to cut one Japanese escape route on 15 December 1943. After this, LCRs were used only for assault waves of subsidiary landings when there were insufficient LVT amphibians available, though they continued to be useful 'where a fringing reef extends a considerable way from the beach and ships' boats are prevented from reaching the beach except during rising tide and high water' (Commander Transport at Tarawa).

Towing LCRs and outboards

The US 26ft motor whaler could tow a string of eight LCRs at $4-4\frac{1}{2}$ knots in calm weather or a string of seven in rougher water. A $9\frac{1}{2}$hp outboard gave the LCR(L) $3\frac{1}{2}-4\frac{1}{2}$ knots and the 6hp outboard on an LCR(S) gave about the same speed. The use of inflatables by underwater demolition teams, as they were called in the US navy, and the underwater clearance divers of the Royal Navy, is described in a later chapter.

The modern Gemini inflatable is a direct descendant of these wartime rubber boats.

LANDING BARGES

British types

The attempt to convert a Thames sailing barge to carry two Matilda tanks was abandoned because of the shortage of tugs, but some 500 engineless (dumb) and other dock-lighter barges were built with stern ramps for ferry and supply work (*Pl 12 and Fig 7*). In addition to those illustrated there were several other types: the LB, Flak with two Bofors 40mm anti-aircraft and two machine guns; the LB, Water, with a large fresh water tank; the LB, Emergency Repair with a truck fitted for maintenance work. The

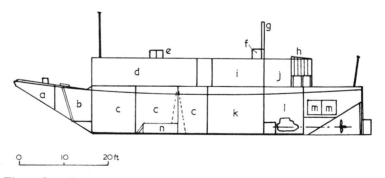

Fig 7 Landing Barge, Kitchen (LBK) (a) coal store (b) toilet (c) bulk and perishable stores (d) crew (e) tanks, sea and fresh water (f) diesel tank (g) vent to galley (h) steering position (i) servery (j) officers (k) galley, four ovens, etc (l) twin engines (m) fuel tanks (n) 10-ton fresh water tank

Plate 12 LBV Mk1 No 44, one of the larger barges, had a wood-on-steel-frame ramp and Lewis gun forward

anti-aircraft guns and maintenance truck were used afloat until the landing area was extended sufficiently for them to be taken ashore while not under fire.

Many of the barges were used in Normandy, and 120 of them were manned by some of the army's 2,000 men in the Royal Army Service Corps (RASC) water transport units. Records show several alternative designations: the LBF was known also as LBG or LBS, and the LBV as AA, BB, or CC according to load capacity, which varied. Most barges were steel or wood, but a few were of concrete.

A very different type of powered barge, the Z lighter (*Pl 13*), was originally intended for ship-to-shore use in harbour. This 134ft raft had a flat iron deck and a gantry to operate the wide ramp. Such barges did not normally become involved in landings until at least the second phase, but in Burma a number were used with a troop of Royal Artillery (RA) 25lb guns. Manned by local crews and Royal Navy liaison officers, they carried their gunners, guns and ammunition into action supporting river crossings.

Plate 13 The 134ft Z lighter carried ten 6-wheeled lorries and drew 28in forward with an 80-ton load; the bow-ramp arrangements shown are of a craft in post-war operation

American types

In the 1941 fleet exercises a 100-short-ton dumb barge was tried out for landing tanks. Four launches were secured as tugs to the corners of the barge and the tank lowered by derrick from the transport's hold. An improvised ramp was fitted when modifying this oil barge but with the advent of LCMs the idea was dropped. Most US barges including those carrying cranes (*Pl 14*) and powered by outboards were made up from the ubiquitous pontoon. The pontoon itself was 7ft × 5ft × 5ft and built from standard plates of varying shapes which could be shipped as components, saving cargo space. US naval engineers estimated 15,000 pontoons would be needed in the Pacific in 1943, and an assembly unit was set up at Ile Nou, New Caledonia, in March 1943. Here and elsewhere the parts were assembled with reinforcing members at the corners of the pontoons; they could be made up into reef-side floating piers, into the 140–175ft double-unit (14ft wide) causeways for use from an LST's ramp to bridge any gap to the beach, and for many other purposes.

The pontoon-barges were often carried as deck cargo, and at Pelelieu, in the Palau Islands, twenty-four were launched from the decks of LSTs. Three were loaded with 80-octane fuel and lubricants for the LVTs and carried a 'gas' banner. Others had cranes fitted and with their outboards could move from their station 1,000yd off the reef, albeit slowly, should enemy fire force them further offshore while transhipping cargoes from LCVPs to amphibians.

Ferrying supplies

By now, readers will have realised how much effort went into the supply and build-up of landing forces. The assault wave was the cutting edge of a very large force; as with any army in the field, there were six or seven men supporting each soldier or marine in the first waves ashore. In amphibious assaults, many of the

Plate 14 Crane on pontoon raft offloading a section of an LCM from a transport in Manus Island anchorage, September 1944

personnel in supporting services spent days if not weeks in unfamiliar conditions, and for many of them their previous experience of boats was limited to trips on lakes and rivers – if they had ever been in a boat at all. Those who have not been far offshore in small boats may not readily understand the effects of wind and waves; the reader must imagine what it is like to sit in a roller-coaster while being drenched by a hosepipe, the whole contraption meanwhile sliding sideways into the unknown. This is how the experience must have felt to ferry craft crews in rough weather. The anchored barge crews may not have had the same doubts over their position in relation to the shore, but they had two hosepipes (as it were) playing over them, and the sickening jerk of the barge against its mooring chain.

The Germans made the greatest use of barge-type vessels, many of their landing craft designs being a platform on several pontoon barges.

3 GERMAN LANDING CRAFT

Sea Lion
German plans for an invasion of England went through a number
of changes, but the final scheme for this operation – code name
Sea Lion – involved some 2,000 large river barges (Prahms),
which would be towed for most of their Channel crossing by tugs
(Schlepper) and motorboats. Half the Prahms had their own engines and could complete the run in to beaches, while the others
were to be pushed ashore by the tugs. Teams of army engineers
experimented with ramps and bow-doors for the barges and
developed rafts, partly submersible waterproofed army tanks,
seaborne flak platforms and methods of mounting machine guns
on the Prahms.

The first wave of Sea Lion was to land from army assault boats
(Sturmboote) (*Pl 15*) and inflatable raft-like craft (Flossacken).
About 16,000 men were to man these barges, after the engineers
had prevailed on the High Command to reduce drastically the
number of horses to be landed. By 15 August 1940 only 200 barges
had been converted out of the 1,600 collected at Channel and North
Sea ports, but by the end of the month – when a further 300
barges, over 400 tugs and trawlers and 1,600 motorboats were in
the ports – it was clear that the port facilities could not cope. The
original landing date was fixed for 17 September 1940 but preparations were obviously not going to be completed in time. British
air raids sank some barges, and division of command between the
Germans afloat and their army headquarters was another and even
greater handicap. After postponing the invasion, the appearance of
preparations was continued as a deterrent to the British though
Sea Lion was abandoned on 10 October 1940.

Plate 15   Sturmboot with motor boat lines intended for first wave
of Sea Lion landings in England

Landing craft organisation

In the subsequent German army operations a number of different types of craft were used. Organised by 1 September 1944 into three regiments based on Denmark, Norway and the Baltic, with other units operating in the Adriatic, the Aegean, the Seine/Oise area of France and scattered independent companies elsewhere. The regiments included assault units, support battalions and beach or wharf-operating elements. The craft used by these units can be grouped in three basic categories: fast motorboats for assault waves; powered rafts and ferries, the larger of which were also used as gunboats; and purpose-built vehicle-carrying craft. There were also amphibious vehicles including a Volkswagen car and river-crossing inflatable boats with outboards.

The assault motorboats were later increased in size and in armament.

Leichte Sturmboot 39: Length 5·98m, 1·58m beam, weight 492kg; an open boat with a small foredeck and a 30PS petrol outboard giving a speed of 25kmph; she carried six men in addition to the 2-man crew.

60

Schweres Sturmboot 42: Length 14·5, 3m beam, draught 0·65m; twin diesels developed 250PS giving 42kmph with forty men and three tonnes of stores; could be fitted to carry torpedoes.

Führungsboot: An adaptation of the Schweres Sturmboot decked over to carry a Zwilling 151/20 heavy machine gun or cannon. A number of these were used in the Adriatic during 1944.

The powered rafts and ferries (*Pl 16*) included small ships with displacements up to 416 tons. Some were merely double-ended pontoon rafts with ramps designed for carrying vehicles across the Channel. Experiments were carried out with single field guns on one type, but it seems unlikely that they would have been able to give accurate support fire to cover assault troops until the raft was firmly beached. Later in the war many of the larger ferries were fitted out as gunboats and could tackle a destroyer in ship-to-ship engagements. Among the types were:

Artillerieträger: An open flat barge with a field gun secured amidships but no protection whatsoever for gunners or crew, and a wide ramp across the front; about 1m deep, 12m long, 6m beam, similar in appearance to the flats used between liners and docksides.

Siebelfähre: Known to the Allies as L-boats and Siebel ferries, this type had a platform deck on a pair of large pontoon hulls with a deckhouse and bridge aft. Various assortments of armament were mounted, one type carrying two 105mm guns, one either side of the ramp between the bows of the pontoons, two 37mm anti-aircraft guns, a twin mounting for 20mm machine guns and four rocket dischargers, the lighter weapons being grouped around the deckhouse roof aft. This MAL-boat in one form had a displacement of 185 tons and carried 250 troops or 60(?) tons of cargo. Overall length was 26·65m, beam 14·06m, and power was from two diesel engines. The Siebel ferries ranged in size from 137 to 170 tons displacement with armament including 40mm anti-

Plate 16 Siebel ferries were of module construction, which led to a variety of forms; the example here, with two pontoon-type hulls, was common

aircraft guns. The SS-Gerät Siebel type was 27·3m long, beam 14·15m and draught of 1·2m; when loaded with 100 tonnes of stores or 250 troops it could make 15kmph on its three diesels.

L-boats and ferries carried up to eight or even ten trucks which they could load in twenty minutes. In the summer of 1943 a number of these boats were dismantled and taken across France to Italy where thirteen Siebel ferries and sixteen L-boats successfully aided the German evacuation of Sicily with the help of seven Marine-fahrprahms (MFP) described below.

There was also a range of artillery barges – the AF, the AFP and the A-MFP – of 335 to 416 tons displacement and able to make 8–9½ knots. They each carried 37mm anti-aircraft guns, two quadruple mountings of 20mm machine guns, and four rocket dischargers. They were used for landing troops and for escort duties at sea and could be equipped to lay mines, and fall into the third classification of German landing craft:

Marine-fahrprahms (*F-lighters*): 50m craft (*Pl 17*) that could beach and make 10 knots with a 100-ton cargo load. Partly armoured and heavily armed against air and surface attacks, MFPs carried at least one 75mm or 88mm gun, a 37mm anti-aircraft gun with one quadruple and one twin mounting of 20mm machine guns, and two rocket dischargers. They could be equipped for mine-laying and were used in escort duties; their shallow draught – only 4ft 6in – saved them from American PT boats' torpedoes in an action in the Mediterranean, though one carrying anti-tank mines was blown up by fire from an American destroyer. The Germans lost 5–600 landing craft during the war.

MNL boats: Described in the British official naval history as 'for use in sheltered waters', these were in many ways similar to the British LCM Mk1, but an early version – the 15m Kleines P-L 39 – was a high-sided, twin-engined vessel that could make 20kmph with a 20-tonne load or 100 men, according to one authority, though there was apparently insufficient room for their equipment in the narrow 4·7m-beamed boat. The Grotzes P-L 40 was longer at 19m but retained the double side-opening bow doors and

Plate 17   Marine-fahrprahm F240 with anti-aircraft gun forward of wheelhouse; stripped of other armament in 1945

separate ramp of earlier types. With a beam of 5·93m it drew 0·75m with a load of up to 40 tonnes, its diesels giving a speed of 20kmph. The later design – the Grotzes P-L 41 – had a ramp door similar to Allied minor craft and a shelter on the aft steering position. The Schweres P-L 43 (43m long with a 8·6m beam) looked more like an LCT, for her three subhulls had low bulwarks and a deckhouse and bridge aft, but the bow was built up with a 37mm or other anti-aircraft gun on a bandstand starboard of the ramp, giving the P-L 43 a distinctive appearance.

Transports and amphibians

Cargo ships were used for transports with minor craft as deck cargo. In the Norwegian campaigns these ships were expertly loaded so that the men coming ashore, knowing exactly what to do, were supplied with priority equipment coming first out of the hatches. There appears to have been no large seaborne landing after those in Norway and Denmark, though there were several major river crossings in the Russian operations.

The first design in 1940 for a true amphibian, as opposed to land tanks equipped for swimming, was the Land-Wasser-Schlepper with a 300-PS diesel engine. This LWS 300 had a boat's hull on a tractor body and was reportedly used as a tug for bridging equipment as it could operate only in sheltered waters. With many similarities in appearance to the British Argosy amphibian, the LWS 300 looks cumbersome by comparison with the American amtrac LVTs.

4 JAPANESE LANDING CRAFT

The first carrier ship
Admiral Maund (RN) saw the *Shinshu Maru* and some 400 landing
craft arrive at Tientsin on the Po Hai (Gulf of Chihli) when these
were operating in China during 1937. There is little doubt that he
was aware of the significance of these craft and the *Shinshu
Maru's* design features, enabling this 9,000-tonner to launch
minor craft two at a time through the stern down a ramp that
could be sealed from the sea by double-doors. She had large loading
ports or doors in her sides, so vehicles and stores could be loaded
into landing craft alongside, and in harbours the craft themselves
might be loaded through these ports. With her heavy lifting gear
and armament, including eight 75mm anti-aircraft guns, she was
the first ship in the world to be built specifically as a landing craft
carrier. Laid down in the spring of 1933, she was completed in
November 1934 and served in the Pacific landings until acci-
dentally torpedoed off Java on 1 March 1942. Raised and refitted
with additional hangar space for aircraft and some rearrange-
ment of her boat holds, she was eventually sunk by US Task
Force 38 while forty miles south-west of Takao on the west coast
of southern Formosa on 5 January 1945.

This carrier – the equivalent of Allied landing ships – was the
outcome of plans laid by the Japanese army who operated all
their own transport shipping, a unique arrangement. Their first
Landing and Landings Defence Operations Manual was prepared
about 1924 and in 1928 3 Company of 5 Engineering Regiment
were among the first troops since 1918 to be fully trained in
operating landing craft. Though landing exercises had taken place
in 1921 and the Japanese had experience of powered landing barges

65

during operations in World War I, there was always some conflict between naval and army requirements which was to give the army shipping units many problems, especially in the later stages of the war.

There were plans to build a further seven ships of the *Shinshu Maru* type; they carried both craft and assault troops, with seaplanes catapulted off, making them ideal for island assaults, but only the *Akitushima Maru* was completed by 1941. She was larger and had more landing craft and planes than the *Shinshu Maru*, and retained the established stern-launching principle to which all Japanese carrier ships were to be built.

Pacific landings, 1941

The Japanese High Command relied on surprise in a political as well as a strategic setting for successful landings in the Philippines and Malaya, so these and the subsequent landings had to be made on a particular day regardless of the weather, with army units coming ashore at many points to achieve landings on wide fronts as well as in depth. This ploy might not have been successful against determined defenders but in 1941 there were few Allied units able to put up serious resistance. The Japanese had planned for a fleet of 600 minor craft and done some research on LCT-type craft, amphibious tanks and troop-carrying submarines, but none of these was operational in significant numbers during December 1941 and the Army relied on their older iron barges, the landing craft Admiral Maund had seen at Tientsin, and amphibious trucks. The landing force included transports manned by civilian crews and fishing boats pressed into service with army crews, with units landed from cruisers or destroyers attacking key airfield and other installations.

After the heavy air raids on Pearl Harbour during Sunday 7 December 1941, the Japanese landed at Kota Baru, a village on the east coast of Malaya, and at Singora and Patani in Thailand, and on the next day at Bataan and near Luzon in the Philippines. Landings took place on 9 December at Aparri and other points in the Philippines including Minadanao, the largest southern island

66

of this group, and at Jolo on the Sulu Archipelago. On 10 December the Japanese captured Guam in twenty-five minutes but coastal batteries on Wake deterred the planned landing, which was not made until 23 December when the assault force was reinforced. By then there had been further landings in the Philippines and the initial Japanese invasions had succeeded with far fewer setbacks than their High Command had expected. Most were by groups of 2,000 or more troops, battle formations in 500 transports spread from the South China Sea to the Marianas and the Central Pacific, distances measured in thousands of miles from Tokyo.

The first opposition to this series of assaults probably came from British fire on the assault fleet marshalled off Kota Baru at 2200 hours on 7 December, but it did not prevent the 5,500 Japanese from beginning their landing at 0030 (still 7 December at Pearl). They came under small-arms fire from units of the Indian army but succeeded in landing although the tanks took more time than planned to be lifted from transports' holds. This delay slowed the advance as the assault wave had to be reorganised and the tanks carried in the second wave. The army supplemented the naval bombardment with fire from the transports and from guns in armoured assault boats, but this supporting fire was not successful. In these and other landings the army engineer beach parties placed landing markers, built piers, and unloaded the landing craft. Although the Japanese had not retained their marine units after World War I, engineers and other assault troops were to become so practised at landings that they were regarded as marines, but as the war progressed the formation of assault forces tended to be on an *ad hoc* basis as most troops had some training in seaborne landings.

The Japanese landings in 1941–2 were successful mainly because they had complete air and sea supremacy and troops with a determination to get ashore. They usually launched their first wave of minor craft some distance from the beach, then the transports moved inshore, shortening the journey for craft ferrying supplies. Landings were on a less lavish scale than those of the Allies, the troops in Malaya, for instance, landing with one month's supply of ammunition but only one week's provisions. Bringing the big ships nearer the enemy coasts meant that a much greater area had to be swept of mines, although fewer landing craft were then needed for the ferry work. Another danger – anticipated at Kota Baru by landing anti-aircraft guns early in the operation – was the possible destruction of ferry craft caught on a beach in an air raid after transports had withdrawn at night. Despite the anti-aircraft cover these losses 'proved staggering' to Lt-Gen Sakurai Shozo, head of the Shipping Section of the Army General Staff, when he reviewed this landing after the war.

By the summer of 1942 the Japanese advances had reached New Guinea, the borders of India and across the Central Pacific to within striking distance of Midway Island. They had occupied Adak, Kiska and Attu in the Aleutians. But the landings on Midway planned for 5 and 6 June never took place as the American aircraft carriers, including the USS *Yorktown*, repaired in four days at Hawaii by 1,400 men working round the clock to make good her damage from the Coral Sea action, caught an over-confident Japanese fleet unaware that their signal code had been broken by the Americans. In the resulting battle of Midway the Japanese assault fleet was forced to withdraw.

Landing ships and craft

The supply and reinforcement of their widely dispersed – not to say far-flung – garrisons was a major preoccupation for the Shipping Section of the army. They had two 59m landing ships built in July 1942 to their designs. This Type ES had bow doors to a ramp with a reinforced lower bow for landing vehicles on a beach, but although described as a landing *ship* the design was closer to that of the British Landing Craft, Tank Mk4 (56·10m) than to the bigger American LSTs. The building of the ES ships was taken over by the Japanese navy and in all twenty-two were built in 1943–4, eighteen of them being lost by August 1945. These ships had a 3,000-mile radius of action but were considered too slow and small for supply and reinforcement of outlying island

68

Plate 18 Japanese Landing Ship Class 1 with rake on after deck
for sternlaunching of minor craft

garrisons, so the faster and larger LS Class 1 (*Pl 18*) was designed
in September 1943 for a speed of 22 knots. This ship could launch
a minor landing craft over rollers down two rails on its ramped
afterdeck while – in theory, at least – cruising below 16 knots, and
forty-six were ordered in October 1943 though only twenty-one
were completed before the end of the war. The need for simple
prefabricated construction forced the designers to use a hull form
of straight lines without sheer or camber, so the vessel could be
mass-produced using electro-welding techniques. Earlier ships had
been riveted or of composite construction, but by 1944, when most
of them were built, there were great pressures on Japanese yards'
resources of men and materials. The Kure navy yard and Mit-
subishi at Yokohama took about six months to build each craft,
much longer than the building times achieved for many American
LSTs that were a little larger than the Japanese LS Class 1.

The Class 1's raked afterdeck obviated the need for doors, but–
no doubt influenced by British LCT designs which after the
Dieppe landings may have been passed in some form from Germany to Japan – the next developments in the naval programme
were the LS types 101 (*Pl 19*) and 103, with LCT-type ramp
bows and in general appearance similar to the LCT Mk1. Although
type 101 had diesels, the 103 was fitted with boilers and geared
turbines giving a better speed but less cargo capacity. Over 100 of
the two types were scheduled for construction in 1944–5, but only

Plate 19 Type 101 Japanese Landing Ship No T149 beached near Kure Harbour, March 1944

fifty or so were completed for the navy and twenty-eight 103s for the army's use in supply but not assault roles.

The Japanese were always short of landing craft and ships despite these programmes, with craft being built in Hong Kong and other overseas ports. As they moved into a defensive stage for the last two years of the war, many of their landing ships were given extra armament for anti-aircraft defence. Other modifications were made along similar lines to the German L-boats and ferries, with four depth-charge throwers and a chute fitted to LS Class 1s. They were given anti-submarine detection equipment and in February 1945 were fitted with radar. The boat hold was adapted to carry two type C or D midget submarines for transport to bases in the Philippines and Okinawa.

The army introduced another fast transport, able to launch a 33ft landing craft over a stern ramp. This army L-type was 33m long with a 5·50m beam and could make 23 knots, but with its crew of twenty-eight was more often used as an anti-submarine boat than an assault craft. Fitted with aero-engines, the L-type had a range of 1,000 nautical miles and although initially armed only with light anti-aircraft guns these were supplemented with depth charges and other armaments.

Brief details of landing ships and craft

The minor craft (*Pl 20*) used by the Japanese army are detailed here according to the descriptions used by the Allies. In addition to the craft listed there are records of a naval '42½-foot' craft of which three were built on the lines of the 46-footer, and a '33-foot' fast motorboat of which twenty were built for use with L-type fast transports. Salient features of the ships and craft were:

Shinsu Maru: A riveted ship of 9,081 short tons displacement, an overall length of 144m and a 22m beam. With two shafts and geared turbines she could make 20½ knots over a reasonable range. She carried various combinations of aircraft and landing craft at different times but was initially designed for some twenty landing craft launched through the stern.

Akitsu Maru and *Nigitsu Maru:* Ships of 13,216 short tons displacement completed in 1941 and 1942 respectively, with two shafts with geared turbines giving 20 knots. Originally laid down as Type M cargo vessels, they were converted during building to launch up to twenty landing craft from the stern and fly off thirty aircraft, but the flight deck was too short to allow aircraft to land. Their armament included two 75mm anti-aircraft guns and ten 75mm field guns (presumably for supporting fire in a landing).

Maysan Maru and *Tamatsu Maru:* 7,800 short tons displacement, completed in December 1942 and January 1944 respectively. They had two shafts and diesels giving 20¾ knots. Each carried twenty landing craft launched through the stern. Their armament included six 75mm anti-aircraft guns.

Takatsu Maru: Laid down in January 1944 as cargo ship but taken over by the army and completed as a 5,600-short-ton landing craft

71

Plate 20 Japanese troops manhandle equipment ashore in the Pacific, December 1941; minor craft in the background show the influence of traditional fishing-boat lines and building methods

carrier for stern-launching twenty minor craft. She had boilers and two shafts with turbines giving her $17\frac{1}{2}$ knots. She carried six 75mm anti-aircraft guns.

Type A landing ships were based on the Type M hull of cargo ships; these four 10,677-tonners – *Hyuga Maru, Kibitsu Maru, Settsu Maru* and *Tokitsu Maru* – were laid down during the war but only the first three were completed by August 1945 and two of them were lost in that year. They carried thirteen '46-foot' landing craft, twelve '56-foot' craft and up to thirty-seven aircraft. Built in late 1943 and 1944, their heavy anti-aircraft defences – eight 75mm and as many as sixty 25mm anti-aircraft guns – reflected the growing need for protection from American torpedo bombers. The ships had stern-launching ramps for minor craft.

Type B landing ships were to follow the Type As but differed from them as they (B-types) had horizontal exhaust stacks on the starboard side to give a longer flight deck for landing aircraft. Only the *Kumano Maru* was completed (in January 1945) before the war ended, and she had similar lines and load capacities to the Type A.

LS Type ES: A steel-hulled ship of 1,062 short tons displacement when loaded, 59m ×9·60m and drawing just over 4m. She could carry four tanks, a truck and 170 men; or three small landing barges with a truck and one tank. These were launched through bow doors. There was accommodation for 208 crew and troops, including the gunners who were carried in increasing numbers as armament was augmented. The original specification included one 75mm gun, four 20mm anti-aircraft cannon, four 7·7 machine guns and one 6in mortar. On some craft the 20mm cannon were replaced by many more 25mm guns. With two 530hp diesels and twin shafts she could make 12 knots loaded and 14 knots when light, with a range of some 3,000 miles.

LS Class 1: This welded 1,680-tonner had a waterline length of 96m overall (80·50m on main deck to the stern ramp) and a beam of 10·2m. She carried four '46-foot' and one '42½-foot' landing craft with 230 tons of cargo, or 500 tons of cargo and 480 troops, or various combinations of light vehicles, men and cargo. Loads could include miniature submarines: six *Kaiten* and over 260 tons of cargo, or two *Koryu* and over 200 tons. Kaitens were 1-man submarines of 8·3 tons submerged displacement, 14·74m × 1m with a designed maximum speed of 30 knots carrying 1,550kg (700lb) of explosives. Koryus were 2-man submarines of 46 tons submerged, 23·9m ×1·85m, with 19-knot speed carrying two torpedoes. Armament included two '5-inch' guns and 25mm anti-aircraft guns mounted as three triple, a double and four single guns. This armament was augmented after November 1944. The single shaft and 9,500SHP geared turbines gave her a speed of 22 knots over 'a large radius of action'.

LS Types 101 and 103: 1,064 and 974 tonners, but strengthening of the original welded hull added some 17 short tons to their weight;

with bow doors and a ramp, vehicles could be driven from the top deck down an inside ramp to the tank deck and ashore over its ramp. The principal dimensions of both types were similar: 80·5m overall ×9·15m – but their propulsion systems differed. The 101's three shafts and diesels, each 400hp, gave her 13½ knots. The 103's single shaft to a geared turbine powered from boilers gave her 16 knots but reduced cargo space. Both types could carry seven medium or fourteen light tanks; the 101 could carry alternatively 320 men with 74 tons of cargo against the 103's 120 men with 74 tons of cargo. The reduction was more a matter of accommodation space than cargo load for the 103 took an all-up load of 242 tons against the 101's 240 short tons. Designed armament was one '3-inch' anti-aircraft gun on both types, with two triple mountings of 25mm guns, though this was increased during the ships' service.

L-type army LS: An 80-ton (length 33m, beam 5·5m) fast vessel with three type 98 aero-engines, each of 800hp and driving a shaft. These ships could make 23 knots carrying a loaded 33ft landing craft, itself carrying 3½ tons, or alternatively more than 25 short tons of cargo. This stern-launching carrier required 37 tons of fuel (petrol) for its range of 1,000 nautical miles. Records show the intention was to build sixty, but the programme was apparently not completed by the end of the war, though at least twenty-eight were built in 1944/5.

46-foot minor craft: This steel craft's actual overall length was 14·25m with a beam of 3·40m, and she drew less than 1m. She had a characteristic high-sided brow with a ramp hinged relatively high over her waterline by British or American standards, and a comparatively small load capacity – 10 tons of cargo against the LCM Mk2's capacity of 25 tons in a craft that was beamier but of the same length. However, the Japanese craft, like all their minor landing craft, carried large numbers of men. The '46-footer' took seventy men on ship-to-shore and inter-island passages, and was closer to a conventional boat than the Allied landing craft; the

Japanese craft needed no special features for hauling them out on davits, and they could be hauled up stern ramps or lifted by derrick. There were six basic variants of the 46-footer with engines varying from single 60hp army diesels to one of 150hp with speed maxima of $7\frac{1}{2}$–$8\frac{1}{2}$ knots. The sides of the craft were armoured against fire from light weapons and they carried twin 25mm or two 7·7mm machine guns; some had a triple mounting of 25mm guns. They were used by both the army and navy, and some naval craft were fitted in the last year of the war with equipment to release two torpedoes and armed for anti-submarine work; others carried depth charges. Over 3,000 were built by 1945.

56-foot minor craft followed the general concept of Japanese minor craft for launching over carriers' ramps, and were designed in 1943 to carry new types of army tank though the load capacity at 18 tons still appears small by Allied standards. There were four basic variants, three having twin diesel engines and one a single 150hp diesel giving speeds of 8 knots for all types; a twin 150hp diesel-engined version could reach 10 knots. Only 163 of these craft were built, and shortage of steel for the hulls seems to have curtailed the programme.

49-foot minor craft: a similar design to the 46-footer (14·5m × 3·35m) but made of wood, with two 45hp Toyota diesels and able to make 7 knots when loaded. She drew just over three feet when loaded with about eight tons of cargo or seventy men. Comparison of these loads with American and British craft shows that the Japanese allowed for fully equipped troops to weigh about the same, man for man, as Allied soldiers, suggesting that the Japanese soldier was not as lightly equipped as some have suggested, even though he carried few rations. Over 1,000 '49-footers' were built, together with a plywood single-engined type that was ·5m longer.

Other assault vessels included fishing boats and also a cargo-carrying submarine which could take up to 36 tons of stores, and at least one submarine class was equipped to launch its own landing craft.

Amphibious vehicles: There are photographs of tanks 'swimming' rivers in China during the late 1930s. During the war several trucks were used as amphibians, including a 2-ton 4-wheel-drive Toyota with a floating body built around a Toyota KCY truck. Earlier models appear crude by comparison with this 63hp Toyota even though it was less boatlike than the DUKW. Under 200 were built, most of them in 1943. About this time, Japanese amphibious tanks had detachable fore and aft pontoons and two counter-rotating screws. The rudder was carried in the aft pontoon. The pontoon attachments were taken off once ashore, but added to the usual air and exhaust breathers for amphibians, the pontoons made the vehicles cumbersome.

5 CARRIER SHIPS

Principal types
Ships that carried minor landing craft can be grouped in three
categories: the vessels carrying assault troops and craft – the LSIs
and American Auxiliary Personnel, Attack; those carrying *only*
craft like the Landing Ships, Gantry (LSG); and purpose-built
LSDs which floated their minor craft and amphibians from stern
ports when flooded down. In addition to the main carriers for mass
landings there were some converted destroyers – APDs – carrying
four minor craft to land a company of US marines or other troops;
a number of Royal Navy destroyers were used in a similar role
from time to time. Most of the LSIs were converted merchantmen
or cargo transport hulls completed as carriers. Before the war, the
British considered using a converted type of deep-sea whaler
along the lines of the Japanese stern-launching carriers, but the
whaler's ramp was found to be too steep for launching craft and
the ISTDC concentrated on methods of hoisting minor craft
aboard liners that would carry them to enemy coasts.

LANDING SHIPS, INFANTRY AND TRANSPORTS
British transports
No work was begun on these carriers until April 1940, after the
German occupation of the Low Countries; the first three converted
were Glen Line ships, *Glengyle*, *Glenearn* and *Glenroy*, earmarked
as potential carriers by the ISTDC in 1938–9. Conversion was a
relatively simple job although the ships had already been modified
from fast cargo liners to supply ships for a proposed Baltic fleet.
Troop accommodation, washplaces, lavatories and storerooms
were provided for army personnel of eighty-seven officers and 1,000

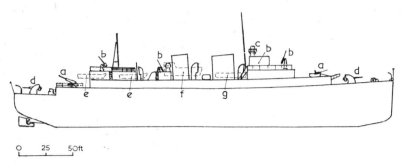

O   25   50ft

Fig 8   LSI(Medium) *Prince David*   (a) Bofors 40mm (b) p and s
20mm (c) rdf aerial (d) twin 4in (e) LCP(L) (f) LCM (g) LCS(M)
Note: minor craft on port side davits three LCP(L) and one LCM

men, landing craft crews (twelve officers and 220 men) and a ship's
company of 291. The davits for hoisting ships' boats were rearranged to include Welin-McLachlan davits to haul up and launch
twelve LCAs; two LCMs were carried for launching by derrick.
These launching arrangements were to be improved later with
the introduction of a luffing davit, described below.

The next British conversions were two cross-Channel Dutch
ferries, *Princess Beatrix* and *Queen Emma* (to anglicise their names)
as LSI(Medium). These ships were almost rebuilt, to enable them
to be used anywhere in the world; practically every feature above
the upper decks was modified and additional fuel and water tanks
were installed. Petrol for their LCAs was carried in cylindrical
tanks with a feed line to positions near the davits, which included
two 30-ton gravity davits for lifting the pair of LCMs on each
ferry. These special davits could not launch a loaded LCM Mk1
and were not fitted on other types of ships. In other respects,
however, the conversions set the pattern (*Fig 8*) for LSI(M)s. The
Dutch ferries were of 4,135 gross registered tonnage but smaller
ferries also were modified as the LSI(M)s proved more suitable
than the larger carriers for raids. There was not, perhaps, the clear
distinction between raiding and invasion that historians might
expect from military advisers of the early 1940s. However, the
Ministry of War Transport requisitioned numbers of troopship/

78

passenger liners as temporary LSIs (*Pl 21*) which needed no major modifications because the LCAs and LCPs could be hoisted on regulation 99-man-lifeboat davits. As craft became heavier, and more were carried, alternative methods were considered. The American three-tiered davit with its strengthening cross-beam could launch two craft chocked ready for swinging out from the deck and also the craft secured for passage on the falls.

On long sea passages in heavy weather, craft carried outboard of ships' sides were liable to be knocked about unless well secured, and even then they were sometimes exposed to such battering that their carrier ship had to reduce speed, a limitation avoided in part on the Glen ships because on their first conversion to LSI(L)s they only carried fourteen minor craft to land 1,087 army personnel. At Salerno, six American LCI(L)s were used to speed up the landing from British LSIs but the Admiralty had devised a luffing davit to improve carrying capacity. This latticed steel rig had two arms carrying a cross-beam with a pair of lifting tackles. The falls and the pivot arms were driven by separate electric motors and could lower an LCA, which might be carried on the luffing davit specially secured for a passage, with two more LCAs in cradles on deck inboard of the davit. With its 25ft arc the rig could be swung

Plate 21 British carrier ship LSI(Large) *Empire Arquebus* with LCAs on davits and lifting gear including crane aft

Plate 22 American AKA transport loading vehicle into ferry LCT during Salerno landings, September 1943

inboard to lift these craft after launching the one it carried on passage. The increase in craft carried on Glen ships as a result of fitting these davits is shown in the LSI(L) specifications following.

The methods of slinging craft by hooks on falls coupled to fore and aft eyebolts on the floors had disadvantages, for heavy boats plunging around in choppy water were notoriously difficult to unhitch without snarling gear or fingers. No satisfactory automatic release was evolved but later the Royal Navy used self-locking moused hooks. The open side of these foot-long hooks could be blocked by a lever-arm pivoted in the shank, the arm keeping the eyebolt in the hook until the lever was raised.

Auxiliary Personnel, Attack ships
These American APAs were mainly 7–9,000 ton transports

equipped to carry LCVPs and some LCMs in davits, with troop accommodation. There were also converted merchantmen. Working with the APAs were AKAs – Attack Cargo Ships (*Pl 22*) – which included 4,000 and 7,000-tonners with LCMs on davits or as deck cargo.

Bulk carriers of minor craft

A number of British conversions for carrying landing craft in bulk were made during 1940. Two ferries (*Pl 23*) were given stern chutes between their propellers after experiments by Thornycroft with a mock-up and system of trolleys on rails to move LCM Mk1s around the cargo deck. The unloaded 28-ton LCM could be moved forward to a transverse trolley carrier that took it from two side tracks to a central track for launching down a third track to the stern. Although these LSSs (Landing Ship, Stern-chute) could carry most minor craft, including the LCM Mk3, they had a range of only 1,350 miles at 11½ knots and were used to deliver craft from the yards to combined operations bases.

The second bulk carrier was an LSG designed to carry LCMs. It had been realised that the increased number of vehicles to be landed made more of these heavy craft necessary than could be carried on the LSIs planned in 1940–1. The design was novel, with three lines of LCMs on the fore and aft upper decks of three converted Dale class Admiralty oilers, *Dewdale*, *Derwentdale* and *Ennerdale*, each of 16,750 gross tons when loaded. The craft were launched by pairs of travelling cranes, one immediately forward and one immediately abaft the bridge house. Designed by Stothert & Pitt of Bath, each crane could traverse the ship's beam and go out on projecting booms over her sides; the booms were hinged for vertical stowage. The LCMs – six forward and nine aft – were carried on a system of rollers so that they could be pulled under the cranes for launching with their loads of ten tons of equipment. The crane gantry's legs straddled the crafts' width, enabling them to be lifted at the four 'corners', and all fifteen LCMs could be launched in thirty-five minutes. The arrangements of rollers were raised above the level of the deck so normal working could go on

Plate 23 HMS *Princess Iris*, an LSS with open stern as fitted out in June 1941; note depth charges aft

in the ships' other role of oiler. Accommodation for landing craft crews was not added until the ships were to go to the Far East, where they were used mainly as fleet oilers.

During the winter of 1941 the Admiralty Construction Department was working on a design for a mobile floating dock-ship that could take a single LCT on longer passages for possible raids beyond the LCT's range. This requirement was outlined in September 1941 but the idea had been considered as far back as 1823 and noted in the transactions of the Institute of Naval Architects for a meeting in 1870. There were also Popper barges on the Danube which launched lighters from side decks when the barge flooded down. The Admiralty designs for this LSD were sent to America, where the Bureau of Ships and subsequently Gibbs & Cox of New York developed them for building in American yards. The British built no landing craft bulk carriers after 1941 but in 1945 some LST Mk3s were given rails on the upper deck for trolleys carrying seven LCM Mk7s transversely, which could be hoisted aboard by derrick and run forward on a pair of trolleys before being jacked down for the LST's passage to the Far East.

Long voyages

Many LSIs sailed tens of thousands of miles during their wartime commissions; the *Royal Scotsman* rounded the Horn; the Glen ships were torpedoed, mined, bombed, burned and stranded at various times but all three survived the war. The crews of some carrier ships were the Merchant Navy men who had manned the vessels in peace time, and the ships still sailed under the Red Ensign; other crews were RN or US navy personnel. Some were from the Australian services. HMAS *Westralia*, for example, began the war as an armed merchant cruiser but completed her refit as an LSI(L) in May 1942 when she had a ship's complement of 500. Her landing craft crews were used in the autumn of 1942 for training troops in landings and acted as a depot ship for minor craft – LCAs, LCPs, LCVs and LCMs – when a combined operations base camp was set up in Australia that December. In July 1943 sixty army engineers joined the ship to work as loading and beach parties. On 15 December that year the *Westralia* took part in the Arawe Peninsula landings on the south coast of New Britain. Her craft's engines made a crescendo of noise as they started up the moment the hooks of the falls were released. All craft were launched in seven minutes and moved to the scramble net stations for troops to climb aboard. Some fifty tons of equipment were loaded into the craft and the ship was ready to leave the dropping area having taken only fifty-nine minutes to launch her assault force.

The saga of the *Westralia* is typical of that of many LSIs. She was in Manus harbour in the Admiralty Islands for Christmas 1944, at the Hollandia, Dutch New Guinea, landings in April when her mainmast crashed while hoisting in the 'after barges', at Panaon in October 1944, Lingayen (Luzon Island) in January 1945, at Tarakan in Borneo in June and Balikpapen in July. She and her sister ships *Manoora* and *Kanimbea* had some of the most comprehensive medical services of any Royal Australian Navy ships.

83

With an operating theatre and secondary theatre, dispensary and dressing station, her wardroom was used as a resuscitation centre when in action and her blood bank was restocked by plasma flown out to the fleet.

In Europe, LSIs were in all the invasion landings when the Allies liberated islands and countries, assaults that had valuable assistance from underground forces. There had always been a danger that local patriots might mistakenly rise against the Germans during a raid and suffer retribution when the Allied troops withdrew. Great care was therefore taken to warn the French Maquis and similar forces when raids were to take place, especially when the LSIs appearing off the coast, as at Dieppe, might have been mistaken for an invasion force. The key operations were: 1941 – Lofoten Island raid in March, Vaagso raid in December; 1942 – Dieppe raid in August and North Africa landings in November; 1943 – Sicily in July, Messina and Salerno in September; 1944 – Anzio in January, Normandy in June, south of France in August, Walcheren in November. Allied carrier ships including the American attack transports and destroyers took part in all these operations and many smaller landings.

In the Pacific, attack transports and cargo ships followed landings which may be grouped geographically as those coming from the South-West, the South and the Central Pacific, although the division of specific areas of command was fraught with inter-staff rivalries and differences between General MacArthur and Admiral Nimitz. In the South-West during 1942-3 landings were made in support of Australian and American land operations in New Guinea. In the South, forces that for a period were commanded by Admiral Halsey came up through the Solomons: 1942 – Guadalcanal and Vella Lavella, both during August; 1943 – New Britain in December; 1944 – Guam in July.

In the Central Pacific the first landings were in the Gilbert Islands at Tarawa during November 1943. Then in 1944 the thrust moved through the Marshalls: Roi and Namur (Kwajalein Atoll) and Eniwetok, both landings during February; on to the Marianas at Saipan in June, where forces from the south landed at Guam;

and across to the Palaus at Pelelieu in September. The liberation of the Philippines began in October, and the Pacific forces could now mount the two great assaults of 1945: Iwo Jima during February and Okinawa in April. This geographical summary shows the lines of the Allied main thrusts though by no means all the battles, nor does it include the British amphibious operations along the Burmese coasts in 1944 and the American landings in the Aleutians, where the first landing was made in August 1942.

The troops on passage in LSIs and APAs found the accommodation cramped and 'few who have not seen troop spaces and latrines have any idea of the indescribable mess which these places become in rough weather'. Nor can the difficulties for men in battle kit readily be realised unless the reader can visualise the narrow passageways along which many men slithered in hobnailed boots towards companionway steps to the boat decks. There, a shuffling delay gave time for last minute checks on gear before the climb aboard the craft to a place on the bench seats, ready for the 40ft drop to the sea. If the matelots bungled their job during the launch, a jammed fall could tilt the landing craft. Even when afloat, the surge of sea under the towering ship's side threatened the craft until she moved off under power and the pitch and toss of a stationary boat eased to a steady roll. At other times troops had an arm-stretching scramble down nets from the boat positions to empty craft bobbing alongside. The tantalising 'If I fall, I'll sink' jump-step brought most men tumbling aboard in rough weather unless they had mastered the landing craft crews' knack of stepping from the net on to the craft's side decks as she rose towards the top of a wave crest. The nets to LCPVs usually extended to the craft's floor, however, so the worst mishap was a hard fall from the nets, not a ducking.

The personal assault equipment which included combat composite-sole boots and para-jackets was never general issue to British forces, although worn by commandos and other special units. American personal equipment, with its many belt-fitting pouches for specific tools like wire cutters, influenced British gear designs towards the end of the war. However, most men landed in

85

fighting order, their kitbags coming ashore days if not weeks after the landing. Complete new kits were held by supply echelons to replace kitbags lost in landing. The only personal amphibious gear every man wore was a simple tube lifejacket inflated by mouth and tied with stout ribbon around his chest. These jackets for landing craft crews and some others could be fitted with a battery-operated red lamp so men in the water might be seen more easily at night. Whether enemy gunners or friendly rescue craft might spot the lamp was a point debated with no final conclusion.

Examples of carrier ships and assault transports

BRITISH LSI(L) HMS *Glenearn*, length 511ft, beam 66ft 6in, 9,880 gross registered tons *LCs carried (after modification):* 24 LCAs or LC Support (Medium) in port and starboard sets of davits (with single-gravity fwd, 1st luffing, two double-gravity, 2nd luffing, and single-gravity aft); one LCM aft launched by 30-ton derrick; two LCMs forward with 50-ton derrick *Assault force:* 65 officers, 1,033 men *Crew (incl LC crews):* 523 *Engines (twin screws):* Two diesels giving 12,000hp for 19 knots max *Range:* 12,000 miles at 14½ knots *Armament:* Three twin 4in guns, four multi-pompoms, four twin 20mm oerlikons.

BRITISH LSI(M) HMS *Queen Emma*, length 380ft, beam 47ft 2½in, 4,135 gross registered tons *LC carried:* Six LCAs (or LCS(M)) and two LCM Mk1 in special 30-ton davits *Assault force:* 22 officers, 350 men *Crew (incl LC crews):* 227 *Engines (twin screws):* Diesels giving 13,000hp for 22 knots max *Range:* 7,000 miles at 7 knots *Armament:* Two 12lb guns (at bow and stern), two mountings for pompoms, six 20mm, four Lewis.

BRITISH LSI(S) HMS *Prince Charles*, length 360ft, beam 46ft, displacement 3,647 tons *LC carried:* Eight LCAs (or LCP(L)s) *Assault force:* 20 officers, 250 men *Crew (incl LC crews):* 207 *Max speed:* 22 knots *Range:* 1,700 miles at 10 knots *Armament:* Two 12lb guns, six single 20mm, four Lewis.

BRITISH LSI (HAND-HOIST) LSI(H) *Royal Ulsterman,* length 340ft, beam 47ft 6in, 3,244 gross registered tons *LC carried:* Six LCAs *Assault force:* 40 officers and 450 men or 865 all ranks for 4-day passage *Additional load:* Six Bren gun carriers and up to 150 tons of stores *Crew (incl LC crews):* 230 *Engines (twin screws):* Diesel giving 5,200hp for 16 knots max *Range:* 4,000 miles at 10 knots *Armament:* Two pompoms, eight 20mm guns.

AMERICAN APA No 117 USS Haskell-class ship of 114 Victory type, 455ft by 62ft, VC2-S-AP5 hulls with displacements of 6,720–873 short tons (unloaded) *LC carried:* LCVPs or LCVs *Assault force:* Varied according to equipment and heavy gear carried as stores for the landing force – could be 500 all ranks *Engines:* Geared turbines of 8,500hp giving 17 knots max *Range:* Over 5,000 miles *Armament:* One 5in and fourteen 40mm bofors Other APA classes included Bayfield in C3-S-A2 hulls (thirty-six ships of 7,845–8,593 short tons displacement); Gilliam in S4-SE2-BDI hull (thirty-two ships of 4,247 short tons displacement); and forty-five other ships, many converted in 1943 from Maritime Commission cargo vessels, of 7,300–13,529 short tons displacement.

AMERICAN APD No 9 USS *Dent,* one of thirty-two converted flush-deck destroyers and seaplane tenders of 1,060–90 short tons displacement (unloaded) Length 314ft 4in, beam 31ft 8in, draught 15ft 11in incl 4ft dome of sound locator *LC carried:* Four LCP(L) or LCP(R) *Assault force:* One US marine rifle company, but 200 men carried on short passages; berths 140 + *Crew:* 112 *Max speed:* 23 knots *Range:* Varied as fuel reduced for increased assault force *Armament:* Four 3in/50s, five 20mm cannon, six depth charge projectors.

AMERICAN APD No 47 USS *Bates,* one of ninety-five converted or modified in building ex-destroyer escorts of 1,400–50 short tons displacement (unloaded) (Fig 9) Length 306ft, beam 37ft, draught 16ft 1in with dome down *LC carried:* Four LCVP *Assault*

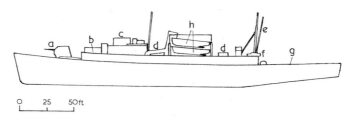

O   25   5Oft

Fig 9 High speed transport destroyer escort (DE) hull (APD)
(a) 5in gun (b) position for p and s twin 40mm (c) bridge (d) position
for p and s twin 20mm (e) lifting gear (f) twin 40mm (g) truck
stowage on deck (h) LCVP

force: 162 all ranks *Additional load:* Carried on aft deck, six ¼-ton
trucks or equivalent with 4,500cu ft ammunition (other loads: four
75mm pack howitzers) *Crew:* 212 *Engines:* Westinghouse
geared turbines (2 shafts) for 23 knots max *Range:* 5,000 miles at
15 knots or 2,000 miles at 23 knots *Armament:* One 5in/38, three
twin-40mm, eight 20mm.

AMERICAN AKA   No 21 USS Artemis-class ship of thirty-two cargo
attack transports in Maritime Commission, S4-SE2-BE1 hulls of
4,087 short tons displacement. Other AKA classes: Andromeda,
thirty Maritime Commission, C2-S-B1 hulls of 6,556-7,132 short
tons displacement; Tolland, thirty-two Maritime Commission
C2-S-AJ3 hulls of 6,318-456 short tons displacement; fourteen
other vessels of 4,036-8,045 short tons displacement.

BRITISH LSS   HMLSS *Daffodil*, length 363ft 6in, beam 61ft 5in,
2,500 gross registered tons *LC carried:* Thirteen LCM Mk1
Crew: 200; (though never in action, these vessels could accommo-
date 105 assault troops) *Engines (twin screws):* Steam reciprocating,
3,000IHP for 11½ knots max *Range:* 1,656 miles at 9 knots
Armament: Four pompoms, five 20mm, five Lewis 120ft loco
gantry added 1944.

BRITISH LSG   HMAuxLSG *Dewdale*, length 483ft, beam 59ft 3in,
16,750 gross tons loaded with cargo of oil *LC carried:* Fifteen

LCM Mk1 *Assault force:* 16 officers, 250 men *Crew:* 92 (assault force provided LC crews) *Engine (single screw):* Diesel of 3,500hp for 12 knots *Range:* Over 10,000 miles at 11 knots *Armament:* One 4·7in, one single and two twin pompoms.

BRITISH LSC A number of Empire cargo ships were equipped to carry twenty-one LCMs and an assault force of 295 all ranks. Typical of many similar adaptations, these ships had heavy derricks but were not extensively modified from peacetime layouts. Twelve US C1-B cargo ships of 5,668 short tons were completed in 1943 as British LSIs.

6 SHORE-TO-SHORE MAJOR LANDING CRAFT

Across the English Channel

Between World Wars I and II, what work was done on landing tanks was directed mainly towards landing a single vehicle from specially built craft like the LCMs in the UK or small numbers from dumb barges in the USA. Only the Japanese, faced with long hauls across the Pacific for their military ambitions, had made deep practical studies of landing vehicles and equipment in quantity. Their solutions were to carry them in transports for ferrying ashore when the enemy coast was reached. The British Landing Craft Committee of the 1920s and 1930s had a design worked out in 1937 for improving the X-lighters that landed mules and men at Gallipoli, and the following year a 150ft pier for landing supplies on open beaches was built for the Committee, but funds were short and part of the RAF's allocation was used to pay for this experimental equipment – a magnaminous gesture of peacetime inter-service co-operation. The tanks of that day in all countries' forces were relatively light and in many armies horse transport was more common than lorries. Only the British had anything approaching fully mechanised armies in Europe, with nearly every unit depending on motorised transports, against the Germans' high proportion of 80 per cent using horse transport.

Not till June 1940 did the British begin to work out methods of landing tanks in the numbers that would be required for a major raid. When Prime Minister Churchill asked what could be done, R. Baker and Admiral Maund settled some broad parameters for a vessel that could load with tanks at a home port and carry them to the occupied coast of Europe. In these shore-to-shore operations the craft had to be able to beach, allowing tanks to roll straight into action on the enemy shore. That June afternoon they decided the craft should meet several basic requirements: carry 40-ton tanks, as 36-ton tank designs were already on the drawing board (before this time only reconnaissance tanks were thought necessary for landings); as the slope of the average UK beach was 1:30 the craft must be able to land tanks on beaches of this gradient or, better, 1:35 (no data were available on Channel and other French beaches, which later proved to have much gentler slopes); the loaded draught forward must be $2\frac{1}{2}$–$3\frac{1}{2}$ft so tanks could wade ashore; and a speed of ten knots was needed. This craft would eventually be about 160ft overall. In three days Baker had a preliminary design and early in July an advisory meeting of principal shipbuilders was called.

LANDING CRAFT, TANK

First trials
John Brown and Fairfield agreed to work out details for the design on which the Admiralty Experiment Works (Haslar) did tests of the hull's likely resistance characteristics. The first craft – LCT Mk1 No 14 – was ready for trials in November 1940, with a 12ft-wide ramp door hinged just above the waterline and a pair of steel doors inboard of this to seal the bow area from the tank well. Along either side of the well or tank deck were storage compartments, wash places and so on, all of which could be sealed in a series of watertight compartments. These added a reserve of buoyancy to the sealed compartments of the double bottom under the tank deck. The side compartments and a tarpaulin cover on cross supports protected the load of three tanks or vehicles from spray and bad weather. The lower-deck crew of ten lived aft in confined quarters where condensation dripped despite the paint-with-cork-chips on the bulkheads. Here below decks astern of the engine room the crew's quarters always throbbed even in harbour when only

generators were running. On the quarter deck was a heavy kedge anchor and powered capstan; the bridge was aptly described as 'a steering shelter' behind which was a small cabin wardroom for the two officers.

The crew went forward on the narrow decks over the tank well compartments to operate the port and starboard ramp winches. The quarter-deck party dropped the kedge already slung on the transom before going into action, this steadying the ship for beaching without risk of broaching though the anchor wire had to be kept taut to avoid fouling the twin propellers. Coming off a beach, the capstan's power was used to help haul the LCT astern but again care was needed to avoid fouling the props. A signaller and the coxswain were with the officers on the bridge in action, while the two single-pedestal 2lb quick-firing pompoms were manned at positions on top of the after cabin.

At her trials, LCT No 14 proved insensitive to steering as she sheered from side to side down the buoyed channel of the Tyne, her shallow draught giving her little directional stability, but her beaching trials were successful and she was accepted as suitable for cross-Channel operations. Baker described the LCT as 'no great novelty' but the success of this prototype led to a flood of ideas.

British developments

Twenty Mk1s and later ten more were ordered and built in four sections for shipment when necessary as deck cargo to the Middle East. There, seventeen LCTs including Mk1s were lost in the evacuations of Greece and Crete. Before these actions, however, the beamier and slightly longer Mk2 (*Fig 10*, p 93) was designed, in December 1940, to carry two rows of 16-ton tanks. The dependable Hall Scott engines were by then in short supply and three Napier aero-engines of a 1918 design were used; these Lion engines were unpopular with the stoker-mechanics and gave the Mk2 a speed of $10\frac{1}{2}$ knots, disappointingly lower than the designed speed of 12 knots. Designed speeds were always suspect in LCTs because conditions in convoys when keeping station on other craft in a flotilla needed a reserve of power, especially in rough or

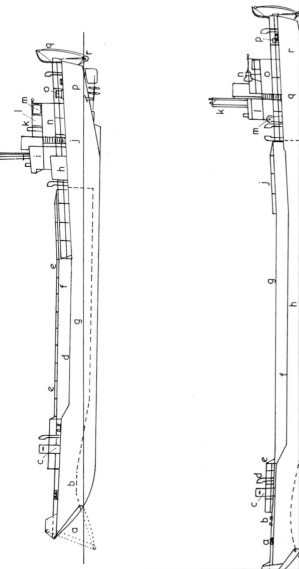
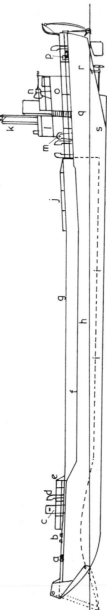

Fig 10 British LCT Mks2 and 3 (*Above*) LCT Mk2 (a) p and s ramp chains (b) ramp winch (c) conning tower (d) deck line (e) portable rafters for well cover (f) top of coaming (g) tank well (h) protective plating (i) bridge (j) engine (k) p and s 2lb gun (l) fw tank (m) ready-use locker (n) deck-house (o) capstan (p) crew (q) hoist (r) kedge anchor (*Below*) LCT Mk3 (a) fairlead (b) bollards (c) bp shelter (d) p and s vents (e) guard rails (f) deck line (g) top of coaming (h) tank well (i) ballast tanks (j) rafters (only four shown) (k) signal halyards and wt aerial (l) bridge (m) winch (n) p and s 2lb gun (o) deckhouse (p) capstan (q) engines (r) crew (s) diesel

0   10   20ft

windy conditions when the ramp bow was buffeted this way and that. The Mk2's range of 2,700 nautical miles (compared with the Mk1's 900) could often take these craft into poor weather conditions on long passages, when the shallow draught tended to make them slip and slide over the water.

Although the first three flotillas of Mk2s had Lion engines, steps were being taken in 1941 to expand production of the Paxman 500hp diesel, an engine that was used in nearly all British major landing craft built after the spring of 1942. This reliable engine – those who struggled with clogged jets or other faults will nevertheless probably accept that the general performance was reliable – brought a degree of standardisation that simplified maintenance problems, though it did not eliminate them. Besides the main engines most major craft had two or more generators supplying electric power; wiring and electrical equipment; radios; and in some major craft an all-electric galley. In addition to the usual ship's equipment, major craft had several features of small warships: ammunition magazines and 'ready use' lockers for ammunition on deck; radio aerials and signal halyards; battery-powered emergency lighting; telephone, tannoy and other communications systems within the craft. These and other equipment needed servicing by the craft's crews, and experts with test equipment and replacement parts that were at first provided by shore establishments though eventually carried on flotilla leaders like the LC(FF)s (Landing Craft(Flotilla Flagship)).

After the first sixteen Mk2s were laid down, all LCTs were prefabricated so that bridge-builders and other structural engineers could make them, a source of labour and management which enabled the Admiralty through the appropriate ministries to reopen disused yards for the assembly of prefabricated sections. While this enabled more craft to be built it was not going to meet the needs of the army in an invasion of Europe. One solution, an interim measure, was the conversion of shallow-draught oilers to land vehicles, but during the winter of 1940–1 there were grave doubts about the chances of beached ships ever surviving an initial landing. Another possibility was tried in John Brown's yard where a 32ft section was added to the Mk1 LCT No 28. This 5-section LCT proved if anything a little faster than the original design, and after her trials on 8 April 1941 she was accepted as the LCT Mk3 (*Fig 10*, p 93). Able to cárry five Churchill tanks, or eleven Valentine tanks, or eleven of the 1941–2 Shermans, most of the 235 built had twin Paxman diesels. However, the craft were too deep-draughted for landings on the very flat beaches of Normandy where they would have dropped waterproofed tanks in some five feet of water when they could wade in no more than thirty inches. This discovery in late 1941 led to various compromises being discussed. A Brunette sectionalised raft with four times the lift of an LCT was considered; it could be built by women, but its four diesels and other features made it uneconomic. A new beamier LCT, the Mk4, was therefore designed specifically for cross-Channel operations (*Pl 1 and Fig 11*), the original purpose of the Mk1, though assault techniques were evolving during 1941 which led to two distinct roles for this type of craft: as a cross-Channel and ship-to-shore large ferry, and as a seagoing vessel able to beach or to offload her cargo of vehicles into minor craft for the final run into the shore.

A raid in force

While new craft were being developed for more specialised roles, plans were approved in April 1942 for a raid on Dieppe, with the principal aim of gaining experience of German defences and mounting landings on a relatively large scale. The raid would also strengthen the Allied threat of a 'second front' being opened in Europe, forcing the Germans to maintain the strength of their western garrisons. There were secondary objectives in boosting morale and possibly capturing German barges to supplement British invasion resources. The value of these aims has been questioned, but there is no doubt that many lessons were learnt which later saved lives in other landings. We have seen something of the plan in the flank landings of 3 and 4 Commando. However, the whole operation involved only light naval forces: eight destroyers, nine LSIs, thirty-nine coastal forces craft and 179

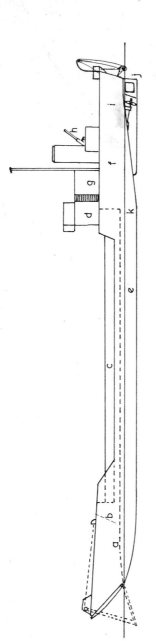

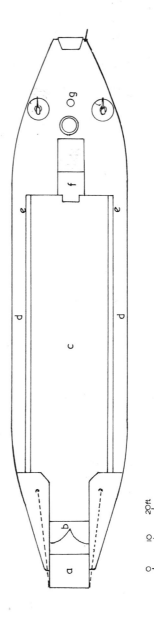

Fig 11   British LCT Mk4 before being stiffened   *(Above)*   Profile (a) tank deck level (b) ramp winch (c) bulwark (d) wheelhouse (e) watertight compartments (f) engines (g) cabin (h) p and s 20mm gun (i) crew (j) rudder guards p and s (k) stores   *(Below)*   Plan (a) ramp (down) (b) wt doors (c) tank well (89ft × 25ft) (d) side deck (e) bulwark (f) bridge (g) capstan

landing craft. Among these were twenty-four LCTs which carried the new Churchill tanks not previously in action. The bulk of the assault troops were Canadians; there were 4,961 of them and 1,057 British commandos and other troops including a small force of US rangers. D-Day was fixed for 19 August when the tide would suit dawn landings at points along the twelve miles of coast around Dieppe.

The flanking forces were to take the inner and outer defence batteries, and those landing against the inner defences were then to join up with the main force. The eastern gun batteries were not effectively destroyed, nor did the commandos manage to link up behind the town as had been planned. The main force had intended to capture the town by frontal assault and then land Royal Marines from the river gunboat HMS *Locust* (585 tons displacement with four 2-pounders and eight machine guns). This cutting-out force would then have attempted to bring back the barges in the harbour.

No sea or air bombardment preceded the landings although sixty fighter and seven other squadrons provided air cover. At the time, it was thought that any such bombardment might block the town with rubble hindering the tanks as well as vitiating any advantages of surprise. But a greater surprise to the Germans was the aircrafts' use of smoke rather than high explosives, for this left their defences intact, and while the southerly breeze persisted it swept the smoke cover several hundred yards clear of the beach.

The three LCTs carrying Churchill tanks for support of the first landing wave were off the town beaches ahead of schedule, but in trying to make a precisely timed run lost their way in the smoke and were late by ten to fifteen minutes. Meanwhile the infantry and assault engineers hit the beach on time at 0520 when the destroyers and fire support craft had stopped their bombardment as planned. Without the Churchills' 6-pounders to help in the destruction of anti-tank obstacles and strong points, the infantry had limited success. The second wave of ten LCTs came in, losing two tanks which 'drowned' when they went off in deep water and one tank which was knocked out before it could get ashore. The weight of

Plate 24 Dieppe beach after Canadian raid, August 1942; Churchill tank (extended exhaust for early form of waterproofing) and burning LCT in background

fire against these craft caused considerable damage, yet among several brought off one was commanded by her First Lieutenant after the Skipper and other personnel on the bridge became casualties along with the senior army officers aboard. A Canadian army officer ran her engines and later a destroyer towed her home.

After landing, thirteen or maybe fifteen tanks got over the promenade wall despite German 37mm anti-tank guns firing at their tracks (the guns were not able to penetrate their armour). The promenade was not passable where an anti-tank ditch had been dug seaward of its centre, but AVRE Fascine Churchill tanks dropped their bundles of chestnut paling where this helped the other tanks to climb from the shingle on to the promenade. They were stopped by heavy concrete blocks on the roadways into the town however. At 0830 General Roberts, the military force commander, landed his reserves, although the confusion of information passed by signal from both the main and flank forces gave him no clear indication of what was happening ashore. Heavy fire from the Casino, pillboxes and other buildings overlooking the promenade contained the assault and only isolated groups of infantry fought their way into the town. The damaged tanks on the beaches (*Pl 24*) and others which withdrew over the promenade fought on in covering the infantry but no withdrawal was possible under the plan until 1100 hours, when the RAF provided more smokescreens. Only one man returned to England from these tank crews, which held out till 1225 hours, the others being killed or captured after 500 men had been taken from the town beaches. Canadian casualties alone were 3,369 including 907 killed or who died in captivity.

The Germans ceased fire at 1358 hours after LCA No 186, the last craft, quit the beach.

After Dieppe

Many valuable lessons were learnt from this landing about the need for close support of assault infantry by landing craft with heavy weapons, the channelling of messages, priority in communications through a floating HQ, and the need to have uncomplicated plans if the assault force was to be flexible enough to react in unexpected circumstances. Since finding the unexpected is about the only certainty of any amphibious operation – to paraphrase the Royal Navy's official historian – this flexibility was an essential feature of all later landings, especially in the American Pacific assaults. After the raid it was learnt that even the destroyers' 4·7in guns had made little impression on pillbox defences, and the light weapons of small fire support craft were totally inadequate. Nevertheless the LCTs had beached and got their tanks ashore, proving the technique could be viable even if a heavy price had been paid in this landing.

In September 1942 the first of the new LCT Mk4s was completed; lightly built and without armament, this design was to go through a number of modifications (*Pl 25*). The tank deck, unlike in earlier marks, was above the waterline so vehicles moved down a slight incline to the ramp, the deep cross-sections of the double bottom being divided into watertight compartments

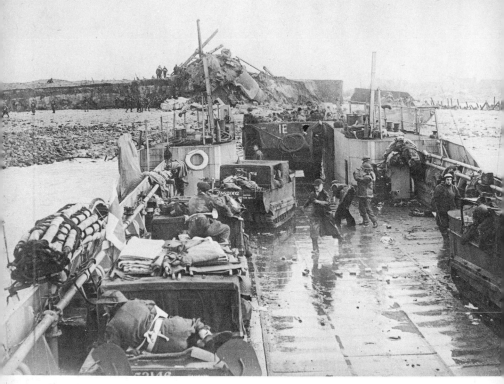

Plate 25 Royal Marine Commandos drive Weasels and other amphibians ashore from LCT Mk4 at Walcheren, November 1944

approximately 15ft × 15ft × 5ft. The extra beam gave more space for crew accommodation and for tank crews who on earlier LCTs had to live on the tank deck while on passage. Seven hundred and thirty-one Mk4s were built by August 1945, most of them in the works of structural engineers using their own drawings and not the working plans which were provided by shipyard drawing offices for the construction of earlier LCTs.

American LCTs

Before the Mk4 was on the drawing board, an idea was put forward in August 1941 by K. C. Barnaby, of Thornycroft, for a double-ended ramp ferry LCT for work with landing ships. This design was considered not entirely suitable for cross-Channel operations but the idea was put to the American Bureau of Ships who designed the LCT Mk5 along the lines of Barnaby's suggestion although with only one ramp. This 112ft craft was broad-beamed (32ft 9in) for her length, with the deck of her tank well above the waterline. She carried five 5-ton tanks, or four 40-tonners, or three 50-tonners. There was no need for troop accommodation and her crew of one officer and twelve men lived aft. Work on details of this design took place when the landing ship programme was under way in the spring of 1942, so these took account not only of sectionalised building for subsequent shipment in three parts as deck cargo, but also for transatlantic shipment in one piece on the decks of LSTs. The complete craft could be loaded (in theory) by a 150-ton crane, though in practice individual craft might be over the designed weight because the steel plating was not exactly consistent in thickness. The Mk5 or her successor the Mk6 could then be side-launched by removing the chocks from the prepared slideways and heeling the LST to about eleven degrees. The three LCT sections shipped on other vessels could be assembled when afloat; as with most LCT designs the parts bolted together and were individually buoyant. Only 470 Mk5s were built, most of them by non-marine structural engineers.

The Mk5s were able to average only 5 knots in anything more than very calm weather, making 7 knots with the wind and sea behind them but only 3 knots driving into moderate seas. They could therefore take a long time to reach an assault area, but once deployed 'they represented the most efficient means of transferring cargo, vehicles and tanks from ship to shore' (Commander, 8 Amphibious Force, Salerno). The Mk6 (*Fig 12*), of which 965 were built on lines similar to but slightly larger than the Mk5, had the further advantage in ferry work of access over the stern so that vehicles could drive forward on to the tank well ready for later landing over the ramp.

Life aboard

Although many of the Mk5s were used for training after 1943, they and the Mk6s could be taken by LSD or towed for long passages to Pacific operations, and at least one flotilla – No 31 with

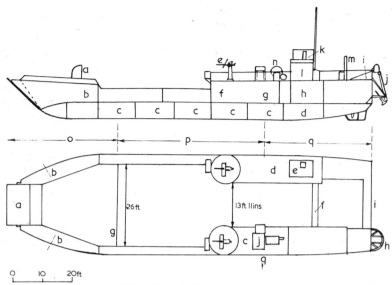

Fig 12 American LCT Mk6 (*Above*) Profile (a) bow anchor hoist (b) vehicle deck (c) ballast and watertight compartments (d) engines (e) p and s 20mm (f) deckhouse (g) crew (h) stores (i) port platform to anchor (j) anchor (k) open bridge (l) wheelhouse (m) vent (port side) (n) winch (port side) (o) bow section (p) midships section (q) stern section (*Below*) Plan (a) ramp (b) winch (c) port deckhouse (d) starboard deckhouse (e) bridge (f) catwalk joining dh roofs (g) bolted joints (h) anchor grid (i) access aft

twenty-four Mk6s – made an island-hopping passage from Pearl Harbour to Leyte under their own power between 15 January and 15 April 1945. Three months later, Groups 91 and 92 of this flotilla had six days of wild seas in a typhoon off Okinawa. By the morning of Friday 28 July they had made only twenty-six miles in the previous seven hours, with men taking short spells at the wheel to hold their craft as she catapulted down 40ft waves into the dark troughs before the next mountain of water. That evening they changed course into the Force 7 gale and some craft stretched the $1\frac{1}{4}$in bolts that held the sections together, but a further change of course put the seas on the starboard quarter and the craft prepared to run before the mounting storm.

In close company, any major landing craft was difficult to hold on station; in a typhoon, trying to stop was impossible as great seas swept one craft hundreds of feet past the ship ahead. Even if the ship ahead was visible in the torrential rain there was little chance of avoiding her once another craft came too close astern, so the LCI flotilla leaders' signalmen risked their lives to flash lights as a guide when the craft spread out. Some LCTs broke down and lay across these great seas in grave risk of being tossed over, nearly all having their radio aerials and much else carried away. But they hung on, repairing engines and rudder cables, until the storm abated a little and all reported themselves still afloat on Monday evening. By 2120 hours on Tuesday the weather had moderated sufficiently to enable a course for Okinawa to be re-set.

Not all life in LCTs was as hectic as this, but from the early days of the Royal Navy's LCT operations supporting the Eighth Army in North Africa, when ill-ventilated quarters made living aboard intolerably hot, through all major and most minor operations, LCT crews consolidated their reputation for delivering the goods. Many will remember the rumble of the ramp door as it juddered down, and the final thump when the winch-man took his foot off the brake. Already the first lieutenant had come down from the bridge and up on to the bows, signalling directions for his skipper as the LCT nosed into the beach. The Number One now watched to see if the ramp splashed into shallow water, while the Skipper turned aft, listening for the kedge-winch party's report of success or a foul-up. In harbour, however, an almost studied lack of routine on many of these craft caused concern to the Admiralty and no doubt to the US Navy Department, though the author can trace no record of LCTs failing to land through indiscipline, but there are plenty of recorded occasions when they landed their cargoes despite bad weather, engine breakdowns, and enemy fire.

Other LCT marks

All manner of bits and pieces were added to LCTs for different jobs from time to time but the main variants began with the Mk3s. Seventy-one were fitted out in the winter of 1943-4 with Sterling

Admiral petrol engines, and firms like Cammel Laird (Birkenhead) broke all production records in finishing them for the European invasion. Other craft were fitted out as hospital ships with cots for seventy-two patients, and operating theatres. There were LCT dredgers to tackle the sandbars, including those which could be created by larger ships' propellers in shallow water. LCT salvage craft helped to recover damaged assault craft and there were LCT tugs that pushed minor craft and barges to and from a beach. There was even an LCT bakery, and some American Mk6s became underwater-mine locators – the AMc(U)s. Minor modifications included a hinged ramp-bolster for Flails, and Mulock ramp extensions for easier landing by all vehicles.

The early Mk4s had 'back troubles' and were strengthened by additional stiffening members in three stages as a number broke their backs in rough weather. Armament was added, and after the landings in Normandy the Mk4's side decks were raised to the height of the original bulwark giving them an extra box-girder form of stiffening, heavier plates being fitted here and on the bottom. The craft were also tropicalised by fitting air trunks with blowers in the crews' accommodation, refrigerated store space and extra ventilation.

Designs for a Mk7 LCT, an American large landing craft, became the Landing Ship, Medium described later. The British designed the Mk8, the first of which was completed by the Sir William Arrol Yard (Alloa, Scotland) in June 1945. She owed something to the LSM design and had troop accommodation, carrying supplies for a week's passage with a range of 2,500 miles at 10 knots. She amalgamated the Mk3's robustness with the shallower draught and simpler construction of the Mk4, though the Admiralty developed and ordered her flooding-down system of pumps for filling ballast tanks, and the machinery for operating bow doors outboard of the ramp. Detailed designs were prepared by Thornycroft and a mock-up of her after-end was built at Pinewood film studios so that details of the forced-draught trunking and other fittings could be worked out. Deliveries of Mk8s were being made when the war ended.

Plate 26 LCT carrying duplex-drive (DD) tanks with flotation screens raised (except tank in foreground)

From the uncomplicated ramped seagoing barge which was the Mk1, the LCT had developed into a warship by 1945. Of the many ferry-type LCTs built in the United States, over 160 Mk5s went to the Royal Navy on lease-lend and seventeen Mk6s went to Russia. After the armistice in Europe a number of LCTs and coasters were fitted with generators for supplying power to Dutch towns and others given large pumps on the tank deck to empty flooded dykes.

Swimming tanks

These duplex drive (DD) army tanks had propellers and detachable flotation screens (*Pl 26*). Made of canvas with a metal frame, the screens could be raised by pneumatic pressure through flexible tubes to the frames' tops. The British 16/17-ton modified Valentine DD tanks (17ft 9in × 8ft 7½in) could use their 165hp diesels to reach about 3 knots when swimming ashore. The 32-ton American medium M4 tank was used with similar flotation equipment and had two propellers when modified as a DD tank. By 1945 the Tare 6 medium Shermans were in use with pontoons providing buoyancy for swimming from LSMs or other assault ships.

The majority of DD tanks were launched from LCTs and expected to swim two or three miles to a beach. In the early trials this proved difficult as water, seeping or washing into the screened area, quickly destroyed the displacement buoyancy. On some occasions the drivers had particular difficulty in getting free from their forward seats in the tank before it sank.

LCT SPECIFICATIONS	MK1	MK2	MK3	MK4	MK5	MK6	MK8
Hull		welded steel, all marks					
Dimensions							
length (ft, in)	152 0	159 11	192 0	187 3	112 4	120 4	225 0
beam (ft, in)	29 0	31 0	31 0	38 9	32 9	32 0	39 0
Displacement (tons)	372	590	640	586	286(sh)*	284(sh)*	895
Draught fwd (in)	36	44	46	42	34	40	45
Loads carried (max tons)	250	250+	300	350	150(sh)*	150(sh)*	350
Crew	12	12	12	12	13	12	22
Troop berths				various			45
Engines make	Hall Scott	(see note 1)	Paxman (note 2)	Paxman	Gray	Gray	Paxman
hp	350		460	460	225	225	460
number & type†	2 P		2 D	2 D	3 D	3 D	4 D in prs
props (× in)	2	3	2	2×21	3	3	2
Max speeds (knots)	10	10½+	9	8	7	7	12
Range miles	900	2,700	2,700	1,100	700	700	2,500
at . . . knots	10	10½+	9	8	7	7	10
Armour							
wheelhouse		15lb	15lb	15lb	2½in	20lb	
gunshields		20lb	20lb	15lb	2in plastic	10lb	

Armament

2lb	2	2	2				
20mm				2	2	2	2
40mm alternative	2	2	2				

1. Mk2 engines were three Paxman 460hp diesels giving 10½ knots or three Napier Lion 350hp petrol engines giving 10½ knots.
2. Numbers of craft built: Mk1 – 30; Mk2 – 73; Mk3 – 164 with Paxman engines, 71 with Sterling petrol engines; Mk4 – 731; Mk5 – 470; Mk6 – 965; Mk8 – 1 only by August 1945.

*(sh)=short tons   †P=petrol   D=diesel

LANDING CRAFT, INFANTRY(LARGE)
Giant raiding craft
Admiral Lord Louis Mountbatten is said to have asked for a large troop carrier which could land 200 men after a 2-day passage to the beaches. The design suited some aspects of combined operations planning for long distance raids in 1941, but the idea was dropped until April 1942 when there was a need for a 17-knot craft to take troops from UK ports to the French beaches, giving the men modest comfort below decks and meals during the voyage. The craft had to beach in water shallow enough for the troops to wade ashore (*Pl 27*), a requirement that Thornycroft studied and concluded must entail a steel hull for this shallow draught. American help was sought and in November 1942 one of the first LCI(L)s was launched at the Barber yard of the New Jersey Shipbuilding Co under the management of Todd Shipyards Corporation. In America as in the UK, the authorities appointed leading manufacturers to oversee the work of smaller firms or those with no particular experience of armaments or shipbuilding.

The all-welded construction and uncomplicated lines made this 158ft vessel fast by landing craft standards. The ship-type bow (*Fig 13*) and powerful sets of diesels driving twin variable-pitch propellers gave her an operational speed of 14 knots and a designed maximum of 16 knots.

The Barber yard itself was an example of wartime improvisation that became a highly organised production plant, 'plant' being perhaps a more apt description of these shipbuilding production

Plate 27 RAF Regiment men land from LCI(L) to protect air-fields; hand-ropes from the ramps prevent men being swept off their feet by inshore currents

lines than 'shipyard'. While the craft was at the design stage a search was made for a suitable site near New York, with its labour supply and sources of materials, and thirty-four acres were found beside the river with the right tidal and other conditions. The site had been an asphalt plant which closed down when the war cut off raw-material supplies from Trinidad. The overhead pipes linking its asphalt pits and tanks had no possible use in shipbuilding, yet in three months the site was cleared and the slipways had begun to take shape. In another three the first craft had been launched.

The prefabricated sections were made in a factory fourteen miles from the yard and moved on special trolleys to be loaded on flat railway trucks for the trip to the slipways. Here they were lifted into prepared cradles, each fabrication being numbered and marked for identification and positioning ready for welding. After each fabrication had been inched into its exact place the hull was welded at position 1, moved to position 2 for the deckhouse to be lowered into place and welded, then to position 3 for the combined pilot house and conning tower to be welded on top of the deckhouse. Thus the craft moved from station to station much as a car moves down an assembly line. At position 4 the electrical and other installations were fitted and at 5 craftsmen completed the furnishings. The new LCI(L) was then hauled into a mobile floating dock which carried her into the river before being flooded to launch her. Two craft were built in November, four the next month, and by February 1943 they were being delivered at the rate of ten a month to the US navy, a rate that was increased before the end of the year when some 2,500 men were employed at the yard in addition to those working for the twenty-three subcontractors supplying parts. LCI(L)s were built along many of the great American rivers by similar prefabrication methods to the British building of LCTs.

The crews of the first flotilla began training in Little Creek, Virginia, in December 1942. LCI Flotilla 1 with twenty-four craft was commissioned in the middle of that month, but renumbered as the 2nd Flotilla before sailing on 1 January 1943 for Bermuda on passage to Europe. The craft were constantly awash in heavy seas so the crew could work only on the bridge with every other upper-deck hatchway closed, but the LCI(L) was tough and sturdy. At Bermuda, however, the 2nd Flotilla had to spend a fortnight repairing leaks in the topsides of the craft – not major faults, for seawater finds the smallest opening around voice-pipe seals in a deckhead, or at other points where holes are made in the plating. The engines also needed patching up before the flotilla sailed with ten LSTs for the UK.

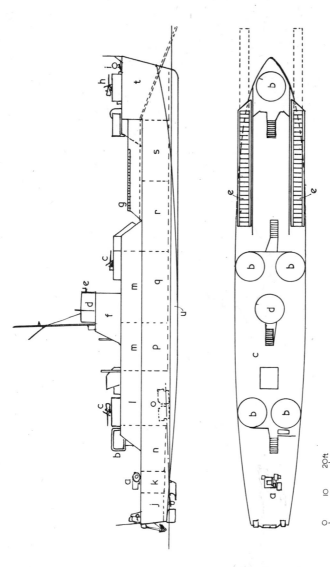

Fig 13 LCI(Large) – LCI(L) class 351 (*Above*) Profile (a) winch (b) liferaft (c) p and s 20mm (d) bridge (e) signal lamp (f) pilot house (g) portable ladder (h) 20mm gun (i) cathead (j) steering space (k) magazine (l) galley (m) mess (starboard) (n) 27 troops (o) engines (p) crew (q) 64 troops (r) 61 troops (s) 44 troops (t) stores (u) diesel and ballast tanks (*Below*) Plan (a) anchor winch (b) 20mm gun (c) officers' quarters, port dh (d) ph (e) 36ft gangway stowed

Propulsion and equipment

The eight diesel lorry engines in two sets of four for each propeller transmitted their power by inflated tyre-like rollers to the shafts. The resulting drive proved satisfactory although all spares for LCI(L)s were scarce in 1942-3. One unusual feature was the tram-handle steering lever in place of a wheel, which proved a simple method of operating the powered steering. Deadlights and other ships' fittings were generally of lighter construction than British equivalents, but nevertheless served their purpose.

North African landings

LCI(L)s were 'very useful and versatile' and 'acquitted themselves admirably as control craft despite their lack of navigational equipment (when special craft were not available during training) . . . and because of their ability to anchor close to a beach are useful as traffic control boats' (Commander, 8 Amphibious Force, Mediterranean). He went on to describe in one report how experiments were successfully made using LCI(L)s to salvage minor craft broached-to on a beach, and the possibility of using them as gunboats. Although not designed for cargo-carrying, they were sometimes pressed into the work of unloading transports.

The American LCI(L)s and other major craft trained at Inverary on Loch Fyne, Scotland, for the landings in North Africa, code-named Torch. The differences between the two localities could not be more marked, as in Africa the target beaches were often backed by featureless coastlines. The assaults, on 8 November 1942, were to come ashore in three widely separated coastal areas: at Algiers, where there was no opposition of consequence; at Oran, also in the Med; and at Casablanca on the Atlantic coast of Morocco. At the time these French territories were controlled by Vichy France under the duress of the Germans, but despite divided loyalties there was no major opposition to the landings except at Casablanca.

At Algiers a regimental combat team captured the Maison Blanche airfield at 0640 and by 0900 hours fighters from Gibraltar were operating from the strip. In the harbour, two destroyers landed US rangers but were forced to withdraw until 1900 when the troops had overcome French resistance. The other landings in the area got ashore safely that morning although many minor craft broached-to across the beaches in strong winds and surf. At Oran, seventy warships covered the thirty-two transports including LSIs which put troops ashore in three sectors, the Americans in the west and British in the centre and east. All three landings were timed for 0400 hours but there were some delays in launching the minor craft and confusion on the run-in. The landings were late – in one case by $5\frac{1}{2}$ hours – but all got ashore, and in the follow-up two of the first LSTs – the converted Maracaibo oilers – landed tanks directly on to the beach. The organisation of shore parties was to become very sophisticated but in the Torch landings each transport landed her own working parties, who slept in foxholes on the beach and took cover in caves from air raids.

At Casablanca the Atlantic coast landing was made by troops convoyed from the United States. Heavy surf wrecked many minor craft and French warships fought gallantly. A battery of 5·5in coast guns in the northern sector held out for two days, and even the American 16in shells were found to have had less effect than expected against the shore battery emplacements, emphasising the need for close support gunnery by special craft.

Principal Mediterranean landings 1943–4

With Torch behind them, the combined operations forces were prepared for the Sicily landings. The Royal Navy was able to draw on the experience of LCTs which had operated in the Mediterranean in support of the Eighth Army, as well as on those who had been in the Torch operations. For Sicily landings, eight months after Torch, the Allies deployed two major forces, the Americans landing to the west of the island's south-east peninsula on Joss, Dime and Cent beaches and the British on five beaches around this point – Bark West, Bark South, and up the east coast at Bark East, Acid South and Acid North. In planning the assault there were found to be too few LCI(L)s and LSIs for the troop lift, so a number of LSTs were adapted for this work with added

'LCVP and troop exits and converted to personnel carriers. The date of D-Day here was 10 July and H-Hour 0630 (on Cent), typical of the timing for a night approach by LCVPs leaving their start line at 0410, accompanied in some assault waves by LCI(L)s. The pre-landing bombardments proved adequate though not exceptionally heavy.

Just before daylight, men of the British 1 Airborne Division were to land on the north-east perimeter of the assaults. The 1,200 men in 137 gliders towed by US Dakotas had a rough ride in the poor weather and about sixty gliders came down in the sea. Those that landed later joined seaborne forces in the capture of Syracuse, a few miles north of the right (north-east) flank of the initial British landings. On this beach, Acid North, a heavy swell made the lowering of LCAs most difficult and although the commanding officer of 50 Division was critical of the delays the fleet commander, Admiral Ramsay, thought the minor craft did well in the blustery weather. At 0500 the LSIs moved inshore to speed the ferrying of troops and all assault battalions of XIII Corps were ashore by 0600 for mopping-up around landing points in Acid North and South. The supporting troops in a second convoy arrived off the coast at 0700.

The convoys had come from Tripoli and the eastern Mediterranean ports. Heavy storms delayed those coming to Bark East and South; 51 Division spearheading XXX Corps was two hours late in landing but met only slight opposition. That afternoon the corps' reserve battalions, including 2,000 men in twenty LCI(L)s, were quickly ashore, for here as elsewhere in the Mediterranean the steep shores made dryshod landings more frequent than wet ones. Around the point at Bark West the Canadian 1 Division and 40 and 41 Royal Marine Commando from Tripoli (in personnel-carrying LSTs) found the coast full of reefs, though they got ashore and again met only slight resistance.

The American forces – General Patton's Seventh Army – included 26,000 men convoyed across the Atlantic to join with troops from Algiers and Oran. Their landing beaches were on a thirty-seven-mile coastal strip, half sandy and half rocky beaches, with distances of ten miles or more between some of the landing points. 45 Division landed on Cent, 1 Division on Dime and 3 Division on Joss. The ships of Joss force had set out mainly from Bizerta on D-2, and in one of several fine pieces of seamanship shown in these landings put their craft on time in the dropping zones despite the buffeting from rough weather nearing Sicily. The Americans, particularly on Dime, met the strongest resistance of the Sicily landings and found the shoreline heavily mined. Due to the rough weather the LCI(L)s and LCTs bringing in the follow-up battalions, anti-tank guns and tanks were two hours late, but despite this the assault battalions, effectively supported by bombarding warships, held off the German counterattacks. The Luftwaffe bombed and strafed the beach areas as American air cover proved inadequate until use could be made of the airstrips taken on the morning of D +2. An unfortunate incident arose because paratroop drops on the nights of D +1 and D +2 were inadequately co-ordinated with the forces ashore, leading to the paratroops being caught in their own troops' fire, a misunderstanding due mainly to lack of time for adequate preparation; the Joss force landings succeeded largely because they were carefully rehearsed.

During the week following 10 July, fifty-six LSTs, thirty-six LCTs and thirty-three LCI(L)s left Malta in a ferry service to Sicily.

The crossing to Italy over the Strait of Messina was covered by 500 guns on the Sicilian coast, and a successful landing made possible a ferry service between points only 3–8,000yd apart across the strait. The ferry service was established in early September 1943 and on 9 September the Italians capitulated, although this political change made little difference to the military situation. The Germans were able to continue a stubborn resistance as they showed on 10 September when the Allies launched their landings at Salerno. The US ranger assault here was strongly counterattacked, though further along the beach the defenders were driven inland after a short but heavy engagement. On the adjoining beach area, confusion caused in part by rockets fired on to the wrong beach led to the first of seven days' hard fighting. There were many ship-to-tank actions, although the main bombardment was hampered on D-Day because no forward observation officers were ashore to direct fire on to specific strong points. The Germans counterattacked the beachhead heavily on D+1 and only effective air and sea bombardment kept the landing force ashore in this week of savage fighting, but after this the Germans began to withdraw as the beachhead was reinforced. The landing had been a touch-and-go affair saved in part by the reinforcements' craft. These the Navy – with a Nelson touch – had retained when they were due for return to the UK, where they were wanted for the preparations for the Normandy landings, a priority that would reduce the Mediterranean fleets.

Towards the end of 1943 plans were made to outflank the German lines south of Rome, and a landing was made at Anzio on 1 January 1944. As defences were slight on this coast, only thirty-three miles from Rome, a night (0200 hours) landing was made which achieved complete surprise, and by 0400 the DUKWs were operating a ferry service. The tank reserves arrived at 0645 in LCTs and the twenty-four LCI(L)s bringing follow-up infantry battalions arrived at 0715 having sailed from Naples. The beach area was congested by this time and LCI(L) No 32 struck a mine in going to help LST No 422 which was on fire. The LCI(L) sank in three minutes with the loss of thirty lives and eleven crewmen injured. Such dangers were an ever-present hazard for craft and ships in the supporting waves even though these landed hours or even days after a beachhead was secured. The Anzio assault was bogged down within a few weeks into trench warfare reminiscent of World War I. Although the initial surprise might have been exploited more successfully, there is reason to doubt whether the Germans would have been completely outflanked even though the initial landing force of one-and-two-thirds divisions had been built up to four-and-a-half divisions. These were opposed by ten German divisions and not until 4 June – two days before the Normandy landings – did the Allies enter Rome, after a series of battles in which the main armies linked up with the men at Anzio.

Modifications to LCI(L)s

The basic design of the hull and superstructure was not altered but many LCI(L)s were adapted both as gunboats and control craft, for 'No 2 troop space made an excellent operations room and additional communications fitted worked well' (Flag Officer (RN), Sicily, where captains RN were in overall charge of craft in each British beach area and used LCI(L)s as their headquarters ships in some cases).

Craft numbered 1 to 350 had a lower conning tower and the mainmast further aft than in Fig 13, though the only major design change was made in craft laid down after 1 June 1944 when a re-arrangement of the engine and troop spaces allowed for a re-designed ramp. A single inboard ramp replaced the external ones and was projected through a pair of side-opening doors below the anchor position in the bow. These changes made no alteration to the craft's capacity for cargo-personnel, though they were less exposed on landing over the inboard ramp which was wide enough to take two files of troops. In all 913 LCI(L)s were built in America as personnel carriers, 220 going to the Royal Navy on lease-lend and thirty to Russia. A further 337 LCI(L) hulls were completed as gunboats, flotilla leaders and other special craft, including the LCI(Demolition) which carried an Underwater Demolition Team.

LCI(L) OUTLINE SPECIFICATION FOR CRAFT BUILT IN 1943 *Hull:* welded steel Length 158ft 4in, beam 23ft 3in *Displacement:* 387 short tons loaded *Draught:* 58in *Loads carried:* nine officers, 196 troops (earlier craft carried seven troops less), and 32 tons of cargo when on ocean voyages *Crew:* four officers and twenty-four men (earlier craft: three and twenty-one men) *Engines:* see text *Range:* 8,000 nautical miles at 12 knots carrying 110 short tons of fuel, 37 tons of water and 5 tons of lubricating oil when loaded for long ocean passages; loaded for beaching, the range was 500 miles at 15 knots, less fuel being carried, or 1,500 miles at 12 knots *Armour:* 2in plastic on gunshields, conning tower and pilot house sides *Armament:* five 20mm cannon but varied with theatre of operations.

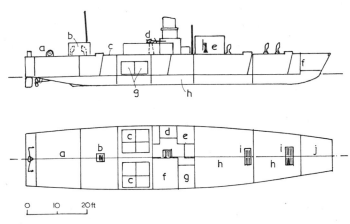

Fig 14 LCI (Small) – LCI(S) (*Above*)   Profile (a) winch (b)
generator house (c) bicycle stowage on deck (d) p and s 20mm (e)
bridge (f) armoured bulkhead (g) petrol (h) fw tanks (*Below*)
(a) sick-bay and troops (b) engine room (c) petrol (d) PO's mess
(e) galley (f) wardroom (g) wt (h) troops (i) steps (j) store

LANDING CRAFT, INFANTRY(SMALL)

Wood construction

This was the largest wood-built landing craft (105ft) and was intended like the LCI(L) to meet the British staff need for long-distance
personnel carriers, though the LCI(S) took only 102 troops of all
ranks and was considered more suitable for smaller raids. The
Fairmile Company, who built coastal forces boats, designed and
built the first LCI(S) (*Fig 14*) ordered by the Admiralty in May
1942, delivering her the following February. Her light construction
was in some respects below the standards for coastal forces craft,
and in a few aspects thought by some Admiralty officials to be too
light for the job. The double-diagonal marine-ply hull was of
laminated strips with armour plate – some in fitted scales over the
wood – protecting the sides, deck, generator deckhouse (aft above
the engine room) and the bridge.

The wooden construction exposed troops to heavy casualties at
Normandy when, for example, 48 Royal Marine Commando
came ashore on the left of Juno beach. The Canadians had landed

here and despite heavy casualties were clearing the beach strong points, but the marines' LCI(S)s came under fire during their run in.

LCI(S) OUTLINE SPECIFICATION   *Hull:* wood with four bow landing ramps   Length 105ft 1in, beam 21ft 5in   *Displacement:* 110 tons   *Draught:* 3ft 8in   *Loads carried:* six officers and ninety-six men with eighteen bicycles on deck   *Crew:* two officers and fifteen men   *Engines:* two Hall Scott petrol, supercharged for 1,500hp (1,140hp in some craft), all engines fitted with silencers; maximum permitted speed 15 knots for short periods only   *Range:* on 4,000 Imperial gallons, 700 miles at 12½ knots   *Armour:* (see text) 10lb D1HT to sides etc and ¼in plate to bridge   *Armament:* two 20mm cannon (more fitted to some craft) and two Lewis guns. (Ten of these craft were converted to LC Support(Large) Mk2.)

7 CONTROL AND HEADQUARTERS CRAFT

Integrated command

The pre-war concepts of integrated command during landings was not matched by adequately equipped ships until 1943. Early British and American landings were made with major warships carrying the naval and army commanders, though these ships often had other duties. HMS *Devonshire*, a county class cruiser with the landing force commander aboard, went off the convoy route to chase enemy ships a couple of days before the Dakar operation, and in North Africa the headquarters cruiser USS *Augusta* was drawn into a naval battle, but in later landings the headquarters ships – converted merchantmen and American AGC flagships – became the nerve centres of invasion landings. Fitted with cabin accommodation, a large operations room, several wireless rooms, cipher offices and all the paraphernalia of headquarters staffs, they provided the means for overall control of all units, navy, army and air force.

In the wireless rooms men of all three services worked their own routines but messages were interpreted into a common 'language'. Gun ranges, for example, were converted from the navy's 'zero-six-zero' for 6,000yd or whatever the range was to the army's 'six thousand yards'. Pneumatic tubes carried the messages to and from the operations room and its adjoining plot. Here, miniature landing craft were moved across the large table marked out to show the landing beach. Also on the plot were symbolic coloured blocks for different enemy units, guns and armour as well as the assault force's deployment. Aircraft symbols were moved on the

Plate 28 Landing Ship, Headquarters HMS *Bulolo* maintained
direct communication with the Admiralty as well as with forces in
the landing area

plot as the ship's radar equipment provided information on these
and many other movements. Towards the end of the war, radar
was a prime source of information for the control of operations
and took up an increasing amount of equipment space.

The headquarters ship was in touch with troops ashore, with the
forward officers, bombardment and others passing back information for the warship's guns, and could call up smaller control
vessels directing minor craft and amphibians working between the
carrier ships, transports and the shore. The staff also had links
through their air force personnel with fighter-bombers and rocket-
firing aircraft, but these – like the support craft described later –
could be in direct radio contact with forward platoon and other
junior commanders when specific strikes were needed in support
of the advancing infantry and tanks.

The headquarters ship's offices produced a stream of directives
formulated by the staffs for changes in the overall plan as the
invasion developed. Bombarding warships were given new targets,

the reserve brigades might be brought ashore more quickly than planned, and there were a host of minor changes affecting such details as meals for the landing craft crews or replacement of lost equipment, minor orders in the stream of messages but nevertheless important to a hungry boot-neck manning the Lewis guns of an LCA or the platoon commander of the signaller with a water-logged set. HMS *Bulolo* (*Pl 28*) handled 2,300 messages a day off Normandy, and she was only one of several headquarters ships in the landing. Communications were vital at all stages, for bad weather might delay LSIs reaching the dropping zone, they could be in the wrong area due to errors of navigation, there might be delays in loading assault waves on their minor craft, or the run to the beach might be put behind schedule by rough weather. In the landing itself enemy obstacles could cause bottlenecks on a beach exit; his counter-boat and defensive fire might catch the second and third waves, leaving the assault brigade unsupported on the shoreline. Whatever eventuality might arise, the headquarters staff expected to have an alternative course ready to follow. Even their own ship was covered by a stand-by LSHQ with staff kept in the picture in case the main LSHQ was sunk, though she should not have gone down quickly as her holds were fitted with empty barrels for added buoyancy.

The LSHQ was sometimes known as an LSH(Large).

The staffs and their personnel worked with all the deadlights closed as if in windowless offices, seeing the landing develop as some gigantic board game with the plot room wall maps sprouting pin-flags and lines of tape, watched by control officers on a raised dais, their desks topped by many telephones. At Salerno one of the British headquarters ships was bombed by the Luftwaffe with radio-controlled as well as ordinary bombs, and was at times exposed to E-boat attack while lying off the beaches. Once the bridgehead was established, the military commander and his staff moved ashore but close liaison was maintained from the new headquarters – through the LSHQ – with naval supply and bombardment ships. At about the same time in an action the air force fighter direction crews also moved ashore, having operated from

Plate 29 Fighter Direction Tender HMS *Boxer*, ex-LST Mk1, with ramp doors replaced by ship's bows and carrying extensive radar equipment

the LSHQ and/or the LSF – Landing Ship, Fighter Direction.

The Fighter Direction Ships on the flanks of a fleet during the assault phase of a landing used radar to guide Allied fighters against enemy air attacks. Several ships – *Antwerp* (2,957 tons), *Ulster Queen* (4,686 tons), *Palomares* (4,540 tons), and *Stuart Prince* (5,000 tons) – were fitted out as LSFs. The three Mk1 LSTs (*Pl 29*) were converted, as were three Mk2s (nos 13, 216 and 217) to RN Fighter Direction Tenders. The ex-LST Mk2s' bow doors were welded up, the hatches covered with armour, and pig iron ballast on the main deck protected accommodation added on the tank deck. They could then carry two VHF fighter direction offices, RDF, R/T and other communication centres, an air control room, a beacon office, a filter room, and extra stores and workshops. Four extra generators were carried for additional power supplies.

Commanders of army brigades and other formations – commandos or ranger battalions – were often carried on specially equipped frigates or similar small warships, referred to as LSH(Small), during some operations. These floating headquarters enabled army commanders to control their part of an assault before going ashore. On occasions specially equipped LCI(L)s were used by commanders; by 1943 these craft had taken on many roles, providing control craft in hailing distance of the minor craft and amphibians operating inshore during a landing.

Control craft

Destroyers and coastal forces craft acted as control boats in both Europe and the Pacific during 1942 but were gradually supplemented in landings by purpose-built LCCs – Landing Craft, Control. The British used converted Fairmile B motor launches and in America the 56ft Mk1 LCC (*Fig 15*) was built with a gyrocompass, an odograph, and other inshore navigation equipment. Even more sophisticated navigational aids were added to the LCC Mk2, which had an NPM microfilm chart projector. By August 1945 ninety-nine LCC Mk1s and 2s had been built. Part of their role was scouting enemy beaches, pinpointing landing places and laying markers before shepherding in the minor craft. With echo-sounders and good radio communications they could set up exact start-lines several thousand yards from the beach. The flotilla leaders of assault and subsequent waves would then follow the established practice and bring their craft on to this line at the precise time to start the run in so that they hit the beach at the moment their troops should land according to the battle plan.

With major craft, a converted LCI(L) might be used as the flotilla leader, forty-nine such conversions being made in 1943–4 to LC(FF). They had accommodation for flotilla staffs and specialists – navigators, engineers, armament, communication and administrative staffs. Additional signallers and radiomen/telegraphists with extra equipment supplemented the usual major craft communications personnel of one telegraphist and one combined operations signalman. Minor craft operated with one of their number as flotilla leader, however, although some British LCP(L)s were equipped with extra navigation equipment and as Landing Craft, Navigation (LCN) could pinpoint landing beaches.

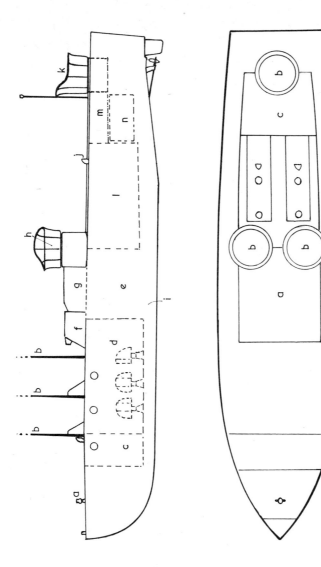

Fig 15 LC Control – LCC Mk1 (*Above*) Profile (a) bitt (b) tcs antennae (c) lav (d) radio room (e) lockers (f) steering position (g) cockpit (h) cockpit (i) p and s positions for twin ·5oin m/g (i) sound detector lowered through hull (j) p and s vent (k) position for twin ·5oin m/g (l) engines (m) cockpit (n) fuel (*Below*) Plan (a) cockpit (b) twin ·5oin m/g (c) aft cockpit

0   5   10ft

The American Scout Craft carried on APA and other transports did this work in North Africa and other landings. Basically an LCS Mk1, this boat had armour protection and engines muffled for a quiet approach.

Normandy landings

Control afloat was closely linked with the work of beach parties as well as co-ordinating the naval and air force actions supporting the landing force, for the offshore operations could last weeks rather than days in an invasion. This factor was fully appreciated by the Allied planners preparing for the Normandy invasion, code-named Overlord, which would involve not only the initial landing of the British Second Army and the American First Army but the build-up and supply of this force with over 550,000 men, 81,000 vehicles and 183,000 tons of stores in the first ten days. Armies ashore had to be supplied and reinforced for over a month before a French major port could be used by transports, and a further two months to the end of August were necessary before sufficient clearance of German demolitions allowed the army's needs to be met entirely through port facilities.

The first objective was to secure a bridgehead along fifty miles of Normandy coast (*Fig 16*) for a depth of several miles. Although the landings all succeeded, the planned depth of the bridgeheads took longer to achieve by several days and even weeks at some points. The initial assault force landing on D-Day, 6 June 1944, came ashore on five famous beach areas: to the east and left of the line were XXX and I Corps of the Second Army landing on Sword, Juno, and Gold beaches, a thirty-mile front from the mouth of the River Orne in the east to Port-en-Bessin; on their right, to the west, the American V and VII Corps landed on Omaha and Utah, a twenty-mile front from Port-en-Bessin to Quinéville in the west. These forces were each supported by naval bombardment groups with a total of seven battleships (two in reserve), two monitors, twenty-four cruisers and seventy-six destroyers including British, American, Canadian, Dutch, French, Norwegian and Polish ships.

125

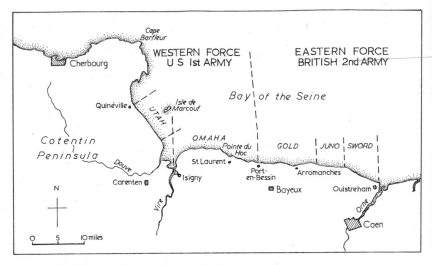

Fig 16 Normandy beach areas, 6 June 1944

The Royal Navy's operational orders alone covered 700 foolscap pages, though Admiral Sir Alexander Ramsay signalled the fleet, to the relief of many junior officers, that they need concern themselves only with those parts which affected their landings.

The plan was to land three or four hours before high water so in the half-light before dawn beach clearance parties could clear lanes in the obstacles which would still be partly exposed at the time of the main landing, although the state of the tide would vary along such a length of coast. Bad weather delayed the landing for twenty-four hours and for 6 June H-Hour was set at: Sword and Gold, 0725; Juno right wing, 0735, left wing 0745; Omaha and Utah, 0630. It was 0300 before the Germans appreciated that a major invasion was under way and for several days Hitler refused to accept that these assaults were the main Allied invasion, for in the months before D-Day the Allies had bombed defences all along the coast and made reconnaissances on beaches they did not intend to use in order to disguise their Overlord intentions. During the night of 5–6 June, over 1,000 RAF bombers attacked the ten most important batteries and at daylight 1,630 American planes bombed the Normandy fortifications though many of their bombs fell inland of the target areas.

The LSIs, APAs and headquarters ships (four with the British eastern force and two with the Americans in the west) arrived at the dropping zones during the night, the British some seven miles off the coast and the Americans eleven miles off beyond the range of batteries on the Cotentin Peninsula. During the crossing the weather was rough and some special minor craft including LCA (Hedgerow) were sunk while being towed by LCTs, but ships and craft of all five groups were moving towards their control ships' start-lines when the naval bombardment opened between 0550 and 0600. This bombardment was not as heavy as those in the Pacific landings after the spring of 1944, and the American landings on Utah and Omaha might have been easier had the bombardment been more effective. Fighter aircraft covering the assault co-ordinated their attacks with the bombing and, although hampered by low cloud, were able to strafe positions up to twenty minutes or so before touchdown.

The eastern Second Army, mainly British and Canadian troops, was deployed in five assault brigades, each with two infantry assault battalions with supporting regiments of mobile artillery and a reserve infantry battalion. The brigades were spearheaded by beach clearance parties of Royal Navy, Royal Engineer and Royal Canadian Engineer teams, the Assault Regiments' RE and other tanks. In close support were Royal Marine tanks in LCT (Armoured). The brigades landed – in panorama as seen by the incoming troops – with 8 Brigade group on the left (eastern) flank beach (Sword). Beach areas adjoined though the distance apart of initial landing points could be five miles or more. The 8 Canadian Brigade group landed on Juno (left) and their 7 Brigade group on Juno (right), 69 Brigade landing on Gold (left) and 231 on Gold (right). 7 Canadian Brigade can be taken as typical of these assault groups, led in by the DD tank detachments of 22 Dragoons, a squadron of 6 Assault Regiment RE, 6 Canadian Armoured Regiment's tanks, and a battery of 2 Royal Marine Armoured Support Regiment; the Regina Rifles and the Royal

Winnipeg Rifles formed the assault infantry with 12 and 13 Field Regiments, Royal Canadian Artillery, in support and 1 Canadian Scottish Battalion in reserve. Brigade groups landing on the flanks were heavily supplemented by commandos: on Sword, two of these formations came ashore to expand the flanks of the landing areas with 3, 6 and 45 Royal Marine Commandos from 1 SS Brigade and 4 and 41 RM Commando from 4 SS Brigade. The DD tanks on the eastern sectors were manned by 13/18 Hussars, 6 and 10 Canadian Armoured Regiments, 4/7 Dragoon Guards and the Nottinghamshire Yeomanry; The Flail tanks from 22 and the Welsh Dragoons landed with 5 and 6 Assault Regiments' AVREs. The East Yorkshire, South Lancashire and (Canadian) North Shore regiments, the Green Howards and the Dorset and Hampshire regiments also provided assault battalions.

The western (American) force landed six assault battalions, two on the left of Omaha, two on its right; two battalions – 1 and 2 of 8 Regimental Combat Team – landed on Utah with 3 Battalion of 22 RCT and 3 Battalion of 8 RCT in immediate reserve. Again, elements of the naval and Engineer Special Brigades' clearance and demolition teams worked with crews of DD and bulldozer tanks to spearhead the assaults. The reserve RCTs and Rangers, with armoured groups and Engineer Special Brigades elements, made up 1 Division group for Omaha and 4 Division group for Utah.

On Sword beach, thirty-two of the forty DD tanks launched 7,000yd off the beach came ashore at 0730 despite the steep seas. They were followed by LCA(HR), intended to fire spigot mortars and destroy mines and wire, but those that were not sunk in the crossing are said not to have been very successful. The first wave of the assault infantry brigade landed at H-Hour and the LCT (Rocket)s fired inshore to clear beach exits and prevent reinforcements reaching the shore defences. However, the defenders contained the assault brigade in a narrow bridgehead, although all its men were ashore at 0943 only eight minutes behind schedule. The tide was higher than expected at points in all the landings and the craft were driven on to obstacles instead of beaching short of them.

The division's self-propelled artillery followed in, firing at targets as they were presented and supplementing the destroyers' fire from the flanks. But 2 and 3 Brigades of the division were not brought ashore in the LCTs, LCI(L)s and the first LSTs until the afternoon, when they suffered some casualties and damage from mortar and other fire although after heavy fighting a beachhead was established. With this reinforcement the area was secured and the troops put ashore despite defences and the weather.

On Juno, H-Hour was delayed ten minutes, again allowing the rising tide to push craft among the beach obstacles. The senior LCT officer considered the sea too rough for the DD tanks and these were carried ashore on their landing craft, but one group was launched 600yd from the beach. Not all the beach defences were knocked out when the Canadians came ashore, but they cleared the beach and in the afternoon 51 Highland Division and 4 Armoured Brigade landed to pass through the assault division and expand the bridgehead. The use of tanks in Normandy – there were some 3,000 in the initial landings – was restricted by the tiny fields with hedge-topped banks (bocages) behind the eastern sectors of the landing; to the south and south-west of Caen the country was 'as easy to cross as Salisbury Plain', being rolling fields with few ditches. Limited firepower and armour hampered many of the tanks. Surprisingly, no air attacks were made against tanks or troops on Juno until the morning of 7 June.

48 RM Commando landed here in wooden LCI(S)s and suffered the heaviest casualties on the beach when their craft came under machine gun and mortar fire from positions not eliminated by the first assault waves.

50 Division landed with the four assault battalions, hitting Gold beach at 0725. On this 3½-mile stretch there were obstacles every three or four yards across the front of the defences, and along many stretches of the coast there were reinforced concrete blockhouses at intervals of about a mile. With each strong point supporting its neighbours and firing diagonally – enfilade – across the lines of incoming troops, the blockhouses were difficult to assault unless knocked out by heavy weapons. It was midday

before Gold beach was no longer enfiladed from these strong points, but the two reserve brigades landed during the morning and 47 RM Commando pushed towards Port-en-Bessin. There were 200 casualties among their 450 men but by D+3 they had taken the village.

On Juno and Gold the sequence of assault followed the general pattern of Sword beach. In the American sectors a number of problems cropped up, partly due to the weather and partly because of well-organised defenders who stubbornly resisted the initial assaults despite heavy bombardment. The battleship USS *Texas* closed to within a mile of batteries on Omaha, firing 250 rounds from her 14in guns, and many destroyer actions were fought against strong points. The first Americans ashore were Rangers who seized St Marcouf Island four miles off the coast, landing at 0430. This action was typical of a number of raids on the perimeter of the landings. These included parachute and glider operations which were made against particular batteries, bridges on the likely route of German reinforcements and other targets.

The worst conditions by far were on Omaha beach where the heavy surf on this piece of exposed coast caused the loss of many craft and DUKWs. On the left the thirty-two DD tanks launched 6,000yd from the beach suffered disastrous losses and only five got ashore. On the opposite flank the LCTs carried fifty-one DDs to the beach and only eight were knocked out or prevented from landing. In the steep short seas the minor craft were forced out of formation, but the British LCAs from the LSI *Empire Javelin* landed A Company of the rangers on the correct beach. The craft had come under fire 500yd from shore and over 60 per cent of this company, landing on the right (west) flank, were casualties within a short time. Other flotillas – mainly LCVPs – had trouble identifying their landing points because of heavy smoke from grass fires caused by the bombardment. Some troops sheltered behind beach obstacles and were caught by mortar fire, others attempting to cross the open beach were cut down by machine gun bursts. The beach became a killing ground. Supporting weapons in DUKWs did not get ashore as only five of the amphibians reached the beach between 0800 and 0900, leaving the assault waves pinned down with only light weapons.

Offshore the follow-up waves were baulked by obstacles now covered partially by the rising tide, for the cleared lanes to the beaches were choked with foundering craft. Then LCT No 30 crashed through the obstructions to get ashore, others followed, and the bottleneck was broken. The support ships came in to beef up the bombardment. At midday, when the defences showed signs of faltering under the renewed assault, the American regimental combat teams of 1 and 29 Divisions were able at last to get across the beaches, and by 1730 a beachhead was secured on Omaha.

Further west, Utah beaches were sheltered by the Contentin Peninsula but a breakdown in Landing Craft, Control led to one of the few navigational errors of the operation, when the assault wave was landed at the wrong points, although fortunately these turned out to be less heavily defended than the intended beaching areas. The landings ran more or less to schedule after the DD tanks were carried to within 3,000yd of the beach before launching. The state of the tide helped, as clearance parties could get at beach obstacles, and by 1800 over 31,000 men with 1,742 vehicles were ashore.

Naval losses were not as heavy as expected during the approach and bombardment; overall, the British lost an LCI(L) and the Norwegians their destroyer *Svenner* when three German E-boats attacked the Sword force. The American destroyer USS *Corry*, four landing craft and a patrol vessel were sunk, probably by mines. On the beaches, however, losses of landing craft were higher than expected, the British alone losing 258 craft.

Allied casualties were 10,300 in the landings and air operations, which were modest – if any casualty can be so described – by comparison with the one-in-three casualties among marines in the much smaller but more bloody landings on Tarawa in the Pacific during the previous November (1943).

Examples of headquarters ships and control craft

AMERICAN AMPHIBIOUS FORCE COMMAND SHIP (AGC No 7 USS *Mount McKinley*, one of nine AGCs (eight commissioned 1944, one 1945), 7,234 short tons displacement unloaded) *Hull:* Maritime Commission type C2-S-AJ1 Length 459ft, beam 63ft *Draught:* 24ft max *Accommodation:* For commanders and staffs of amphibious force with 130 officers and 869 men on some AGCs *Equipment:* (see text) included multipurpose radar, communications radios, etc and operations rooms *Engines (three shafts):* Geared steam turbines giving 15½ knots *Range:* Over 5,000 miles *Armament:* Two 5in, twelve 40mm *Note:* Four other AGCs built in C2-S-B1 hulls, one in converted transport of approx 10,000 short tons and one in seaplane tender of 1,710 short tons.

AMERICAN LANDING CRAFT, CONTROL MK1 *Hull:* steel Length 56ft, beam 13ft 7in *Displacement:* 30 short tons *Draught:* 47½in max *Equipment:* SO radar with VPR scope, two echo sounders, odograph, underwater sound location gear, radio direction unit, two TCS-type radios, two FM radios (all radios transmitter/receivers) and gyro compass *Crew:* 14 *Engines (twin props):* Two 225hp diesels giving 13½ knots max *Range:* On 550 US gallons, 240 miles at 13½ knots or 500 miles at 10 knots *Armour:* ¼in STS to bridge and gun cockpits *Armament:* Three twin ·50in machine guns on ring mounts; smoke pots *Note:* The Mk2 had improved equipment but only two twin ·50in machine guns.

BRITISH LANDING CRAFT, NAVIGATION *Hull:* LCVP with superstructure to provide covered wireless room/control position and an engine room *Equipment:* BO13 Radar antennae (on strut-supported bipod mast aft – this could be lowered to stow on deckhouse cradle), WS Radar, Loran or Decca navigation receiver that could fix craft's position, echo sounder, and reel of nine *miles* of wire for 'taut wire' measurements *Crew:* 9(?).

8 SURVEY AND BEACH WORK

Intelligence

Two years of planning and intelligence work were needed to launch the Normandy invasion armada, and earlier reconnaissance began in 1940 when commandos landed on French beaches after coming inshore in canoes. These men and later the British combined operations pilotage parties with the SAS Boat Section (who also carried out sabotage raids) were looking for underwater rock ledges, shingle banks and natural obstructions as well as enemy obstacles. They collected sand and other samples for analysis and determination of a shore's capacity to carry heavy vehicles and/or the types of roadway that would be needed. Some landed with crude but effective measuring instruments like the spiked shooting stick on which a RNVR sub-lieutenant sat to assess the sands' firmness below the surface. From this and more sophisticated measurements the conditions and topography of the shore and its hinterland would be carefully studied, for an 'ideal landing' beach in aerial photographs could prove less practical on site inspection.

Photographs provided data on likely defences, wave heights in particular conditions of wind and tide, and other information, though the impression of low-lying strong points given in such panoramas were deceptive and might not reveal that these positions could have commanding height over the shoreline. Nor did aerial photographs always show, even to highly trained interpreters, the extent of enemy defences. At Manus Island (200 miles north of New Guinea in the Admiralty Group) during the winter of 1943–4 the Japanese commander had enforced a rigid security against telltale signs of defences. There were no paths to latrines, no washing on lines or other indications of a troop concentration, and American planes were not fired on, but American Intelligence nevertheless estimated that there were 4,000 troops on the island. At Iwo Jima there were unseen gun emplacements, revealed only when they fired on Underwater Demolition Teams working inshore on D-1. With these UDTs were reconnaissance companies of twenty men and an officer from each assault division, and observers from B Company, Amphibious Reconnaissance Battalion. These men swam inshore to get firsthand knowledge of landing points, then reported back to regiment and battalion commanders on the conditions to expect, a tradition that went back to the patrols of mixed army, marine and navy personnel with LCRs who might spend three weeks ashore reconnoitring islands in the earlier Pacific campaigns. Six-man patrols could learn a good deal, as they did before the Vella Lavella landings (August 1942), and in those areas where the Japanese were thin on the ground a backup team of twenty-five men could be landed a week before the operation to mark out channels and beaching points. In similar operations in Burma during the 1945 ambush war among the mangrove swamps 500 miles south of Akyab, Royal Navy and Marine Pilotage Parties with army and RAF support scouted ahead of the advancing Fourteenth Army.

More extensive use of air reconnaissance became possible after 1943 when the Americans had air supremacy in the Pacific. Air observers, flying from carriers, reported on targets and tactical progress, a technique first used by 4 US Marine Division in the Gilbert Islands during January 1944. Despite some initial naval objections to the divisions' officers flying off carriers, the scheme worked well, the observers flying low over the assault areas. A similar technique was used at Normandy when Spitfire and Mustang pilots, working in pairs (one plane spotting, the other protecting the observer), covered the fifty-mile front with 104 aircraft finding targets and reporting on the progress of the assault.

Information before and during landings was of course vital to commanders, and, from the hydrographic data collected by submarines to the radioed reports of forward company commanders in an assault, all had to be sifted and brought to the right command for action, a major task of the headquarters and AGC ships.

Beach location

Before the war the ISTDC experimented with infra-red beams from the control ships along which craft could be guided towards a target beach, each flotilla officer observing the beams with special binoculars, but the idea was abandoned, apparently because there could be navigation errors by a control ship, in favour of the more certain though more risky method of sending in scout boats. With the advent of radar the control ships could give much the same guidance as the original beam provided, as long as they could keep in radio contact with flotilla leaders. The Decca navigation system and new radar control techniques were first used by the Royal Navy at Normandy, and since 1943 radar had been used by control destroyers to follow crafts' passage inshore. They still had the guidance of lead (landing) lights and daytime markers in all major operations, however.

On 6 June 1944 two midget submarines, X20 and X23, showed their green lights to seaward on the limits of the landing zones. They had lain submerged with their five-man crews for most of their three-day wait off the beaches, then at 0500 their lights were shown from the correct positions.

Beach location parties made overland trips in New Guinea to place beacons, and the underwater demolition teams placed markers for daylight landings. These methods might suggest to some yachtsmen that landing craft officers and coxswains were not good navigators, but the featureless, flat coasts of North Africa, for example, made inshore pilotage tricky, and landing craft could not move as much as a cable or two to attempt to identify a coastal feature without fouling up someone else's approach run.

Clearing underwater obstacles

The British Clearance Divers and American Underwater Demolition Teams did much the same work. Coming close inshore hours or perhaps a day before an assault, landing craft dropped these swimmers tens of yards from the obstacles. British teams had wet-suits and 'air' tanks but American teams used snorkels, on occasions working in swimming-trunks and flippers, with the long diver's knife their only personal weapon underwater. They also wore light lace-up boots with thin rough soles to protect their feet from the coral, and a silver body-paint on the chest helped recovery crews to spot a swimmer in distress as well as assisting members of a team to find each other. After swimming to the first line of obstacles the clearance divers defused mines and prepared demolition charges to knock flat the wood or metal obstructions. They might then check the seabed for rock ledges, coral pillars and craters from past bombing if such survey work had not already been done.

British LCOCUs (Landing Craft Obstruction Clearance Units) were used to clear obstacles, working mainly when the tide was out, thus exposing mines and shells clamped to German obstructions. Recruited from Royal Navy and Royal Engineers, with Royal Marine Engineers forming LCOCU Nos 7–12, each of these commando teams had twenty-five men and an officer. Two LCOCUs cleared 2,400 obstacles in three days on the Normandy beaches. All obstruction clearance parties aimed initially to create a clear lane ashore to the landing berths, and in the Pacific this became an essential part of the 1945 landings.

Twenty-one American UDTs, each with five to twelve men and an officer, were trained at Camp Perry, Florida, which was opened on 1 June 1943 by the navy CBs and later taken over by Amphibious Operations Command. The average age of the enlisted men in these teams was $21\frac{1}{4}$ and of their officers 24 years. Supremely fit after expert training, they were taken with their LCP landing craft by APDs to the assault area. There, at Okinawa for example, the LCP(R)s with inflatable LCRs lashed alongside as diving platforms took two teams further inshore, leaving 200yd or so for the swimmers to cover to the reef while the craft withdrew. The action was supported by gunboats – converted LCI(L)s – which could get close to the reef and pour heavy fire on to the enemy strong points. The swimmers worked systematically despite enemy snipers and roar of their own ships' quick-firing cannons, and always at risk of being killed by underwater explosions or being run down by their craft. One man worked along the reef to record water depths, coral heads and pothole locations, making notes on a sand-blasted plastic 'slate'. Two other men swam out to check depths on the seaward side of the reef. The three of them might take an hour or more to collect data on 200yd of reef, the full team covering three such stretches.

After the survey the men swam back to be picked up by the LCP(R)s and might then – as the teams did at Okinawa – go back inshore with packs of Tetrytol. In 2½lb blocks, this explosive had a greater shattering effect than the 2lb blocks of TNT they used at other times, or their C-2 plastic explosives. A block of Tetrytol was fixed by the swimmers to the base of each obstacle and a strip of instant fuse led up the post or obstacle support. The tie-in fuse strips were then connected by a trunk line of fuse laid by other swimmers who connected up the 400 or so obstacles in a 400yd stretch prepared for demolition. As this line might be in water only sixty-five yards from enemy pillboxes the work was not only cold but incredibly dangerous. While other swimmers might buoy shoals and mark channels, at Iwo Jima two men swam to the shore itself to collect sand samples.

After laying the charges and markers the men swam back to their craft which picked them up at speed. Crewmen in the inflatables secured to LCPs, used a special armhold to snatch each swimmer from the water. Once the swimmers were clear of the obstacles, the charges were blown and the three LCP(R)s carrying two teams withdrew from the beach area. These small craft, in addition to their normal crews, each carried two radio operators, though an LSM of over 500 tons carried only one radioman. Also in the UDT craft were two lifesaver swimmers, a pharmacist's mate and reserve divers.

The Americans tried out radio-controlled explosive boats to destroy underwater obstacles in the south of France (August 1944) and elsewhere but apparently without satisfactory results. In New

Britain, Australian army engineers cleared a sixty-foot gap in anti-boat obstacles at Linkas (August 1945) while their artillery on Sandau shelled the beach defences. Many other jobs in clearing underwater mines and demolition obstructions along the French Channel coast and the Far East ports were tackled by Royal Navy clearance divers – the frogmen – and American UDTs, sometimes called 'webbed feet', a name used also for US Special Engineer Brigades in general.

Anti-tank obstacles and shore mines

Assault engineers landed a few minutes before the first wave of infantry and relied on DD tanks or the amphibious gunned tractors, LVT(Armoured), for protection during the first few minutes in action when – as happened to 5 Assault Regiment RE, at Normandy – they could also be caught by a shortfall of shot from the army's self-propelled guns firing from incoming LCTs, or other support fire. The Royal Engineers used assault vehicles with crews of six, twenty AVREs to a squadron and four squadrons to an assault regiment, RE. These regiments, when landing at Normandy, had to be self-sufficient in many ways and their B Echelon supply trucks were not scheduled to come ashore until five weeks after the landing. Their A vehicles – the fighting units – were specially adapted tanks which included: Petards – Churchill tanks with large spigot mortars (*Pl 30 and 31*) firing 40lb bombs to breach concrete strong points; the Fascine, with its chestnut paling bundles; and road-making tanks, some of which improvised roads by laying a continuous strip of 'matting' from large rolls, while others had bridge sections they could lower over wide ditches. With the AVREs at Normandy were squadrons from the Welsh and 22 Dragoons with Flail tanks – Scorpions. These were Shermans with flailing chains ('crabs') to explode mines ahead of the tanks.

The British RE assault engineers and their counterparts in the US army's Special Engineer Brigades and navy CBs also made expert use of bulldozers with armour plated blades. The first bulldozer out of an LST at the Empress Augusta Bay landings ob-

Plate 30 Spigot-type Petard 40lb bombs with vacuum (Piat-type) heads drawing blast 'into' concrete or other protection of enemy strong points

literated a Japanese strong point by burying it under a mound of earth. Less startling but almost equally dangerous work was done by bulldozer drivers in improving landing points for craft to off-load more easily. On occasions – at Guam, for example – eighteen CBs and an officer used a bulldozer landed at H − 4 minutes to help moor incoming craft against the reef, then unloaded fifty LCMs and five LCTs in nine hours, plotting a track waist-deep from the reef to the shore for LVTs and tanks. Establishing such 'safe'

Plate 31 Churchill tank AVRE (79 Squadron, Royal Engineers) equipped with Fort Buster spigot mortar for Petard bombs

routes could entail clearing minefields not only of anti-tank but also anti-personnel mines with their nasty trick of throwing up explosive canisters to spray ball-bearings waist-high among the engineers. Wire was cleared with perhaps a 'Bangalore torpedo' drainpipe length of explosive. Every stretch of cleared pathway had to be taped along the edges as a guide for infantry and tanks.

Beach organisation

With the army, marine and naval personnel ashore some overal direction was essential. The British used a system of Beach Masters, naval lieutenants landed with naval commando signallers and a small shore party who could direct incoming craft (*Pl 32*) and set up a central point to clear information. The parties came ashore with the assault wave and were in radio contact with the headquarters ships as well as major craft coming in. Within four hours of these initial landings an army beach 'brick' of 2,000 men was established ashore to handle stores, improve roads and set up all those vital backup services essential in keeping armies in action. The American organisation was on similar lines, with elements of the Engineer Special Brigades joined by naval Beach Battalions (after the spring of 1943) to handle these supply services. They also provided the DUKWs for much of the ferry work but this and other duties of the beach parties were passed to the US army's ordnance and land supply echelons within a few days of a landing.

Communications in the Pacific after the middle of 1943 were the responsibility of Joint Assault Signal Companies (JASCOs) with their beach party communication teams, shore fire control parties and air liaison parties, all landed early if not with the assault waves. Other work in any landing, after the initial beachhead was established, followed familiar routines of setting up supply dumps, improving roadways and handling stores. The bulldozers could now clear off scrub and build earth quays. Marston matting designed for airstrips came ashore in fifty-foot concertina packs weighing 325lb, with seven packs to a skid towed by tracked LVTs.

Plate 32 Beach Master's shore party calling in craft to landing points (Sicily, 10 July 1944); note loudhailer and flags, often a more direct means of communication than radio

Working in teams of a dozen or so, engineers laid these 14in strips of metal mesh, picketing down the edges and/or covering the strips with sand to form a roadway. Others put up signposts to dumps, and manhandled stores.

Beach ports

The supplies to be landed for the British Second Army in Normandy during the week to D +7 required sixty ships for which the logistics of loading were worked out along with other supply details by a RASC 'top' team. A sales manager, a senior civil servant, a newspaper publisher and a chartered accountant in civilian life, the men in this team typified the sort of administrators who did excellent staff work throughout the Allied combined operations commands. In June 1943 a 24-hour ration of dehydrated food, matches, cigarettes and toilet paper was devised in a water- and gas-proof pack. Five million were used and fifteen million held in store in New York in case the English ports were devastated by 'doodlebug' flying bombs or rockets. Rations which could have fed the whole of the UK for two days, a million 'tommy cookers' and the same number of water-sterilization kits were procured, and 32-day rations in 2-, 3- and 5-man packs provided to fit lockers in tanks and other AFVs. These were just a few of the stores required for D-Day. Landing craft crews and cargo personnel had to be fed; on the LCI(S)s this meant daily deliveries from D −4 but other craft and ships could carry at least forty-eight hours' rations for their cargo personnel and some were victualled for feeding prisoners they would bring back from the beaches. Food rations for French civilians were landed; ashore, eight field bakeries each with a daily output of 29,000lb, seventeen smaller mobile field bakeries and fourteen butchery cold-stores were deployed.

To land these supplies and a great deal of heavy equipment the Allies needed a port, and as they were unlikely to capture one undamaged two Mulberry harbours were prefabricated in England and floated to Normandy. The American A Mulberry off the western beaches, and the British B Mulberry off Arromanches in

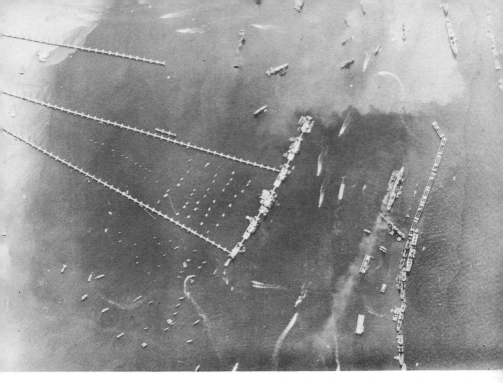

Plate 33   Mulberry harbour with roadways to floating piers and concrete caissons as first offshore breakwater

the eastern sector, arrived on D +3, 9 June. Plate 33 gives an aerial view. At the seaward side there was a floating breakwater of steel 'Bombardons' each weighing 1,000–1,500 tons, ninety-three being used altogether outside both harbour areas. Inshore of the floating caissons were, first, a line of specially prepared and scuttled old warships, and thirty freighter blockships which formed five 'gooseberry' breakwater shelters, added because the navy doubted if the bombardons would be effective in their positions half a mile from the shore. The harbour itself was formed by an inshore breakwater of 'Phoenix' concrete caissons; 167 of these 1,600–5,780-ton monsters, some as high as a five-storey house, were positioned and sunk. Protected inshore of these were pier-heads (*Pl 34*) and floating piers (collectively called 'whales') which could move into position under their own power and lower legs to the seabed. On these 'spuds' the pierheads could be raised

Plate 34 Seven pierhead 'whales' forming one wharf of Mulberry; the tops of the 'spud' legs on which the pier floated can be clearly seen rising above the wharf's roadway

and lowered as the tide flooded or ebbed. Some whales had 100-ton Baker floating 'dolphins' extending seaward and all were linked to the beach by floating roadways – ten miles altogether (with innumerable pontoons) to carry vehicles. Cargo ships and LSTs could come alongside the piers or were discharged on to 'rhino' ferries. One of these 175ft × 45ft raft pontoons could be locked to an LST's ramp for loading and was then pushed (by the rhino's own detachable tug-unit) to the piers. The Mulberry harbours took only six months to build but absorbed five per cent of the Admiralty's and Ministry of Supply's total output during the first half of 1944. Towing them across the Channel was a demanding job, needing 10,000 men and 160 tugs to handle some 400 different units in the breakwaters and harbours. This does not include men laying the underwater petrol pipe line 'Pluto' from the UK to the beaches and beyond.

The American Mulberry was off the St Laurent on Omaha beach and the gooseberry breakwaters were in place by D +2 for the LCI(L)s' and LCTs' protection, but German shelling delayed the completion of these breakwaters until 11 June (D +5) off Utah beaches.

On 19 June a gale blew up, gusting to forty knots, and at least 800 craft were driven ashore, as were some floating bombardons. Floating roadways were smashed and the ferry service from the UK suspended, but on 21 June fourteen LSTs beached in a Force 6 gale, unloaded and got off safely. During the next week repair squads brought over from the UK made good most of the damage.

Less elaborate, but serving much the same purpose, were the pontoon piers and jetties assembled by US naval CBs and army pioneers in the Pacific. These pontoons were brought in on LSTs, but as soon as possible in the island landings all construction work was brought under a single command ashore to speed the building of airstrips, PT-boat bases and other installations. The main supplies for the amphibian forces were carried in the fleet trains serving as mobile bases: thirty days' fuel supply for the fleet; medicine for 20,000 men; three units-of-fire in ammunition for anti-aircraft guns, stores and sufficient fuel to supply the amphibious force for fifteen days.

9 AMPHIBIANS

The pros and cons

There were – and are – obvious advantages in being able to carry men straight from the LSIs and APAs across the shore to the perimeter of a beachhead without exposing them to small-arms fire and mortar bomb fragments. Mention has been made of the Japanese and German amphibious tanks and the Allied DD tanks: there were a number of technical problems to overcome before such vehicles could be used in any number, not least of which was their slow speed on water, exposing them to enemy anti-boat gunfire. Amphibious lorries for ferry work offered equally great advantage in handling stores without transhipment in the later stages of a landing, however, and did not usually run the risks of direct fire from enemy positions.

SEAGOING LORRIES

The DUKW

The D = model year, the U = amphibian, the K = all-wheel drive and the W = dual rear axle: the DUKW (*Pl 35*), pronounced 'duck', was a 2½-short-ton lorry with 6-wheel drive, a boat's hull, rudder and propeller (*Fig 17*). Designed in conjunction with Sparkman & Stevens, the naval architects, it was built around a General Motors truck chassis and the final design was standardised in October 1942. On land its topsides were nearly six feet from the roadway; at sea it could have as little as eighteen inches freeboard. Despite these drawbacks in each of its environments, there were apparently never enough DUKWs to go round although over 21,000 were built by the summer of 1945. The first DUKW trials had been made three years earlier by Engineer Special Brigades at Cape Cod and the British ordered 2,000 in January 1943, sufficient numbers being supplied by the following July for their first operational use in the Sicily landings. Shepherded by a motor launch, 300 of them 'were most successful' in ferrying supplies across the Strait of Messina, and at Salerno the US army's 105mm howitzers were brought ashore in DUKWs to be in action far sooner than if transhipped from landing craft. But the naval commander felt the vehicles' full value could not be exploited here because 'they diverted to Army use at such an early stage'.

Such thinking may have delayed their use in the naval-dominated commands of the Pacific, for they did not appear in numbers in this theatre until January 1944 when sixty DUKWs landed army howitzers and forty landed stores. In this operation, at Roi and Namur in the Marshall Islands, the DUKWs were carried on LST upper decks and driven down an inside ramp to the tank deck for launching over the bow ramp while the LSTs were still

Plate 35 The amphibious DUKW, a bulky but useful land vehicle, is shown here on the steel-mesh road of the Sicily beachhead

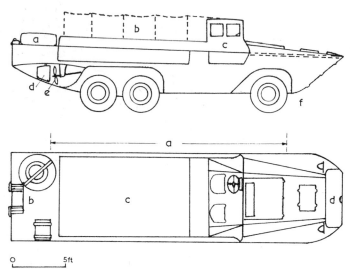

Fig 17 Amphibious truck – DUKW (*Above*) Profile (a) spare
wheel (b) portable canvas cover (c) collapsible hood (d) rudder
(e) prop (f) ground clearance 18½in loaded (*Below*) Plan (a)
spacing for lifting, 21ft 3¾in (b) roller (c) cargo space 12ft 6in × 6ft
9¾in (d) hinged plate could be raised as breakwater

offshore. The DUKWs landed their cargoes of guns, hoisting these
out with A-frames and tackle fitted to some vehicles which backed
against others for unloading. These then returned for stores – two
cargo nets or pre-palletted loads per DUKW – in bulk from the
LSTs. At other times DUKWs yoked in pairs by a removable
platform could carry light vehicles ashore. Marshalling them – the
RASC used motorboats and the Americans LCVPs – was particularly difficult in rough weather when many DUKWs were
lost, but ashore their large wheels could negotiate rough terrain
although some, like many other vehicles, needed bulldozers' help
in the volcanic sands of Iwo Jima.

Although not designed as fighting vehicles, two of the first
DUKWs in the Pacific were adapted by US army engineers to
carry 120 4½in rockets with an 1,100yd range. These were then
fired to cover landing troops to within 150yd of Arawe beaches
(New Britain – December 1943). RASC, US army and/or marine

DUKW companies took part in all major landings after 1943 and many river crossings – XXX Corps's RASC DUKWs lifted many Arnhem paratroopers to safety back across the Rhine. The vehicles were complicated to maintain and the two US army and one marine DUKW companies at Iwo Jima had to have 200 spare shafts and propellers urgently flown from Hawaii before that operation. Although some DUKWs were carried in transports' davits on a few operations, it was the close link between LSTs and all Allied amphibians which made possible the vehicles' use in great numbers.

There were several other Allied wheeled amphibians, included in the following outline specifications.

DUKW SPECIFICATION (US vehicle, 2½-ton, 6-wheel drive amphibious truck) *Dimensions:* 31ft × 8ft   *Weight (loaded):* 18,600lb   *Loads carried:* 25 troops, or 12 stretchers, or 5,000lb (but loads limited to under 5,000lb in rough seas)   *Crew:* 2 (although one driver handled vehicle when necessary)   *Engine:* 6-cylinder; max land speed 50mph, and 5½ knots in calm water   *Range:* Ashore, 400 miles at 35mph   *Armour and Armament:* Not normally fitted (but see text).

AMPHIBIOUS JEEP SPECIFICATION (US vehicle, Ford jeep with flotation body and propeller) *Dimensions:* 15ft 7in × 5ft 4in   *Load carried:* Up to 800lb   *Crew:* 1   *Max speeds:* 50mph on land and 4·7 knots in calm water.   Design standardised in Sept 1942; over 5,000 built by mid-1945.

TERRAPIN MKI SPECIFICATION (British vehicle, 4-ton, 8-wheel drive Morris Commercial with Thornycroft-designed flotation hull and prop) *Dimensions:* 23ft × 8ft 9in; height with cab screens down, 8ft 3in   *Weight:* 37,682lb   *Loads carried:* In two holds fwd and aft of central cab, total of 4 tons   *Engines:* Two Ford V8s   Approx 500 built; handling reputedly not as good as DUKW; feature of MkI was front pair of wheels suspended above ground level.

TERRAPIN MK2 SPECIFICATION (British vehicle, 5-ton, 8-wheel drive improved Mk1) *Dimensions:* 30ft 8in × 8ft 10in, waterline 15ft 3in *Loads carried:* Up to 11,200lb in single hold behind fwd cab   Only prototypes built, apparently.

GOSLING TRAILER SPECIFICATION (Hand trailer used by Royal Signals) *Dimensions:* 8ft × 3ft, height 3ft 9in *Weight:* 448lb *Engine:* Outboard, for use in calm water.

LANDING VEHICLE, TRACKED

Amphibious tractors
These amphibians, sometimes called amtracks or amphtracks, were developed from swamp buggies. Originally designed for rescue work in the Florida swamps, the tractors swam as their cleated tracks scooped water in a paddling action while their watertight hulls gave them buoyancy. Donald Roebling of Florida built a private venture prototype of one of these rescue vehicles in 1935, and after many trials and much development work by Roebling and a design team from the Food Machinery Corporation the design was adapted for military use and 200 (as LVT Mk1) were ordered from FMC. The first of the production models was

Plate 36   Early LVT with gunners exposed in forward positions; the track blades can be seen as they move forward to begin paddling action

built in July 1941, the Florida and California plants of FMC completing 11,251 LVTs by the end of the war. Several designs were evolved, but early marks (*Pl 36*) did not have a ramp, exposing troops coming over the sides and making stores and guns difficult to offload.

One of the first LVT actions was fought by five Alligator LVT Mk1s from 3 Platoon, A Company, 2 Amphibious Tractor Battalion of the US marines. In the first wave ashore in the Marine Corps, landings at Tulgai, they beached at 0900 on 7 August 1942, only eight months after the Japanese raid on Pearl Harbour, the battalion's LVTs starting a history of unique operations by amphibians. One of the LVTs, without armour plating, used the fire from its single ·30in and ·50in machine guns to destroy an enemy strong point while protecting wounded infantry before evacuating them to an LST offshore, one of several techniques developed rapidly from the battalion's success in this landing.

Armour was added for the Mk2 of larger dimensions (*Fig 18*), the Water Buffalo, still without a ramp. Over 4,000 Mk1s and 2s were built, Borg Warner of Kalamazoo, the St Louis Car Company and Graham Paige Motor Corporation joining FMC in production. By 1943 the Mk3, with a ramp, was in full production (2,964 were built), but this LVT had a water-cooled engine and the final wartime design reverted to the basic Mk2 configuration with the air-cooled engine moved forward to behind the cab. As the Mk4, this had a stern ramp. Over 8,000 were built by August 1945.

Gilbert Island landings

On 20 November 1943 assaults were made on two islands in the Gilbert group. On Makin, an atoll base defended by only 800 Japanese, some of whom were construction pioneers, the landings were effected, 'the 50 LVT Mark 2s . . . clearing wire and knocking down apparently heavy obstacles . . . freeing stranded boats and recovering drowned vehicles' (Commander, 5 Amphibious Force). This report also stressed the need for LVTs with heavier armament. The defenders held out against 6,500 marines (1,500 more than would land at Tarawa) for three days, but on 23 November the

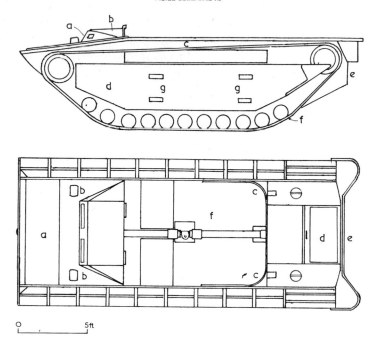

Fig 18 LVT Mk2 (*Above*) Profile (a) 20lb plate, cab front and sides (b) 10lb plate, cab top (c) 10lb plate, inboard of track (d) pontoon, 10lb plate (e) 10lb stern plate (f) track (cleats not shown) (g) steps (*Below*) Plan (a) 20lb bow plate (b) p and s lights (c) 10lb plate in hold (d) radiator grille (e) 10lb plate (f) hold 10ft 8in × 7ft 10in

island was secured, giving the Americans a base near the Marshall Islands.

The second landing on the same day was at Tarawa, a heavily defended atoll (*Fig 24*) some seventy-five miles south of Makin and one degree from the equator. Tarawa is roughly triangular, its east and south sides strips of many islets and the west side an almost continuous reef completing the boundaries of the atoll's lagoon. The Japanese had heavily fortified the two-mile-long, 800yd-wide Betio Island (nowhere more than 10 feet above sea level). At the south-west corner of the atoll, 4,800 Japanese, including the 6 and 7 Special Naval Landing Force and 3 Special Base Force, all units with many experienced troops, had prepared the defences. A double apron of barbed wire about seventy yards from the high water mark, mines, log walls, concrete blocks and other obstacles formed a barrier behind which were 13mm machine gun strong points and some 75mm anti-boat guns. On the reef around Betio, anti-tank and anti-personnel mines were laid along the shoreline. The defenders intended to knock out assault transports by fire from the 80mm coastal batteries. Any craft getting inshore would then be caught by the log walls along which enfilade fire could be brought from the beach strong points. There was no defence system inland but the ammunition dumps were in bombproof shelters, protected at least from the American bombs available, though if the 2,000lb 'daisy cutters' had been used as was at first suggested the results might have been devastating.

The bloody battle that ensued has, like the Dieppe raid, been criticised as an unnecessary operation, yet wars are not fought in the knowledge of hindsight or we might all have kept our heads down until the atom bomb was perfected. A New Zealander, with knowledge of the islands, Major F. L. G. Holland, had warned the amphibious force staff of the natural hazards in landing among the reefs and no doubt they took account of this in their planning. Whether or not these factors and other considerations should have led to a different strategy can be debated, but what is not in doubt is the value of lessons learnt at Tarawa which later saved many lives. For at some point in any campaign the attacker has to face and defeat enemy troops, since the occupation of territory can never be secure while the enemy has fighting armies in the field.

The preliminaries to Tarawa followed a now-familiar pattern: transports at the dropping zone at 0320 after a navigation error, so they had to be repositioned, delaying the launching of craft; at W-Hour, 0620, the naval bombardment opened on schedule although some counter battery fire had begun earlier when the transports were shelled; the bombardment lifted to allow an air strike against the defences. The air strike was late, allowing the Japanese a half-hour shoot at the transports before they were obscured by smoke covering the minesweepers clearing beach approaches. During this time the defending troops were also able to concentrate behind the target beaches.

At 0715 the destroyer USS *Pursuit* set the start line for the first wave of forty-two LVTs. They were now to beach at 0900, a quarter of an hour later than planned due to the delays in launching the LCVP from which troops were transferred to the amphibians. The first two assault teams were to land on palm-fringed beaches 500yd long either side of the island's jetty. In the second wave of twenty-four LVTs and in the twenty-one of the third wave was a reserve assault team. All fire from the bombarding warships stopped on schedule at 0854 but the LVTs, making little better than four knots, came under uninterrupted fire as they emerged from the minesweepers' smokescreen. A scout sniper platoon landed on the jetty, clearing it of riflemen who could have enfiladed the beaches. On the right beach the LVTs got ashore but only thirty-five were still operational and most of the LVTs' gunners had been killed. This left too few amtracs to go back for all the reserve company troops on the reef.

The craft bringing in further reinforcements grounded as far as 600yd from the beaches. Many marines were hit crossing these open shallows or were drowned by the rising tide as they waited for LVTs to get out and bring them ashore. A third of the 5,000 marines landing were casualties, but by nightfall two toeholds on the original 1,500yd front had been established, with one perimeter 150yd inland and the other 200yd inland. On D+1, artillery was landed on Bairiki Island to support the Betio advance and by D+2 the defenders were forced into the western corner of the island as the marines fought off three counterattacks. By D+3 organised resistance ceased although many bunkers had to be reduced by hand-placed TNT charges during the next few days as the sickly smell of death smothered the island.

The lessons of Tarawa

The first and most salutary lesson of Tarawa was the need for effective prelanding bombardment; only 2,400 tons of shells had been used. The second lesson was in the development of assault techniques: clearing obstacles so that LVTs were not forced into congested landing points; the use of infantry to locate targets for tanks; the need for heavier weapons in immediate support of the assault waves.

The use of heavier weapons in LVTs was under development some years before these landings and led to the marks of LVT (Armoured) detailed here. The firepower of ordinary LVTs was increased by multiple machine-gun mountings on some tractors. At Pelelieu, US 1 Marine Division tried out the navy's long-range flamethrower, newly developed in the autumn of 1944. The device – designated Mk1 – could throw a stream of napalm up to 150yd and was fitted in three LVTs with a backup amtrac, but the height of these tractors probably did not suit the weapon as well as the lower-profiled tanks to which it was subsequently fitted. The LVTs were needed to find safe routes for tanks crossing reef shallows or shore swamps, however.

The Royal Engineers' 5 Assault Regiment and other British units were equipped with Buffaloes (LVT Mk2s) for their action at Westkapelle in the Walcheren landings. They were joined by 11 Royal Tank Regiment, also equipped with LVTs, and with other amphibious British vehicle and tractor companies operated in river crossings in the liberation of north-west Europe.

LANDING VEHICLE, TRACKED(ARMOURED)

Fire support

The techniques of fire support were introduced to many US marines in the LVT(A)s of 4 Division who made their first assault as part of the January 1944 landings to 'capture and develop Kwajalein Atoll as a fleet anchorage and Roi and Kwajalein Islands as air bases' before Admiral Nimitz could extend his Central Pacific operations to other islands in the Marshalls. These covered 800sq miles of ocean, with thirty-two atolls and 867 reefs among some 2,000 tiny islands, none more than twenty feet high. A number of new methods were tried in these landings, including

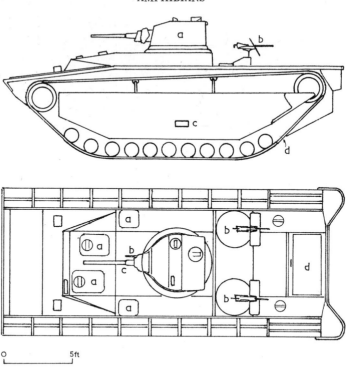

Fig 19 LVT(Armoured) – LVT(A) Mk1 (*Above*) Profile (a) 37mm gun turret (b) ·30in m/g (c) step (d) track (cleats not shown) (*Below*) Plan (a) hatches (b) ·30in m/g (c) 37mm gun (d) radiator

1 Joint Assault Signal Company with a shore fire party co-ordinating information for target and ranges to be used by fire support craft. These gunboats and the LVT(A)s carried heavy weapons and fired at strong points as the assault waves came in after the naval bombardment had moved to targets behind the beach. Support craft led the line of LVT(A)s until they were close inshore and then both forces usually moved to the flanks, allowing the assault engineers and infantry craft to land while – in theory at least – the close-support guns kept the enemy's heads down.

The idea of putting army guns in amphibious tractors was tried out in 1941 with a 37mm gun in a Ford Swamp Buggy and a 75mm gun in a Studebaker Swamp Buggy. From these experiments an LVT(A) Mk1 (*Fig 19*) was built with a 37mm field gun mounted coaxially with a ·30in machine gun in an armoured turret on an LVT Mk2 hull. This Mk1 LVT(A) (*Pl 37*) also had two single ·30in machine guns in ring mountings behind the turret and armour plate. The layout of this armoured amphibian allowed only a limited supply of ammunition, but 510 were built. A version of the armoured LVT Mk2 was designated the LVT(A) Mk2 although it did not carry a heavy gun, but only 450 were produced, and designs for a Mk3 on the Mk4 ordinary LVT's hull did not go into production.

The LVT(A) Mk4 reverted to the Mk1 tractor's hull design but carried an army M-8 75mm howitzer and single ·50in machine gun. The need for ammunition was met by using ordinary LVTs carrying reserves of shells, and the howitzer was able to fire in high trajectory at mortars on the reverse slopes of hills behind a beach. After the landing foothold was achieved, the LVT(A)s could be used ashore as a form of light tank although not able to match a true tank's performance. On land they had a maximum speed of 25mph and at sea could do 5·2 knots in calm water. By August 1945, 1,890 had been built, as they were accepted as an integral part of the landing forces, although the LSTs taking them to the beaches had to be convoyed under separate escort and their slow speed meant they were off the enemy coast some time before the main assault force. However, in the invasion landings of 1945 they proved invaluable, and by then the prebombardment of landing areas tended to reduce the element of surprise.

Landing preparations

The US 4 Marine Division's tractor and armoured amphibian battalions had 240 LVT Mk2s and 75 LVT(A) Mk1s when they sailed from San Diego for landings in the Marshalls that were typical of many operations mounted on a more limited scale than the invasion landings. The division created a tractor force in thirty days, underlining the urgency of battle preparations as the tractor battalions were expanded to these numbers. New recruits

Plate 37 LVT(Armoured) Mki with hatches open, showing 37mm M-6 gun in turret

replaced some men in 4 Amphibious Tractor Battalion and 1 Armoured Amphibian Battalion, then these trained soldiers with other recruits formed a new 10 Amphibious Tractor Battalion and later also A Company of 11 ATB. The old and new battalions had to train their recruits, armour the tractors and carry out weapon checks in a way typical of how amphibious forces were expanded in all units. Senior officers of these battalions also had to attend planning meetings with the artillery, however, but the CO of the armoured amphibians was unable to get detailed landing plans or the prearranged radio frequencies for the forces to land at Roi and Kwajalein. The overall plans were being made in the central Pacific and had been started seven weeks before the Tarawa landings in the Gilberts, since planning in September (1943) for a 31 January landing gave all too little time when forces have to be brought 5,000 miles by sea to the action. Yet the momentum of the thrust must be maintained in any campaign if the enemy is not to recover his balance. The CO of 1 Armoured Amphibian

Battalion was no doubt well aware of the need to keep up the momentum, but his companies would be attached to various infantry battalions without adequate direct links to his command. The amphibians were combat-loaded in LSTs, another job for the overworked battalions before they sailed early in January.

Landings in the Marshall Islands

The close co-operation between LST and amphibians' crews was unfortunately soured during a practice landing when the LSTs went 'by the book'. They refused to refuel any LVT that was not from their ship and one LST ran down an amphibian. The bad feeling carried over into the actual operation but in time the relationships were to settle down and marine and navy crews worked well together. Perhaps some friction could be expected in such a complex force for V Amphibious Corps was part of an armada of craft ranging from battleships to coasters (later the Fifth Fleet) under Admiral Nimitz. For the landings in the Marshalls the troop-carrying naval force had three divisions, each lifting a battalion landing team with support elements and headquarters personnel. Three transports carried the assault troops of each battalion, a fourth transport carried the support and headquarters troops, and a cargo ship carried the battalion's supplies. The transport divisions were to link up with the LSTs and other craft in the operation which carried divisional artillery (105mm guns with ammunition preloaded in fourteen LCMs). The craft were themselves carried to the dropping zone in one LSD. The 75mm pack howitzers were preloaded in LVT Mk2s carried on LSTs. The armour was divided, with thirty-six light tanks in the APA transports and fifteen medium tanks each in an LCM on a second LSD.

The landings took place in two separate operations timed to coincide on the morning of 31 January 1944. In the north the objective was the islands of Roi and Namur, and in the south it was the islands forming the south east corner of Kwajalein Atoll. Both landings were in areas with several small islands that could be used as fire bases, for artillery on one to support an assault on the next. Although both initial landings met relatively light resistance, 196 marines were killed and 550 wounded before the northern objectives were taken, and the southern assault force lost 177 killed and 1,000 were injured. Some 8,000 Japanese troops were killed. In tracing the LVT and LVT(A)s' part in these landings, the lack of time for adequate training shows up, but with experience the amphibians' crews were to form some of the finest units in combined operations.

The assault companies of marines in the northern operations had an 0330 reveille for breakfast of 'battery acid' fruit juice, cold meat and coffee before boarding their LCVPs from the transports. There was a 19-knot easterly breeze and choppy sea as they moved to tranship to the amphibians. Once aboard the LVTs there were delays because in these conditions the amtracs could only make two knots, so the landings on Mellu and Ennuebing Islets were postponed from the planned 0900 hours. Air strikes went in on schedule, however, against Roi and Namur 8,000yd to the north, while 4 Division's air observer, flying below a 1,000ft cloud ceiling, reported no signs of the enemy on the marine's immediate target islands. The news of the postponement of H-Hour to 0930 did not reach B and D Companies of 1 AAB before they followed the leading line of LCI gunboats across the start line set by the destroyer USS *Phelps*. There were only twenty-five defenders, and after an LVT had capsized in the surf more sheltered beaches were found on the lagoon side of the islands.

Ennuebing was secured by 1042 hours and Mellu by 1125. Four further assaults were made that afternoon when the *Phelps* was intended to set each start line, but she moved inside the ring of islands to support the gunboats for which she acted as control ship, and some aspects of the overall control communications broke down. Despite this and some poor discipline among LVT crews landing artillery, a job they botched, all four little islands – Obella, Ennubir, Ennuennet and Ennugarret – were taken between 1515 and 1915 hours. The LSTs were then to pick up their amphibians and take them inside the inverted V of islands with Roi and Namur forming the northern apex, the largest islands, each some 1,000yd in diameter, joined by a causeway. But before the LSTs completed this manoeuvre, six amphibians were lost because individual LST skippers refused to take aboard other ships' LVTs. A further seventeen of these had been lost during the day through damage on coral pillars, faulty bilge pumps or being swamped in the surf. Next day, 1 February, landings were made on Roi and Namur with support from artillery on islands captured the previous afternoon, the nearest to Roi being under 1,000yd from the final objective. The landings met little resistance, fortunately, as they came in piecemeal with 500 LVT and craft crews milling around on the lagoon in rough weather.

The bombardment had stunned the defenders in their sixty-five pillboxes and eight or so larger blockhouses, neutralising the six mobile guns, but 300 Japanese away from the beaches later fought the assault troops from 23 RCT, although most of the marine and Japanese casualties were caused by the explosion of an ammunition dump being demolished by US army engineers.

The southern force on 1 January used major support craft rather than LVT(A)s though the LVT machine-gunners and later 37mm artillery (landed in DUKWs) supported the infantry. Three small islands were secured – Gea by 1310, Ennylabegan by 1310, and Enubuj by 1210 hours – after landings touched down at 0915 on all of them. Only the Enubuj landing included LVT(A)s. On the same day, over 100 miles to the east of Kwajalein, Majuro Atoll was occupied, its solitary Japanese postmaster, the only Imperial presence, highlighting the impossibility of defending so many islands without complete command of the sea and air.

Admiral Nimitz's first objective in the Marshalls had been achieved and he was now able to move on Eniwetok, a major island in the north-west corner of the group and potential base for later operations against the Marianas, 600 miles WNW. He used it to bypass Truk Island, a large Japanese base to the south-west of the Marshalls once described as 'the Gibraltar of the Pacific' though not in fact as well defended as the Allies believed it to be. As carrier aircraft were still too few to support major landings, these stepping stones for airfields were necessary in the thrusts towards Japan. On 18 February, within three weeks of securing Roi and Namur, V Amphibious Corps landed at Engebi and Eniwetok; the first gave little opposition but at Eniwetok the Japanese in well-camouflaged foxholes and trenches put up stiff resistance. They counterattacked the marines and brought down heavy mortar fire on the beachheads, but the pre-landing bombardment, with UDT clearance and survey of beaches, had enabled the marines to land quickly and establish a beachhead. By D+3 the island was secured, and the lessons of Tarawa proved in practice.

The Fifth Amphibious Corps – 2 and 4 Marine Divisions with the army's XIV Corps artillery – sailed from Eniwetok in early June to seize Saipan and Tinian (*Fig 24*) in the Marianas and break the Japanese inner ring of defended islands. At Saipan on 15 June over 8,000 men were landed in twenty minutes on eight beaches along a four-mile front. The islands in the Marianas were very much larger than those in the Marshalls and the period of assaults on sizeable if limited land areas had begun. Here, rocket-firing aircraft were first used in covering the landings but had less effect than was expected against well-camouflaged defenders who, despite the speed of the initial landings, were able to bring heavy fire down on the fourth assault waves from fifty or so field guns undiscovered in pre-assault reconnaissance. The Japanese Command had allowed aircraft from these islands to be diverted as reinforcements for the New Guinea defences, and American air support was therefore unhampered at least in the early stages of the battle. On 22 July napalm was dropped for the first time in Pacific air attacks but was not very effective until later in the war. The battle for Saipan lasted six weeks, during which a Japanese seaborne counterattack was routed when most of their barges were sunk and 'banzai' suicide attacks by their infantry were repulsed.

The islands were not considered secure until 10 August, but before then – on 24 July – the marines had landed on Tinian. There is a five-mile channel separating Tinian from Saipan, so the landings could be covered by artillery from Saipan. The ledges on the reefs would have blocked the amphibians if two vehicles had not been specially equipped, however. I-section girders were carried on each side of the tractors and positioned at an angle to form the supports for a ramp to the reef top. Attached to each pair of girders were eighteen baulks of timber joined almost edge-to-edge and laid across the LVTs. When the girders were secured in position the vehicle backed, allowing these timbers to fall and thus forming a 25ft ramp that could carry a 35-ton tank. Pre-loaded lorries were ferried across the channel and the island secured by 1 August, but here and on Saipan a further three months of mopping up was needed to overcome isolated resistance.

On 21 July III Amphibious Corps had come up from Guadal-canal in the Solomons to land on Guam (*Fig 24*), an island in the Marianas some seventy miles south-west of Tinian. This force had 180 LVTs of 3 Amphibious Battalion and 178 LVTs of 4 ATB, as well as III Army Corps's Motor Transport Battalion with sixty DUKWs assigned to 3 Marine Division and forty DUKWs (C Company) supporting 1 Provisional Marine Brigade. *Figure 2* shows the deployment of some of these amphibians in the assault. The transports, protected by Task Force 53, had been at sea four weeks and their landings were further delayed by three days because of naval and other commitments in the Saipan area. The landings were made after one of the longest bombardments of the war: for a week the 19,000 Japanese defenders were under more or less constant bombing and shelling. Four days before the landings, UDTs 3, 4 and 6 first reconnoitred the landing beaches and then, after these night operations, worked under smoke cover and support-gunships' fire to clear some of the most difficult obstructions found in the Pacific. Off Agat beach in the south were palm log cribs filled with coral and joined by cables; in the north – Asan beach – 4cu ft cages of coral were cemented in blocks. Nearly 1,000 of these cribs and cages were cleared before the landings.

The beach areas offered some natural defensive features; Agat beach was overlooked by cliffs and Asan by a semicircle of hills.

Both had good gun positions which the Japanese exploited despite the bombardment. The south and north assault forces' amphibians were launched at about 0600 and 'disintegrated into waves behind their LCI(G)s and LVT(A)s'. There were nine LCI(G) support craft with each force. The heavy naval bombardment lifted from the beach to inshore targets when the LVT(A)s were 1,200yd out but destroyers and LCI(G)s continued to fire on beach targets. An air strike by eighty-four fighter-bombers and sixteen torpedo bombers went in, then LCI(R)s fired 4,536 rockets minutes before the first LVT(A) hit the beach. At 0832, 1 Brigade's LVT(A)s hit the southern beach three minutes after 3 Division's amphibians touched down in the northern landing. Already the brigade had lost ten amphibians and the division nine from the leading waves on the run-in, as mortar fire was heavy despite the navy's bombardment. The intention on both beaches was to use LVT(A)s as support for men carried 1,000yd inland by the LVTs, but only two amphibians got B Company of the brigade this far. There they were isolated ahead of the main force for about two hours. Many LVTs and some LVT(A)s were running short of ammunition and had to go back to sea for more. This and the loss of twenty-four more amphibians forced the assault forces to limit their initial perimeter well short of the 1,000yd target.

On D+1 a Japanese counterattack on the northern Asan landing was beaten off, and on D+4 the decisive battle was fought when the full weight of a Japanese attack was broken and the Corps could break out from its bridgeheads, but another nineteen days of heavy fighting were needed before the island was secured on 12 August.

US army Pacific landings

Through 1942–3 and into 1944 the US army were in action with Australian and New Zealand troops clearing the Japanese from northern New Guinea, the Bismark Archipelago and adjacent territories. As these Allies fought back to a position where they might free the Philippines they carried out several major and many minor amphibious landings. These broadly followed the pattern of operations already described, although the New Guinea landings were typical of operations to support land forces. In autumn, 1944, however, the invasion of the Philippines could not begin until the threat of air attack was removed by taking the last Japanese bases near the proposed landings. Their airfields were on Peleliu, Angaur and Mgesbus, three of the largest of the Palau Islands some 500 miles east of Mindanao; III Amphibious Corps linked up with the army's 81 Division to capture these islands, elements of the division landing on Angaur (17 September) against light opposition, mainly mortar fire. A feint by one of the Beach-Jumper diversion groups against the island's north coast may have delayed the Japanese concentration of troops for a counterattack as the division consolidated a deep beachhead on the southern coast, but despite the rapid build-up of divisional strength there was a month of hard fighting before the Japanese were cleared from the island's north-west corner.

At Peleliu 24,300 marines from III Amphibious Corps, with 19,800 soldiers of 81 Division, landed on 15 September, two days before the Angaur landings. On Peleliu's ridgeback island there were indications that the Japanese had begun to think in terms of inland defences to avoid pre-landing bombardment, but the assault combat teams came ashore on the south-west coast to stiffening opposition. Over 1,000 mines had been laid by the Japanese, a defending crack force of 10,500, and guns had been carefully ranged on these minefields' perimeters. Nevertheless, the assault teams established a beachhead, though the defenders' resistance stiffened further as they retreated to prepared defences on the high ground of the interior, and it was on Peleliu that the Americans suffered most of their casualties among the 1,792 killed or missing in the Palaus campaigns. As events turned out, the Japanese air strength was too weak to have been effective even if these islands had not been attacked.

American air raids began that September – 1944 – on the Philippines, and despite Japanese naval activity one of the largest Pacific convoys of 701 craft was assembled to carry the Sixth Army's 200,000 men to the Leyte landings. Here, Rangers seized two islands at the entrance to the gulf and on 20 October the assault began. The Philippines campaign was to entail many land battles and landings against the 387,000 defenders, but the American transports had a fortunate escape early in the actions. At Leyte their protective force – the Third Fleet – was drawn after the main Japanese naval squadrons in that area. This left the assault transports exposed to a second Japanese naval force though it did not take the opportunity to destroy them.

Amphibious tractors' outline specifications

The Philippines campaigns were not over when the landings on Iwo Jima began. By then, February 1945, the amphibious tractor was a tried and successful vehicle. All LVT and LVT(A) marks continued in use and a number of other tracked amphibians, both British and American, were used in the war.

LVT SPECIFICATIONS	MK1	MK2	MK3	MK4
Hull/ramp	no ramp	no ramp	ramp's max load 5,000lb	ramp
Tracks	all marks, cleated type for swimming			
Dimensions				
length (*ft, in*)	21 6	26 1	24 $1\frac{1}{2}$	26 1
breadth (*ft, in*)	9 10	10 8	10 10	10 8
max ht (*ft, in*)	8 2	8 1	8 $5\frac{1}{2}$	8 $2\frac{1}{4}$
Weight (*lb*)	16,900	25,200	28,000	23,350
Hold space				
l × w (*ft*)	$8\frac{1}{2}\times7\frac{3}{4}$	$10\frac{2}{3}\times7\frac{5}{8}$	not known	as for Mk2
depth (*ft, in*)	3 11			
Load				
men	20	24	24	24
cargo (*lb*)	4,500	6,500	8,000	6,500
Crew	3	3	3	3
Engines (*all petrol*)	Hercules	Contin'l	Cadillac	Contin'l
hp	146	200	110	250
nos and type	1 w/cooled	1 a/cooled	2 w/cooled	as for Mk2
max land speed (*mph*)	15	25	25	
max sea speed (*knots*)	4	5.4	5.2	
Range				
fuel (*US galls*)	80	110	150	
land miles	75	150	150	
sea miles	50	75	75	

LVT SPECIFICATIONS	MK1	MK2	MK3	MK4
Armour	none	portable 20 and 10lb	portable	portable pin-up kit
Armament				
·30in m/gun	I	I	I	I
·50in m/gun	I	I	I	I

Protective wrap-round shields were added to give gunners extra armour, a change of detail that led to differences in reported specifications. The prototype aluminium-hulled LVT was technically the Alligator, but Mk1s were known by this name. After 1945 a modified Mk3, with its many transmissions and engine parts common to M5 and M5A1 light tanks, became the standard amphibian in US.

WEASEL SPECIFICATION (US Studebaker modified M29 cargo carrier with swimming tracks and cable-operated rudder (*Pl 25*)) *Dimensions:* 16ft × 5ft 7½in, lowest height 39in *Loads carried:* Up to 1,000lb as mini-LVT without ramp *Engine:* 6-cylinder 65hp, 3½ knots max Over 15,000 in service 1945.

ARGOSY OUTLINE SPECIFICATION British heavy tractor with boat hull, tracks and two 24in props; designed by Morris Motors to carry 20,160lb (*Pl 38*).

Plate 38 British *Argosy* amphibian, designed in 1942; too heavy for initial assaults but used for beach recovery work

NEPTUNE OUTLINE SPECIFICATION   (British tractor with track-shoes for swimming) *Dimensions:* 30ft × 11ft 6in, height 9ft 6in *Loads carried:* Up to 11,200lb   Although designed in 1944–5, no record of operational use before the war ended.

LVT(ARMOURED) MK1 SPECIFICATION   (US tractor with gun in LVT Mk2 hull) *Dimensions:* As for LVT Mk2, height 10ft 1in *Weight:* 32,800lb   *Load carried:* In addition to guns, 1,000lb *Crew:* 6   *Engines and ranges:* As for LVT Mk2   *Armour:* $\frac{1}{2}$in under bow, to cab sides and turret; $\frac{1}{4}$in elsewhere   *Armament:* In turret, one 37mm M-6 gun with ·30in machine gun coaxially mounted; two single ·30in machine guns in ring mountings behind turret.

LVT(A) MK4 SPECIFICATION   As for Mk1 but with army M-8 75mm howitzer and only one ·50in machine gun in ring mounting behind turret   *Weight:* 38,000lb   *Load carried:* 2,000lb ammo *Crew:* 5   Other details as for Mk2 LVT, but speed on calm water 5·2 knots   *Armour:* 1in to turret, $\frac{1}{2}$in to cab sides, $\frac{1}{4}$in elsewhere.

10 ASSAULT FIRE SUPPORT

Naval bombardment

By 1944, naval bombardment was a refined skill used in support of both European and Pacific operations, and the assault troops had – barring some unfortunate shortfalls of shot – reasonable confidence in its accuracy and destructive powers. One LCPL flotilla officer is said to have signalled the bombarding warships firing over his head: 'Enough, Admiral. Leave us something to land on.' But a different attitude persisted in inter-service discussions before the war. At that time, the British army had understandable doubts about the accuracy of naval gunnery, for the roll of a ship could give an unsteady fire base before the days of electronic controls in small warships, and even battleships' half-ton projectiles could not be used with toothpick accuracy. Throughout the war no complete solution was found to the problem of closely supporting advancing infantry by ships' guns, as even the specially developed fire support landing craft could not always identify small targets quickly enough to prevent them firing on the assault troops, and the LVT(A), although able to work ashore, had limited 'vision'.

The typical bombardment shells were American navy 6in and 8in with an added potency of extra-high explosive from prewar projectiles. Three different heads could be used on the standard calibres of larger shell: a pointed army-type with impact-detonating fuse for ship-to-shore bombardment; one with a mechanical fuse for anti-aircraft fire; and a dummy plug for use against lightly armour-plated craft. A different shell, with a steel plug head and its fuse in the base, was used to destroy bunkers. Before a landing the navy carried out counter battery fire against long-range coast guns, and softened the beach defences by at least neutralising them so that defenders could not man their guns even if the strong points were not destroyed. But naval gunfire and aircraft bombing had to lift from the beaches as assault waves came inshore or the blast from the bombardment would have caused casualties among assault troops.

In the 1930s the interval between bombardment and beaching was to be covered by blanketing the defenders in smoke (or possibly gas?) and engaging entrenched troops with machine gun fire from small craft. After Dieppe and with the increased use of tanks, heavier weapons were put in minor craft during 1942–3. Before then, however, the need for better anti-aircraft defences led to the arming of major craft which could also provide support fire, as a small number did at Dieppe. Destroyers – at Salerno among other landings – engaged in ship-to-shore actions against strong points and were often used in this way, particularly by the Americans, but they were expensive to build and could play more valuable roles. The Allies therefore built a number of different fire support craft using major landing craft hulls.

MINOR FIRE SUPPORT CRAFT

Smoke cover
The first British fire support craft was devised in 1938 and built to a Thornycroft design developed on one of their ALC prototype hulls carrying a 4in smoke mortar devised by the ISTDC with help from Porton Gas School. It was a weapon with a range of 600yd and origins that will not surprise readers who remember the strong conviction – at least among civilians – that the coming war would involve gas attacks. This mortar was in the forward well of the LC Support(Medium) Mk1, which had similar lines to an LCA though with a snub bow. Several configurations in proto-types were tried with this mortar and Vickers ·50in machine guns on two single pedestal mountings: LCS No 1 was a motor-boat-type hull with the steering position forward and the mortar astern of the Vickers; No 2 had a somewhat similar arrangement

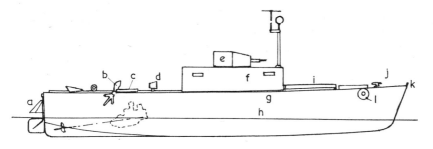

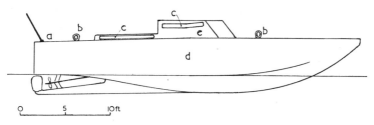

Fig 20 Minor Support Craft (*Above*) LCS(M) Mk 3 (a) rudder guards (b) p and s cowl (c) escape hatch, p and s (d) extractor vent, p and s (e) power turret, twin ·5oin m/g (f) conning position (g) wt to starboard (h) desk for Bigsworth board to port (i) position for 4in mortar (j) cleat p and s (k) roller fairlead for bow mooring (l) drum windlass in cockpit (*Below*) LCS(S) Mk1 (a) smoke pots aft (b) lifting eye (c) m/g tracks (d) cockpit (e) p and s rocket projectors here when carried

in an ALC hull. The Mk1s ordered had the mortar forward, the Vickers staggered in the well (forward gun to starboard), and the steering position aft. Two ·303in Lewis guns were also carried and a small search-light fitted atop the steering position.

These craft could be launched from davits or derricks of LSIs, as could the LCS(M) Mk2 with the twin Vickers in a power-operated turret over an armoured control position amidships. This hull kept many LCA features, presumably for advantages of standardisation, but was given a pointed bow. The 4in mortar was retained in a forward well. These and earlier LCS(M)s were launched from the LSIs at Dieppe, came inshore to lay smoke and engage shore targets, and stayed near the beaches until the withdrawal; LCS No 25 shot down a German aircraft. Despite their rapid fire the weapons were too light to be effective. Nevertheless an LCS(M) Mk3 (*Fig 20*, p 171) with its improved hull design was in production until 1945.

None of these LCS(M)s carried anti-tank weapons, so Thornycrofts were commissioned to design an LCS(Large) Mk1 carrying a 2-pounder in a Daimler armoured car turret with coaxially mounted BESA, the turret being forward of the control position from which a periscope was used to view ahead. A 4in breachloading mortar was mounted on the deck level, which was chest high to control room crew. This mortar, and a power-operated twin Vickers mounting further aft, were behind the control position. When the first LCS(L) Mk1 was completed in April 1943 the 2lb anti-tank gun was already outdated by increased armour on German tanks, though in April 1945 LCS No 144 with HDHL No 1394 destroyed two Japanese barges in what was probably the last amphibious operation in the Arakan (Burma) campaigns.

The Americans used a converted LCP(L) as a carrier-borne support craft; this LCS(Small) was first produced as the LCS(S) Mk1 with an open cockpit-bridge amidships (*Fig 20*, p 171) protected by ¼in shields. A variety of armament including rockets could be carried, and all craft had eight Mk3 smoke pots. An improved LCS(S) Mk2 was introduced, with diesels replacing the Hall Scott petrol engines for which special fuel supplies had been carried on the transports. At Salerno the transport ship commanders had raised the special fuel problem, and found the LCS(S) cumbersome to launch. Eighth Amphibious Force commander reported that the crafts' rockets effectively silenced machine gun fire and their smokescreen covered the incoming LCVPs, but he went on to point out that LCI gunboats could achieve a better result. A policy of replacing the LCS(S) with the more effective LCI gunboats was subsequently adopted, enabling more LCVPs to be carried in the maximum number possible. Only 558 LCS(S) of both marks were built.

A number of other general-purpose minor craft were modified as support craft. The LCA(Hedgerow), for example, was an LCA with reinforced floors and four lines, each of six spigots, firing mortar bombs and mounted in the well. Intended to cut wire and explode beach mines, these LCA(Hr) were not as successful at Normandy as had been hoped, a failure partly due to the mortars punching through the floor unless the craft was very firmly beached when the spigot bombs were fired. Mention has already been made of the 'unofficial' modification of LCMs as gunboats in the Philippines. Other LCMs were fitted in the tank well with the Woofus Mk24 launcher with 120 launching rails. An LCM(R) could fire this number of rocket-powered bombs with a 7·2in demolition head. The launchers with this particular bomb had a range of 280yd from the 2¼in launcher and 420yd from the 3¼in.

Minor fire support craft outline specifications
The principal types of support craft launched from LSIs and APAs, and other small support craft, are shown below with their official armament. These weapons were often supplemented by extra guns and modifications made by flotillas.

MINOR SUPPORT CRAFT SPECIFICATION	LCS(SMALL) MK I	LCS(MEDIUM) MK I	LCS(LARGE) MK I
Hulls: All of wood to designs of	LCP(L)	LCA-type	motor boat
Dimensions			
length *(ft, in)*	36 8	41 2	46 11
beam *(ft, in)*	10 10	10 0	12 7
Displacement (long/short tons)	11(st)	10·8(lt)	24·5(lt)
Draught (in)	42	23 max	51 max
Crew (all ranks)	6	4	5
Gunners (all ranks)	3 or 4	7	8
Engines	Hall Scott	Ford	Gray
hp	250	65	165
nos and type	1 petrol	2 V8 petrol	2 diesel
props	1	2 × 19in	2 × 27in
max knots	12	10	10¾
Range			
fuel *(US/Imp galls)*	180(US)	64(Imp)	146(Imp)
miles	112	60	100
knots	10 +	9	10

MINOR SUPPORT	LCS(SMALL)	LCS(MEDIUM)	LCS(LARGE)
CRAFT SPECIFICATION	MK I	MK I	MK I
Armour	¼in	10lb	15–20lb
	bridge	sides etc	vitals
Armament			
anti-tank			1 2lb &
			BESA m/g
machine guns	1 ·50in	2 ·50in	2 ·50in
	2 ·30in	2 Lewis	2 Lewis
rocket projectors	2 bar'ge		
smoke	8 Mk3 pot	4in mortar	4in mortar

1. Mk2 LCS(S) had 225hp diesel for 11½ knots, twin ·50in machine guns and 24 rails to launch 7 salvos of 6 rockets each.
2. LCS(M) range increased to 90 miles at 9 knots in Mk3; equipped with 10lb HE bombs from mortar and twelve Type 18 smoke generators.
3. LCS(L) Mk2 was a major fire support craft.

LCA(HEDGEROW) SPECIFICATION *Hull:* Strengthened LCA with performance and other characteristics similar to LCA *Armament:* Four rows each of six spigot mortars.

RIVER GUN CRAFT TYPICAL SPECIFICATION *Hulls:* Teak for HMS *Pamela* and HMS *Una* blt by REs for RN use in Burma *Dimensions:* 52ft long, 13ft beam *Displacement:* 25 tons *Draught* 27in *Crew:* 10 *Engines:* Three Ford giving 10 knots *Range:* 200 miles *Armament:* One 40mm, one 20mm, four Lewis or other machine guns.

MAJOR FIRE SUPPORT CRAFT

The basic types
The British, aware after the Crete evacuations of the devastation air attacks could wreak among troops concentrated on a beach, converted two LCT Mk2s in June 1941 to anti-aircraft flak ships. One carried a pair of 4in high-angle naval guns and three 20mm oerlikons (in single mountings, one at the bow and two on the roof-deck of the after cabin). This LCF No 1 was a mini-monitor, more powerful in weaponry than many ships several times her

size. The second conversion was more prosaic, with eight single mountings of 2lb pompoms staggered port and starboard on her gun deck with four single-pedestal oerlikons (two in line in a small bow well and two on bandstands – circular platforms with low bulwarks – aft on the deckhouse). Both these craft had the LCT tank well decked over, providing a gun deck with ample space below for the Royal Marine gun-crews' accommodation, magazines, wireless room, stores and the wardroom. After living in the cramped quarters typical of most major landing craft, going below on some Flakkers was like walking in a dance hall of a mess deck, albeit with a low deck-head ceiling.

From these early conversions stemmed three types of support craft: the LCF for anti-aircraft defence, though they also engaged shore targets at times; the LC Gun(Large), with two 4·7in naval guns, derived from LCF No 1 during the autumn of 1942 as a substitute for monitors to shell coastal batteries in Sicily; the LCT(Rocket), based on an idea put forward by Col Langley when (in 1943) 792 rocket launchers of the army's 5in type were fitted over the well of an LCT. A completely new design was brought out in 1943–4 with characteristics that met the navy's need for support craft with long range for Far East operations, and had either two army 25lb field guns or two 17lb anti-tank guns. These were the LCG(Medium) intended to provide the equivalent of axle-to-axle gun bombardments the army were using in land battles. The 25-pounders could also fire in high trajectory on mortar positions behind hills, and the 17-pounders could out-gun most strong points or tanks on a beach.

By 1944, however, British designs were in some ways outdated by the American fire support craft developed on an LCI(L) hull. The first two were converted in the Pacific during October 1943, though up to this date the Americans had preferred to use destroyers, minor support craft and LVT(A)s for immediate support of assault waves. The advent of these two very successful LCI-gunboats led to a number of other LCI(L)s being converted before the LCS(Large) Mk3 could be designed in an LCI(L) hull. In 1945 an even larger support vessel, the LSM(Rocket), was built on the LSM's hull, with plans at the end of the war for forty-eight super-LSM(R) which would have had a capacity of launching 500 rockets in the first minute and *sustain* a fire of 300 a minute thereafter, using continuous reloading 5in rocket launchers with variable elevation remotely controlled on the mountings designed for twin 40mm guns.

Developments in the theory of close fire support

Support craft led in the LVTs and 'soft' waves of LCA or LCVP, then the support craft and LVT(A)s moved to the flank to continue engaging beach strong points and lay smoke. There were two serious problems with early techniques, however. First, the lifting of the bombardment and air strikes to a prearranged timetable could extend the five-minute gap when only support craft and LVT(A)s covered the assault brigade's last 1,000yd of approach and getting ashore. If this wave was late the defenders had time to recover and shoot up the support craft before firing on the landing troops and assault tanks. The second problem was the assault casualty rate from mortar bombs fired in high trajectory from the reverse slopes of hills. These mortar positions were shielded from the direct (flat trajectory) fire of most ships' guns and quick-firing weapons.

The timing of bombardments was improved by rolling the barrage forward on to defined areas or 'blocks' ashore; a single block could be repeated although the general line of the barrage had moved forward. In this and other ways the interval between beach bombardment and landing was cut to three minutes, putting it only 3–500yd ahead of the first wave. The indirect high-trajectory fire at positions out of sight of the guns was met by mortars on LCI-gunboats, and the LCG(M)s' 25-pounders which could be fired 'howitzer-style'.

Support craft were also expected to cover the assault until the army's mobile guns, the British 'rams' and 'priests', or American field pieces landed from amphibians, were deployed ashore, a period of twenty minutes in theory and often longer in practice. During this time support craft might first engage preselected targets, and perhaps others that observation officers spotted. These men were Royal Navy forward officers, bombardment (FOBs) and British army forward observation officers (FOOs) who were ashore and in radio contact with bombarding warships, support craft and incoming army guns. (Such guns could be loaded on their landing craft to add to the covering fire during the run-in.) The American JASCO shore fire control parties carried out similar gunnery observation. The FOO or his counterpart radioed back information on the fall of shot: how far a shell fell away from its target and in which direction. In North Africa the FOOs and FOBs were parachuted in a day or so before the landings, but they usually landed with the assault wave. An FOO might then not only direct fire on to preselected targets but also against strong points he saw were holding up the infantry. There are some delightful stories, all probably apocryphal, about targets army FOOs selected for big ships' guns: the British battleship, for instance, that had fired a series of 15in shells, each at 1,000yd greater range than the previous shot, before querying the FOO's grid references by which he gave the gunners a point of aim. The gunnery officer asked 'What's the target?' and was not amused to find his precious 1-ton shells had been chasing a German dispatch rider. On another occasion, a ship's power was used more effectively when HMS *Rodney's* big guns shelled German tanks seventeen miles inland from the Normandy Gold beach area on D + 24 *days*.

After a landing, the support craft were used to protect the anchorage from air raids and against surface attacks. At Normandy, for example, support and other major craft formed a 45-mile ring each night to deter E-boats and drop anti-personnel mini-depth-charges against German divers with limpet mines and other devices.

LANDING CRAFT, FLAK

The Flakkers
Apart from LCF No 1 described earlier, LCFs all had quick-

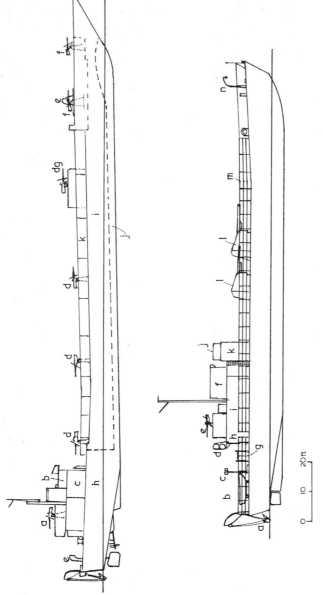

Fig 21 Major Support Craft (*Above*) LC Flak Mk3, based on LCT Mk3 hull (a) p and s 20mm (b) bridge (c) wheelhouse (d) 2lb gun (e) vent (f) 20mm gun (g) port side 2lb guns only shown; four starboard guns matching but staggered (h) engines (i) crew accommodation (j) fuel and ballast tanks (k) splinter screen, 15lb plate (*Below*) LCG(M) Mk1 (a) kedge (b) dinghy (c) heater flue (d) tanks, fw, sw (e) p and s 20mm gun (f) bridge (g) capstan (h) heads (lav) (i) wardroom (j) guard rail (k) control room (l) 17lb (or 25lb) gun in armoured turrets (m) fwd guard rails, collapsible (n) hoist

firing anti-aircraft weapons with which they also engaged shore targets on occasions. Except for Nos 1 and 2, all LCFs were on LCT Mk3 hulls (*Fig 21*, p 178) with the following outline specifications.

LCF 'MK3' SPECIFICATION   *Hull:* As for LCT Mk3 (as used in this craft's name) Length 192ft, beam 31ft *Displacement (light):* 470 tons *Draught:* 6ft 9in *Crew:* Two officers, ten ratings *Gunners:* Two RM officers, forty-eight marines *Engines:* Two Paxman 500hp diesels giving 9½ knots max at 1,100rpm *Range:* 2,700 miles at about 9 knots *Armour:* 15lb D1HT to gunshields and splinter screens, plastic to bridge *Armament:* On LCF Nos 3–6, eight 2lb pompoms, four 20mm; on Nos 7–18, four 2lb pompoms, eight 20mm   The 2lb pompom used a cordite powder propellant (not made in USA) for mv 2,350ft/sec; the oerlikon was a Swiss design built in the USA, with big magazine, easily changed barrel and simple mechanism firing 450 rounds a minute of solid, tracer or explosive cannon shells 20mm in diameter.

LANDING CRAFT, SUPPORT(LARGE) MK2

Anti-tank fire
In the spring of 1942 the British combined operations staff agreed that minor support crafts' weapons would be inadequate against heavy tanks, and an anti-tank 2-pounder was being fitted in the LCS(Large) Mk1. To carry the weight of gun needed for actions against heavy tanks, a major craft was necessary, and therefore the idea of carrying 'anti-tank minor craft' on LSIs was abandoned. Ten LCI(S)s were converted (*Pl 39*) and given 6-pounder tank turrets with extra armament and armour.

LCS(L) MK2 SPECIFICATION   *Hull:* Wood, as for LCI(S)   Length 105ft 1in, beam 21ft 5in *Displacement:* 116 tons *Draught:* 3ft 8in *Crew:* Two officers, twenty-three RMs, POs and ratings *Engines:* Two Hall Scott, some supercharged, developing 1,500hp and driving two 31in propellers for a maximum speed of 14 knots

Plate 39 Fairmile LCI(S) hull converted to LCS(L) Mk2 with forward turret and bow well for mortar

Range: On 4,000 Imperial gallons, 700 miles at $12\frac{1}{2}$ knots *Armour:* 10lb D1HT to deck, hull sides and gun position; $\frac{1}{4}$in plating to bridge *Armament:* One QF 6-pounder in turret forward of bridge, twin oerlikons abaft the bridge and a power-operated mounting for twin ·50in Vickers on the after deck; 4in BL smoke mortar carried in a bow well.

LANDING CRAFT, GUN(LARGE)

Combined operations 'big guns'

The experiment with LCF No 1 proved most successful, allaying the doubts of those who thought such heavy guns for a light craft would make her as dangerous for her crew as for the enemy, so twenty-three LCT Mk3s and ten LCT Mk4s were converted to LCG(L)s. The first group – Mk3s (*Pl 40*) – were given either two 4·7in quick-firing or breach-loading guns of the type used on British destroyers.

The conversion of Mk4 hulls into LCG Mk4s involved strengthening the comparatively flimsy hulls. Armed with two 4·7in breach-loading guns, these LCG(L)s were similar to the previous design though both guns could fire forward. All carried large quantities of ammunition above the waterline and the separate cordite charges of the breach-loading guns added to the dangers of explosion. They did not therefore close the beach but anchored beyond the range of mortar fire from the shore. The many water-tight compartments of their LCT hulls, on the other hand, made them difficult to sink with solid shot.

After the major landings in Europe, a more elaborate conversion of the LCT Mk4 was designed as an LCG(L) with a ship's form of bow, 2in or 1in NC armour over magazines, engines and other vital machinery, and improved accommodation. These 'tropicalised' LCG(L)s were intended for operations in the Far East, but only one was completed as the war ended before the programme was fully under way.

LCG(LARGE) 'MK3' SPECIFICATION *Hull:* As for LCT Mk3 Length 192ft, beam 31ft *Displacement:* 491 tons *Crew (incl. gunners RM):* Three officers, forty-four men *Engines:* Two Paxman 500hp diesels giving approx 10 knots max *Range:* 2,700 miles at 9½ knots *Armour:* 25lb plate to vitals *Armament:* Two 4·7in BL or QF naval guns (Mk1 gun had 50lb shell for mv 3,000ft/sec using charge of 11¾lb); two or four 20mm.

LCG(LARGE) 'MK4' SPECIFICATION *Hull:* As for LCT Mk4, to which LCG(L) Mk4s closely corresponded in dimensions and

Plate 40 All major craft and landing ships could be fitted with smoke generators, used here by LCG(L) Mk3 to cover her repositioning off the beach

performance though individual craft varied according to strength-ening etc   *Displacement:* 570 tons approx   *Crew and RM gunners:* Three officers, forty-eight men   *Armour:* 25lb general   *Armament:* Two 4·7in BL guns, three 20mm.

LANDING CRAFT, TANK(ROCKET)

Use of rockets
The first experimental salvo fired from an LCT(R) was said to have devastated her bridge; certainly her successors were an awesome sight in action (*Pl 41*). Colonel Langley's idea for craft with 5in army rockets, when first taken up in 1943, led to the fitting of 792 rocket-launchers on an LCT Mk2. On later LCT(R)s rockets were fired in twenty-four salvos in quick succession by a system of electrical triggers, so a pattern of explosions 750yd × 160yd could be laid on a beach or its exits. These British rockets, falling one every 100sq yd, carried high-explosive heads with 29lb charges and 7lb bursters. Rockets could also be fitted with a CSA smoke head or an incendiary head for ranging by day and night. The launchers, in stands of six, were at a fixed angle of 45 degrees from the deck and had a range of 3,500yd. They were aimed by positioning the craft relative to its target, this constant range determining where the LCT(R) must be at the time of firing, a manoeuvre calling for pinpoint navigation.

The tailless rockets were not accurate enough for more than a blanket attack on the target, though the fifteen-tons-plus of explosive dropped on enemy beaches could be a great morale booster for assault troops preparing to land, provided that no rockets collided in flight and fell short of the target. During a landing, the LCT(R) was not intended to reload, a job that took several hours, but after a second flight of rockets had been used from her cargo space the crew could remove the rocket stands from over the well to provide space for ferrying stores. Six LCT(R)s surprised the Italians on the Sicily beaches on 10 July 1943, and after the Salerno landings the senior American naval commander reported that they 'showed remarkable possibilities

Plate 41 A covey of death and destruction: a salvo of rockets leaves an LCT(R) shrouded in smoke and flame

. . . though more experimentation and training (was) necessary to realise fully the capabilities of this type of craft'.

Types of LCT(R)

After the prototype, all LCT(R)s were conversions of the LCT Mk3 hull, with special navigation equipment including radar with its lattice tower mast abaft the bridge. A substantial blast screen protected the bridge and after deckhouse from the rockets' fire. These craft had the hull dimensions and machinery of the LCT Mk3 and carried either 1,080 Mk1 projectors or 936 Mk2s with two single-pedestal oerlikons aft. The crew of two officers and fifteen men did much of their training at the RN Assault Firing Establishment in Dorset, the craft and most other British major fire support gunboats using Studland Bay near Poole for practice shoots while lying off the Milkmaid Bank.

LANDING CRAFT, TANK(ARMOURED)

Royal Marine armoured support regiments

Although orders were placed in May 1943 for the LCG(M) with army field guns, too few could be completed by 6 June 1944 to cover the Normandy landings, and as an interim measure tank hulls were to be used in a specially adapted LCT Mk5. General (later Viscount) Montgomery decided that these tanks should be able to land, so Royal Armoured Corps drivers were drafted to regiments formed in 1943–4 as 1 and 2 RM Support Regiments and 5 Independent Armoured Support Battery. Each regiment had two batteries with four troops of tanks to a battery – twenty Sherman and eighty Centaur tanks in all. The troop commanders had Shermans, and four Centaurs (with 95mm guns) made up the troop.

The troop commander's tank was positioned in the after part of the LCT's tank well, but he controlled the fire of the three tanks on board from the craft's bridge. There, he could follow the captain's instructions during the run-in and was better able to see shore targets. Although his own tank could not fire directly ahead, the pair of Centaurs were side by side on a raised platform in the forward part of the well. Under this ramped position was extra ammunition, fed to the tanks by a corporal and two marines working through a hatch in the platform. Ammunition for support craft was always limited, and if a tank was to fire on the run-in it needed immediate reserves to draw on when ashore. For this the Centaurs had Porpoise No 2-type float sledges with forty-eight rounds they towed ashore. The sledge was connected by telescopic bars fixed to the tank but these could be cut by a small charge fired electrically from within the tank. The bars were also crossed diagonally to form a satisfactory tow.

These tanks landed at Normandy and were ashore for nearly three weeks. They penetrated at least ten miles inland and one – to the commander's surprise, for he claims he was lost – received the mayor's civic honours for liberating a French village. Among these tank crew officers and on the LCG(M)s were a number of

South African Royal Artillery officers who had served in North Africa and were seconded to the Royal Marines. The regiments came back to the UK on 24 June and were disbanded in October 1944.

LANDING CRAFT, GUN(MEDIUM)

Army requirements

Although most major support craft could beach without much harm they were not normally intended to do so. The Royal Navy's LCG(M)s did, however; they were an armour-plated box with sharp and blunt ends added in 1½inch plate. The 'box' carried two 25-pounders (*Fig 21*, p 178) or two 17-pounders in 5in armoured turrets. In flotillas of three craft and squadrons of three flotillas, they were intended to place the equivalent of troops and batteries of field guns along the waterline of defended beaches. Crazy? Certainly this broke the golden rule of combined operations: get off the waterline as quickly as possible, either ashore or back to sea. But the LCG(M)s' armour was considered heavy enough to resist Japanese 6in shells, though German 88mm high velocity armour-piercing shells could jam the craft's turret or worse. The first craft were delivered in June 1944, by bridge-building and other firms on Tees-side, after the John Brown yard had done much of the development work.

Both 25-pounder and 17-pounder craft engaged targets on the run-in, and then by partially flooding their tanks they reduced buoyancy before dropping the kedge in beaching. There they flooded down – that is, filled the buoyancy tanks further – to provide a firm gun platform. From this they engaged predetermined targets in direct fire and targets of opportunity. The 25-pounders could also be used in indirect fire, when an army-type dial sight measured the required angle of aim from an imaginary line to an identifiable feature onshore. The crews also trained in working with FOOs and firing rolling barrages, but these 25-pounders were never used in action. The craft came off a beach by using a powerful pump which shifted nearly 16,000lb

of water a minute from the tanks; with buoyancy restored they
went astern and were winched off to the kedge.

Walcheren landings

In the winter of 1944 the Germans had strongly fortified
positions in the Schelde estuary, denying the Allied armies the
use of Antwerp and smaller ports needed for the thrust into
Germany. But by the end of October the Canadian First Army,
fighting over the flooded Dutch countryside, had cleared the
coastal areas south of Flushing. During that month plans were
also made for 4 Special Service Brigade (Brig B. W. Leicester
RM) to land here and at Westkapelle, both on Walcheren. The
brigade of 41, 47 and 48 Royal Marine Commando and 4 Army
Commando, 2,135 all ranks, had been fighting as infantry on the
Allied left flank. Now they were to make two amphibious assaults
on the morning of 1 November. Landing at 0545, 4 Commando
achieved complete surprise at Flushing and were quickly reinforced
despite stiffening German resistance until the town was secured
by the early morning of 4 November.

At Walcheren the Germans had created a fortress with ten
batteries mounting some forty 78–220mm guns defending the
high sea-dykes of this island, twelve miles across from east to
west and ten miles from north to south, with many strong points.
Nearly a month before the landing – back on 3 October – the
RAF blasted a 100yd gap in the dyke at Westkapelle, the flanks
of which were the Royal Marines' target beaches. The assault
was spearheaded by twenty-seven close-fire support craft including two LCG(M)s with 17-pounders, LCT(R)s, LCG(L)s
and LCFs, this support squadron being commanded by Cmdr
K. A. Sellar RN. These craft were to draw most of the German
fire.

At a few minutes past 0900 the naval bombardment began
though low cloud cover hampered aircraft spotting for it, while
the support craft came in before the LCTs carrying the commandos' LVTs and Weasels. Despite the bad weather, Typhoon
aircraft made rocket attacks on the batteries just before the Royal

Marines touched down at 1000 hours, fifteen minutes later than the planned H-Hour. An LCT(R) on the southern flank had fired her salvos when hit by German gunfire. The rockets, off target, were mistaken by the northern LCT(R) for her ranging shots, and this and an error in her navigation caused her salvos to be fired short and partly among the assault wave. The other support craft began to draw most of the German fire, with the two LCG(M)s closing to destroy preselected target bunkers either side of the gap. One knocked out her target but the captain and his officers were killed. Their last signal suggests they probably stayed on the open bridge until the craft was right below the German batteries. The second LCG(M) also knocked out her first target and withdrew, her first lieutenant being killed as he tried to chop free a fouled kedge wire. In repositioning her for an attack on the second target the skipper had been given, he found the craft riddled with solid shot. Out in deeper water she rolled over and sank, and only half the ship's company survived the action.

The commandos got ashore around the gap, suffering heavy casualties especially from machine gun fire, but few assault vehicles, tanks and armoured bulldozers could land to support them as they began to fight their way along the dyke. By 1030 three waves of 41 and 48 RM and the Inter-Allied 10 Commando were ashore. The fire support craft continued to engage strong points, however, and the LCG(M), still beached, kept her less-damaged turret in action though only two of the crew were able to fire from it, the rest being dead or badly wounded. One marine from this turret was awarded the DCM for his part in the action. Having been wounded when keeping the gun firing, he was swimming ashore when a German flamethrower tank trundled down the beach to destroy the LCG(M). He was captured but later released by the advancing commandos, the only survivor from his craft. Later that morning when Cmdr Sellar withdrew his squadron, only seven support craft were still afloat.

That night the naval force withdrew because of the dangers of firing among their own troops in any night bombardment when the fall of shots could not be clearly identified, and the risks of submarine attack. Next day a monitor returned to support the commandos, then, with cover from army guns across the estuary and fifty Spitfires, the beachhead was extended. On D + 2-3, 2-3 November, the Canadians took the South Beveland causeway in an action that used minor craft to outflank the defenders by coming over the shallows. The causeway linked Walcheren to the mainland, and on D + 7 (8 November) the Germans on the island formally capitulated. The Allied casualties were about 7,700, including two out of every five commando troop officers and one in four of the support craft crews. Nearly 30,000 Germans were taken prisoner.

LCG(M) designs

The early LCG(M)s had an unusual, not to say strange, trim on the water: minus 6in draught forward and only 1ft 6in of freeboard aft. A rumour at the time suggested that someone in the naval architect's office forgot to include the weight of her armour plate in his calculations; certainly, her low centre of gravity imparted a momentum to her roll which could reach forty-five degrees in rough weather unless she was headed into the sea for a time 'to get the roll off her'. The LCG(M) was not therefore sent on passage without ships in company. Their low silhouette and after deckhouse led to mistaken identification as U-boats on occasions, and the Dover guard-ship hailed one on passage as she was thought to be sinking. The rudder hung partly in the turbulence between her two props, making the Mk1 slow to turn to port, and she might take up to four minutes to respond to a wheel change. Nor was the crew accommodation adequate for her designed complement of four officers and thirty-two ratings, which was reduced to the figures shown in the outline specification following. She had some interesting machinery, however, with a gyrocompass repeater in each turret, an all-electric galley, and 'mod cons' added to most craft during tropicalisation, but the oil-fired water heater aft will be remembered by most crews for the size of the soot flakes it floated over clean dhobi (washing).

However, later Mk1s had improved trim.

A Mk2 design was produced with the same lines but less armour and without the beaching capabilities, and it was intended to add two or three twin ·5oin Vickers guns in hand-operated mountings, but the only hull apparently completed by August 1945 was the one used for the first LCS(Rocket).

LCG(M) MK1 SPECIFICATIONS *Hull:* Mainly welded; these were among the strongest vessels ever built   Length 15oft 6in, beam 22ft 4in *Displacement:* 380 tons *Draught:* see text *Crew:* Three officers (including RM gunner), twenty-eight hands – the rating of specialists in major support craft crews varied with flotilla needs but typical was a PO coxswain, three ABs and two OSs (one a co-ops signaller) and a telegraphist; engine ratings included a PO and four stoker mechanics with two wire-men (electricians); the RM gun crews had a sergeant (always 'CSM' afloat), with a corporal and five RMs in each gun-and-magazine team, and an RM signaller *Engines:* Two Paxman Riccardo 5oohp diesels (three generators), designed maximum 11¾ knots *Range:* Over 1,500 miles; craft carried fresh water and supplies for 3–4 week passages *Armour:* 8olb, 4olb and 15lb with heaviest plate on turrets *Armament:* Two 17lb or 25lb army guns and two single oerlikons on aft bandstands; the 25-pounder craft carried 400 cartridges and 400 shells of HE, smoke or solid shot; the 17-pounders had 300(?) fixed shell-cartridge high-velocity ammunition with armour-piercing shells; two Lewis guns for mountings in control position; RMs' rifles etc also carried   On some craft a CO's cabin was welded on deck forward of the control position.

LANDING CRAFT, SUPPORT(ROCKET)

Royal Navy plans for 1945
By August 1945 the British had begun to increase their assault fleet of support and other craft/ships for operations in the Far East. These vessels included the LCG(L) Mk4s with ship's bows,

the LCG(M) Mk1s refitted for the tropics, and the LCG(M) Mk2 designs intended to give better sea-keeping qualities. With a normal ship's waterline and the armour reductions already mentioned, the hull was ideal for inshore bombardment craft and at least one was fitted with banks of rocket launchers as the first LCS(R) to arrive in Poole during the late summer of 1945.

The combined operations staff were organising three British forces of landing ships and craft – Forces W, X and Y – each able to lift an assault division to meet South East Asia Command's requirements. These forces were to have their own squadrons of support craft, but only elements of Force W had reached the Far East by August 1945.

LANDING CRAFT, INFANTRY(LARGE) GUNBOATS

Pacific support craft
When Capt Roy T. (Slim) Cowdrey, the senior ship repair officer of Admiral Halsey's fleet, modified two LCI(L)s – Nos 24 and 68 – he began a new line of support gunboats (*Pl 42*) that was one of the most successful innovations in combined operations. These first two craft had added armour and a range of quick-firing light weapons: two 20mm oerlikons, three 40mm Bofors and five ·50in machine guns. They were used most successfully at the Treasury Island (South Pacific) landings on 27 October 1943 and elsewhere in this theatre during actions in the Empress Augusta Bay area. The craft could bring a greater weight of fire against beach strong points than the much smaller armoured amphibian LVT(A)s, and the gunboats could manoeuvre more rapidly to meet changing situations. Forty-eight LCI(L)s were therefore converted to gunboats with various armaments until the LCS(Large) Mk3 could be brought out in 1944, when sixty LCI(L) hulls were fitted with rearranged accommodation below decks, and armament that included a 3in/50 dual-purpose gun. The armament was arranged on the main deck with the 3in forward and a twin-40mm aft, with two single 20mm guns (port and starboard) immediately astern of the deckhouse. On the roof

Plate 42 LCS(L) Mk 3: these LCI-type gunboats could give sustained automatic fire for comparatively long periods, though overheated gun barrels needed changing or cooling

of the deckhouse were a twin-40mm forward and two single 20mm (port and starboard) just forward of the control position, but later LCS(L) Mk3s had increased firepower with added rocket-launchers and other armaments.

Fire support from LCS(L)s was not confined to actions during the landing, their shallow draught enabling them to run inshore to cover beach clearing parties working a day or so before the major landing. Craft designations were used to show principal armament, with the LCI(G) a converted LCI(L) with a 3in gun, the LCI(M) with mainly 4·2in mortars, and the LCI(R) with rockets; all had 40mm and 20mm quick-firing guns.

Iwo Jima

The techniques of close-fire support by the time of Iwo Jima landings (19 February 1945) (*Fig 24*) were highly sophisticated, 5 US Marine Division's action report stating that 'these fires (by support craft and ships) made it possible for the assault waves to land'. Yet thirty months before at Guadalcanal in August 1942

191

the very idea of 'supporting fire' was completely new to many gunner officers of the amphibians, and 'naval fire support' a new subject for discussion.

Iwo Jima was a Japanese fortress island $4\frac{1}{2} \times 2\frac{1}{2}$ miles in area with the bleak appearance of dead lava and dominated by an extinct volcano 550ft high, but with geysers still active in some parts of the island. Only 660 miles from the mainland of Japan, the island was regarded as home territory by many Japanese. Deep underground bunkers linked with natural caves had reinforced concrete protection and some were on as many as five levels. None of these bombproof shelters had less than thirty feet of earth over the roof. Before the landing bombardment there were more than ten weeks of shelling and air attack with 6,800 tons of bombs, 203 rounds of 16in shell, 6,472 of 8in and over 15,000 5in rockets. But gun emplacements with walls between four and six feet thick, and bunkers, protected 21,000 highly-trained and experienced Japanese defenders.

Before the landing on 19 February (D-Day), Underwater Demolition Teams went inshore on D − 2 to reconnoitre the east coast beaches and clear obstacles. The swimmers were covered by fire from the gunboats of 3 Flotilla of LCI(G) group 8, and in the forty-five minutes from 1045 when the swimmers went inshore, nine of the twelve craft were put out of action and the other three were damaged. The flotilla came out with bloody decks and the bodies of gunners in fire positions pitifully draped with sacking. The swimmers had only one casualty and that afternoon made a reconnaissance of the west beaches, covered by destroyers' fire; all came out safely but next day two men of UDT 15 were killed and twenty swimmers with eleven crewmen of USS *Blessman* injured when a bomb hit this APD. This was the only air attack that day to reach the assault ships, but on the other hand the defences were attacked in 226 air strikes on D − 1 and D − 2, in support of UDTs and against anti-aircraft and other batteries.

H-Hour was set for 0900 on 19 February and at 0640 the final phase of the bombardment began. In the next hour and a half the

nine LCI(R)s fired over 9,500 5in rockets, mainly against the
Motayana Plateau inland, while naval guns drenched the coastal
and beach defences. Also in the support group were twelve LCS(L)
Mk3s, three LCI(G)s and eighteen LCI(M)s which at 0730
joined the bombardment with fire on to the high ground to the
north of the beaches. By 0805 these craft had begun to move
towards their covering positions for the actual landing, a manoeuvre protected by a strike of 120 carrier and other fighter-
bombers during the next twenty minutes; then the naval
bombardment resumed. The LVTs of the assault waves moved
through their start line at 0830, having half an hour for the
4,000yd run to the beach. As they passed bombarding warships
in the boat lanes, the ships' gunners switched from airburst high
explosive to impact fuses.

Sixty-eight LVT(A)s led in the 482 amtracs carrying 4 and 5
US Marine Divisions' eight battalions. At H−3 minutes a naval
air strike came in, moving 'the bullet impact area' 500yd ahead
of the LVT(A)s, which hit the beach at 0902; three minutes later
the LVTs, from some 250yd behind the LVT(A) first wave,
brought ashore the marine infantry on a 3,500yd front. A 15ft-
high terrace masked the LVT(A)s' line of fire and they had to
put back to sea in order to engage targets. The infantrymen found
volcanic ash ankle deep on the beach, bogging down men and
amtracs under heavy fire, the Japanese gunners catching many
marines as they crouched behind the slight protection of the
terrace slopes. Of the 30,000 men landed that day, 2,400 were
casualties by nightfall; the beachhead was 700yd deep but only
500yd wider – at 4,000 yd – than the landing area. The congestion
of vehicles, jib-cranes and other gear set the beach masters almost
an impossible task. LCMs and LCVPs had brought in essential
supplies of water, ammunition and radio equipment, however.
On D +1 the flamethrowing battle of attrition began as marines
inched forward, losing many more men killed in hand-to-hand
fighting in the caves. By D +4 the marines were established ashore
and that day reached the summit of the volcano, but the island was
not secured until D +25 (16 March) and there was a further six

weeks' isolated resistance. Marine and naval casualties were 26,001 including 6,812 killed; the Japanese lost over 19,000 killed and 867 taken prisoner. By 7 April, seven weeks – not the planned five days – after the landing began, American fighter planes were operating from Iwo Jima in support of their Super-Fortresses flying incendiary raids which caused heavy damage in many Japanese cities.

Mortars and rockets

By the time of the Iwo Jima landings, mortars and rockets had added considerably to the firepower of support craft. These weapons are complex, and the following explanations of their operation are simplified. A conventional army mortar bomb is fired when the charge in its base strikes a fixed pin as the bomb is slid down the barrel; spigot mortars have a rod spigot holding the tube tail of the bomb ready to fire, and it is launched when a ballistite or other charge is triggered off at the tip of the rod; rockets are launched by igniting the solid propellant motor in their base. The British developed Capt Blacker's Bombard spigot mortar, and the Americans had a Mk20 Mousetrap launcher for rocket bombs. The California Institute of Technology developed this to throw a 20lb bomb 1,100yd, carrying a 6lb charge of high explosive which, although it did not always completely fragment the case, proved a useful weapon against troops in the open. A Mk22 double-decked launcher was built, and by 1943 one for sixteen bombs had been developed.

The breach-loading (BL) mortars on British minor support craft had a trigger-fired charge to launch the bomb, but the American 4·2in mortar was muzzle-loaded, with a rifled barrel firing smoke, time-fused airburst and high-explosive bombs of 25½lb (up to 4,400yd) and 32lb bombs (maximum range 3,200yd).

Rockets were of two types: the 5in barrage rocket (British type) and the 4½in (American type) with fins to help stabilise its flight; and American spin-stabilised (SS) rockets rotated in flight to get stability and had greater accuracy than barrage rockets. The spin was imparted by the setting of the rocket motor's nozzle. For all these rockets a simple rail could be used for launching, and although some had elevation adjustment the most effective bursts came ashore when a rocket dropped at its extreme range. Developments from anti-aircraft and air-to-ground rockets of several sizes were used not only on LCS(S)s but in many other ships including PT-boats with a 4½in rocket launcher, for the rockets had no equivalent to a gun's recoil when firing a shell. The Mk7 single-rail launcher with a gravity feed (for 4½in barrage types) fired twelve rockets in four seconds, and with the Mk8 launcher one LCI(R) could get off 480 rockets without reloading its forty launchers. The rockets were armed with a standard Mk137 fuse and had a small propeller which rotated in flight and released the safety stop so that the rocket burst on impact.

A 5in American air-to-ground bombardment rocket was tried with some craft, but its low take-off velocity and long fins for stability when launched from aircraft made it inaccurate in ship-to-shore flight. An SS series was developed during the summer of 1944 in America, and the 3½in and 5in types put into production. Using a Mk51 launcher with a gravity feed, the 5in SS rockets with a 5,000yd range were fired from sixteen of the LCI-type support craft, each with six launchers, at the Iwo Jima landings. Further developments came with the Landing Ships, Support.

LCI-TYPE SUPPORT CRAFT SPECIFICATIONS *Hulls:* As for LCI(L) with LCS(Large) Mk3 below-deck accommodation rearranged and slight variations of performance, dimensions and displacement from standard LCI(L) *Crew:* Varied with armament, but typical was five officers, sixty-eight men *Armour:* 2½in plastic on early conversions, 10lb gun and weapon shields on LCS(L) Mk3 *Armament:* Initially installed on first conversions and as designed for Mk3; included variations:

	LCI(Gun)	LCI(Mortar)	LCI(Rocket)	LCS Mk3
3in/50 DP	1	–	–	1
4½in mortar	–	3	–	–
40mm Bofors	1	1	2	2 twin

	LCI(Gun)	LCI(Mortar)	LCI(Rocket)	LCS Mk3
20mm oerlikon	4	varied	4	4
·50in machine guns	6	varied	6	varied
rocket launchers	–	–	10 Mk7	varied
			2 Mk22	

1. Bofors, of Swedish design, fired clips of 40mm shells. (Half the suicide planes shot down in the Pacific are estimated as Bofors kills.)
2. The 3in/50 dual-purpose gun fired fifty rounds a minute, using a mechanical loader, for a firepower equal to five Bofors, on one estimate.
3. Craft built/converted: 172 LCI(G); 59 LCI(M); 52 LCI(R); 130 LCS(L) Mk3.

SUPPORT LANDING SHIPS

Rocket firepower

The first eight LSM(Rocket) (*Pl 43*) built in December 1944 and January 1945 were equipped with simple launchers for 5in aircraft rockets. Although they could launch 480 rockets in thirty seconds, they took two and a half hours to reload. The next four LCM(R)s had Mk51 launchers for 5in SS rockets and could fire 1,040 rockets in the first minute of action. To reload took forty-five minutes and the ships carried sufficient rockets to fire three full 'shoots'. These ships were in action at Okinawa, where the banshee shriek of their rockets was 'an unforgettable sound'.

Plans for the super-LSM(R) were drawn but no ship was completed before the end of the war. All LSM(R)s were in LS Medium hulls and had loaded displacements of approximately 1,000 tons. Crew complements varied with the type of rocket launchers carried, from 138 all ranks on the less-automated ships to as few as eighty-one on others. The ships carried four 4·2in mortars, at least two 40mm Bofors and a 3in/50 at the stern. Some were fitted with a Kirsten cycloidal propeller so they could turn through 360 degrees on one firing position. Fifty-two LSM(R)s were built or being built by the end of the war.

OTHER FIRE SUPPORT FROM LANDING CRAFT

The self-protection theory

Major landing craft and ships needed sufficient firepower to protect

Plate 43 Most sophisticated of the close-support ships of amphibious fleets, the LSM(Rocket)'s fire exceeded many pre-war cruisers in destructive power

themselves against air attack, especially when on unescorted passage to supply forward areas. To some extent they had also to protect themselves from the enemy's light naval forces during such operations, and there are a number of ship-to-ship actions that were fought by some support and other landing craft. In the spring of 1944, for example, an American LST convoy on exercises off the Devon coast was attacked by nine E-boats and suffered over 600 casualties.

The LSTs described in the next section used their weapons not only in self-defence but also in support of troops ashore. The potential firepower can be appreciated from a table of armament carried by the LST echelon moving in to Bougainville (Solomon Islands) on 6 November 1943:

LST No	37mm	40m	20mm	·50in m/gun	3in/50 DP gun	Total
207		4	13	6	1	24
70		3	12	5	1	21
353		5	18	4	1	28
488		4	14	18	1	37
341		3	11	15	1	30
395		4	16	13	1	34
354	3	4	18	9	1	35
339		4	14	10	1	29
	3	31	116	80	8	238

This firepower was 'augmented by automatic weapons of combat
load suitably mounted on the main deck for use' (Commander,
LST 5 Flotilla) in Empress Augusta Bay area. The captain of
LST No 395 commended the men from 35 Combat Team who
'although not experienced with 40mm guns . . . steadied well on
the targets and behaved throughout as if they were fighting their
own ship in the landings at Vella Lavella . . . their action provided
invaluable protection during heavy (air) attack . . .'

11 LANDING SHIPS ON THE BEACH

A key to victory

By 1944 the Allies were landing 100,000s of tons of supplies in amphibious operations. These loads required ships to be able to beach and offload their vehicles and stores across short causeways or on to improvised quays of prepared banks bulldozed out of the beach. At other times amphibians carried in the ships had to be launched through the bow doors to swim ashore. Always there was pressure when unloading cargoes to build up strength for the breakout second phase of a landing, followed by the steady supply of foods, ammunition, fuel and often drinking water for the armies ashore until they had captured – or built – a port for the transports. A great deal of this work was done by LSTs, LSMs, LSVs and those mobile floating-dock-type ships the LSDs. Principal of these was the LST, with her origins in a British design and owing her numbers to American production skill.

LANDING SHIP, TANK

Early doubts

Although LCT designs and a prototype craft were completed in the winter of 1940–1, Prime Minister Churchill demanded ships that could land the heavy tanks which were to be built during 1941 and put them ashore anywhere in the world. The last requirement meant the vessels had to have sufficient speed to keep station in transport convoys and therefore needed ship's bows. There would also be a gap between the beached ship's bow ramp and shallow enough water for tanks to wade ashore. To these design problems was added the difficulty of finding yards with the capacity to build such ships in the UK, and the more bewildering problem of a ship's survival on enemy beaches. This was the most intransigent feature of the whole concept, for ships of the size envisaged would take time – hours, at least – to discharge bulk cargoes, and vehicles would not all get ashore in less than forty-five minutes. During this period she might be stranded by enemy action or simply because delays in unloading meant she missed the tide. In the event these fears were not realised because of the Allies' air power, although LSTs did on occasions get stuck on a beach longer than intended, despite many efforts to speed unloading.

As a stop-gap measure to meet Churchill's demands the Admiralty found three shallow-draught Maracaibo oilers – *Misoa*, *Tasajero* and *Bachequero* – built to cross this harbour's shallow bar. Greenwell's of Sunderland completed a conversion of the *Misoa* (4,890 gross tonnage) in July 1941 as the first Landing Ship, Tank in the world. She had a double ramp arrangement (*Pl 44*) devised by the Department of Naval Construction and developed by the firm of Clarke Chapman; the ramp extended through double-flap bow doors hinged at the base. On a 1:35 beach, with her forward draught of four feet, she could land a 40-ton Army tank across the 8ft-wide retractable causeway. Her eighteen Churchill tanks or other vehicles were carried in rows on the turret deck over the oil tank spaces, now used for accommodation and large water-ballast tanks. The sides were built up above the turret deck and a new deck added to protect the tank cargo, housed in an enclosed space needing special ventilation.

The trials of the *Misoa* proved ships of her size could be kedged off a beach, and although she was not strictly a prototype of the purpose-built LSTs the Department of Naval Construction gained valuable experience in a number of aspects of tank and vehicle cargo landings on beaches. The *Bachequero* was a sister ship to the *Misoa*, both being 382½ft long with beams of 64ft. The *Tasajero* was slightly smaller – 3,952 gross tonnage, 365ft long, with a 60ft 2in beam – but could carry virtually the same cargo. The

Plate 44 One of the first LSTs, a converted Maracaibo oiler, extends her retractable causeway on to a beach

three ships each carried two LCMs, had heavy derricks and armament of three pompom guns, six 20mm oerlikons, two smoke mortars and two Lewis guns. There was accommodation for tank crews or other army drivers (207 all ranks) and a ship's company of eighty-three.

The ships' 9–10 knots was not considered fast enough for work with transport convoys but the limitation had to be accepted, although the first British purpose-built LSTs of the Boxer class were designed for a speed of 17 knots. These ships caused the DNC to exercise considerable thought over the design of a ramp that could reach across a 100ft gap to very shallow water from the bow drawing 5ft 6in on a 1:35 beach. The complicated solution was a double-cantilever ramp with a 71ft main section and a 54ft extension. The device took up a large area of the tank deck on these 400ft vessels. The heavy vehicle deck was carried over into later LST designs and ran nearly the full length of the ship.

Vehicles could also be carried on the upper deck and were taken by lift to the tank deck, along either side of which were accommodation spaces. The two sets of Foster Wheeler boilers with 3,500SHP turbines were placed just aft the centre section, with the funnel off-centre to allow room for a 40-ton crane. She had side ports for offloading vehicles into LCMs, ventilation of the type used on the Maracaibo conversions with exhaust trunks joined by flexible connections to vehicles' exhausts, and features to facilitate possible use in carrying crated aircraft, a contingency plan the DNC wisely made as there was no experience of such vessels in action when the first was ordered from Harland & Wolff (Belfast) in January 1941.

Harland & Wolff had been involved in the project from an early stage in the design, and it was their suggestion to use a pair of vertical bow doors. The ramp-causeway was developed by Stothert & Pitt (Bath). The Boxer class were by far the fastest LSTs; the ramp-causeway in the shallow-draught hull, other design innovations and German air raids resulted in the first ship not being launched until early in 1943. By then her original role had been taken over by the LST Mk2s, and the three Mk1s – HMS *Boxer*, HMS *Bruiser* and HMS *Thuster* – were converted to other uses (*Pl 29*).

Invasion ships

When the LST Mk1s were being designed there was still a measure of distant raiding in their intended role, but by the winter of 1941 this had been largely replaced by invasion plans and work was concentrated on an Atlantic tank landing craft which could sail from American yards to Europe. She was a 300ft vessel designed to land heavy tanks direct on to the beach, and because of her size was renamed LST Mk2. The details of her design (*Fig 22*) were worked out by the Department of Naval Construction and American authorities in the winter of 1941–2 and the first ships were ordered in February 1942. President Roosevelt approved the building of 200 Mk2s – although little over half this number came into Royal Navy service – for supply under lease-lend, along with

Plate 45 An LST Mk2 with doors open discharges cargo on to the volcanic ash beach of Iwo Jima, February 1945; on her port hand is an LSM; LVTs in the foreground

200 LCT Mk5s, and the same numbers for the US navy. He also approved on similar terms the building of seven LSDs, in place of the original British requirement of LST Mk1s, and seven for the US navy.

In the Mk2, tanks were carried just above the level of the water-line and parallel to it throughout the ship's length, an arrangement that gave convenient machinery space aft for the locomotive-type diesels below the main tank deck. At the bow the LCT-type ramp was protected by a pair of vertical doors (*Pl 45*). The ship's machinery included a variable-speed power winch for the kedge, a simple lift from the upper deck for vehicles, and fan-trunk ventilation of the tank deck. Some major modifications were made, starting with LST No 513, and all later ships except No 531 had a ramp from the upper to the tank deck, but no lifts. Ships numbered in the series 1 to 541 were as shown in Fig 22 and are some-

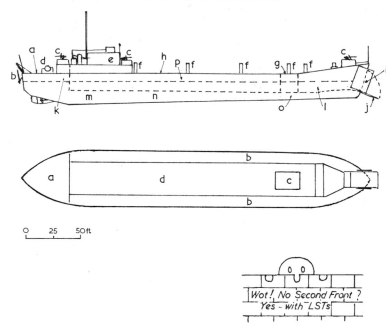

Fig 22 LST Mk2 (*Above*) Profile (a) before winter of 1944,
kite balloons flown from after deck (b) kedge (c) p and s 20mm
(d) winch (e) bridge (f) fan exhaust (g) hatch 20ft 9in × 16ft (h) top
deck (i) doors (j) ramp (k) crew (l) tank deck (m) fw tanks (n)
engines (o) ballast and fuel (p) 2nd level through side decks   (*Below*)
Plan (a) stores and magazine (b) troop accommodation (c) elevator
(d) tank hold/deck 288ft × 30ft

times called 'US Mark 1' in American references. The 542 class took
less payload to compensate for increased armament, a seawater
distillation plant with a capacity of 4,000 gallons a day, and other
added weight; in this way the draught of both classes was kept
within the same parameters. The loading of these ships was varied to
suit either an ocean passage or the shallower draught needed for
beaching. With 33·3 tons per inch immersion, they carried 2,100
short tons (1,900 tons on the 542 class) for an oceangoing draught of
8ft forward, and with 500 tons for landing they drew 37in at the
bow. When light, they drew only 18in. A causeway carried out-

board of the sides allowed vehicles to land in shallow water on a beach when it was floated into position.

Their main feature was their vast tank deck, 288ft ×30ft with a clear height of 11¼ft from the deck to the underside of the electric lights, giving a volume of 92,765cu ft after allowing for ship's equipment on this deck. The noise of engines and tracks reverberated in this vast soundbox. The spaciousness made the handling of any vehicle reasonably easy, including bulldozers. Though the fire risks were obvious, there were no Board of Trade or Maritime Commission regulations to observe when steaming towards an enemy beach with petrol-laden vehicles on the upper deck and the great undivided area of the main hold chock-full of tanks or highly inflammable stores. There were sprinklers in the hold and fire mains on the upper deck, and later US navy LSTs had water curtains and drenching equipment fitted. That there were comparatively few major fires is a tribute to the discipline of soldier passengers and LST crews, many of whom had no previous experience of the stringent fire precautions needed at sea. Passenger troop accommodation was lavish by major landing craft standards. The troops had multiple two- and three-tier bunks with heads (lavatories) and a seawater shower in each accommodation area.

Construction programme

The invasion of Europe and the defeat of Japanese forces were entirely dependent on the rapid building of the Allied armadas in which the LST played a major – if not *the* major – role. The date of the Normandy landings was not fixed until the supply of such vessels was assured, and the Pacific operations could not have been mounted so rapidly without LSTs. Over 1,000 LST Mk2s were built by 1945, many constructed in very short production times even by comparison with the records set for all manner of armament manufacture at that period. The first thirty built at the Baltimore yards of Bethlehem Steel were delivered in ten months, only nineteen days outside the contract schedule, yet the LST took more man-hours to build than a Liberty ship which was about five times larger: 10,600 tons deadweight to the LST's 2,286 tons. The original British designs allowed for flat plates to form the turn of the sides under the hull, but this hard chine added 16–25 per cent more resistance compared with the rounded bilge chosen for a 10-knot speed. The technical decisions were complex. A flat deck was quickly assembled but a curved deck readily drained water. However, it took longer to build. Such compromises, saving building time, made work more difficult aboard ship.

The longitudinal strength in the Maracaibo oilers was carried through to the Boxer class and later LST designs despite the all-welded construction of the Mk2. The electric welding used advanced techniques in 1942 and firms like the Dravo Corporation of Neville Island, Pittsburgh, drew on their industrial experience. Dravo were – and are – a firm with long experience of river barge construction, among other skills. They used clusters of generators on skids to provide power for the arc welders moving around the site, with suspended staging and other mass production methods. The prefabrications included box sections of the main hull with plates tightly flanged at the edge for smooth lap joints, giving little resistance to the water. Each section had lugs temporarily welded for jacking it into position, where it was held by a screw bolt during the welding, this tight construction making strong ships. Even the washbasin supports, the bow-door assemblies and hinges were welded. On the upper superstructure, tubed guards were shaped and welded around the gun positions, preventing accidental fire into the ship's own decks or upperworks. These guards were fitted on all major craft and other warships.

During the war, Dravo, with 2,400 employees in 1941, was appointed a lead yard and drew some 60 per cent of their fabricated steel from subcontractors. This enabled them to expand building not only for 150 LSTs worth $205 million but also twenty-seven escort destroyers, sixty-five LSMs, ninety-six dry dock and floating cranes, two shipyards, power plants and much other equipment in all worth $490 million up to February 1945. The cost of LSTs was a measure of their complexity. Although the contracts for 300 Mk2s had been placed by May 1942 for delivery before the end of June 1943, in January that year at the Casablanca conference their building had to be given priority over destroyers and other escorts.

Cargo handling

On ocean passages the LST Mk2 could carry an LCT Mk5 or 6 for side-launching, and this feature was used on occasions for carrying LCTs to the dropping zone for a landing. A method of bridging the gap between ramp and beach was not satisfactorily found till the Sicily landings in July 1943, when pontoon causeways designed by Capt John N. Laycock, of the US navy, were used. With a section on each side of the LST, these 140–75ft roadways were dropped and then floated inshore to overlap, forming a causeway of adjustable length in shallow water, which could ride the waves on a shoreline. When first used, the causeways had been towed in astern of LSTs, as were LCT Mk5s and 6s and other equipment from time to time, but as far as possible such cargoes were carried rather than towed because of the handling difficulties a tow creates. The causeways were used in all theatres, although early experiments with coconut log causeways were made in the Pacific. There also, at Tarawa, the LSTs carried multi-pontoon sections for floating jetties to be assembled by US CBs into a pier alongside a reef. The use of piers and jetties resulted in sophisticated prefabricated ports off Normandy. Before that, the LSTs at Anzio – working to bulldozer-prepared mounds – supplied Allied armies with such tonnages that for a short period Anzio was one of the largest 'ports' in the world, although the ships' own propellers caused sandbanks they and LCTs had to surge over.

There was so much more cargo to unload than on LCTs, for example, that even with a causeway the work took time. At Empress Augusta Bay, when LSTs were shaking down in their first Pacific operations during November 1943, some carried as much as 1,400 tons of cargo and vehicles and the average load was 700 tons, 200 more than the designed beaching load. Once vehicles had been driven ashore the bulk cargo was offloaded by backing lorries into the cargo space and manhandling the loads, a job that could take up to eight hours to clear a ship with an average cargo. Vehicles – especially the 2-wheel drive British lorries at Salerno and elsewhere – could not be driven quickly over the 1ft drop off an LST ramp even when plank extension ramps were used, so this unloading time was not unreasonable. Faster times were achieved by manhandling the stores ashore and at Finschapen (New Guinea – also spelled Finchhafen) a hundred men were carried on each LST to clear an average of fifty tons of stores and twenty vehicles an hour. Other loading methods were tried, one in which a 50ft gap was left on the tank deck between cargo stowed aft and the other bulk cargo, so that once the vehicles had landed from the tank deck seven lorries at a time might be used for offloading. Their movement was co-ordinated with the offloading of light vehicles from the top deck, allowing cargo-handling to go on while these were driven ashore.

One method of speeding up cargo landing to meet the optimum 1-hour limit for discharging was to preload trucks or trailers, a method tried with limited success at Cape Torokina in Empress Augusta Bay as the space taken by the vehicles seriously reduced the load capacity of 2 Echelon LSTs. By 1945 the loads were often carried on pallets, with LSTs – reminiscent of the tiny LCVPs at Peleliu – each carrying specific stores and materials for the amphibians to collect as though moving from bay to bay of a floating warehouse. Other LSTs brought amphibians to the dropping zone, though as they exceeded the 10-ton gross vehicle weight for which the upper deck was designed they had to be carried on weight-spreading chocks or in the tank hold. They could be driven down the inboard ramp to offload through the tank deck, a simpler drill than using the elevators of early LSTs which needed special maintenance and could get stuck (a mishap that meant going alongside another ship to drive upperdeck cargoes across to her lift). At Iwo Jima in 1945, LSTs carried in addition to their primary load of LVTs the stores needed as soon as the VAC (V Amphibious Corps) was ashore: drinking water in water trailers; two 'infantry battalion's unit of fire'; concertina wire; 2,000 C and K rations; 1,200 D rations; petrol and lubricating oil.

LSTs brought all manner of equipment needed as soon as the assault troops had a toehold on a beach: marston matting – 8½ miles of it at Iwo Jima; 6-wheel drive and 4-wheel drive trucks; vehicle service trailers; mobile cranes and anti-aircraft guns. The tractors were the first vehicles ashore and trucks were loaded from the cargo hold in a sequence that did not jam up dumps and enabled it to be sent to different points ashore, avoiding congestion. The offloading plan had to be taken into account in stowing bulk cargoes before a landing. A typical manifest for an LST was: twenty-six 6×6 trucks; four jeeps; six 4×4 cargo trucks; one 4-wheeled machine-shop trailer; one Imsley 5-ton crane; two New Zealand prime movers; two 40mm Bofors on the gun carriages; 'dead' cargo of 115 tons of rations, 200 tons of fuel in drums, 40 tons of ammunition and 12 tons of 'organic' gear. All these – as on any craft or ship – had to be 'secured for sea', using chains and chocks so they did not shift position as the vessel rolled.

Several craft were given a short flight-deck and flew off OY-1 light spotter planes from Brodie equipment. Once unloaded, a number of other LSTs remained off the beach area in many Pacific landings to act as clearing stations for casualties waiting to be taken further out to the hospital ships. In Europe several LSTs had railway lines fitted for taking rolling stock to France.

The only other LST – the British Mk3 – was a transport ferry. This class of ship was intended to meet British needs in the Far East, as in 1943 there were some difficulties over allocations of Mk2s to the Royal Navy. Exact copies could not be made of the Mk2 because no suitable engines were available, nor were the welding facilities. This Mk3 class was given heavy steam reciprocating engines intended for frigates. The cutaway hard-chine hull, flat decks, steam – not electric – machinery except for that working the ramp and bow doors, and other features were intended to make production reasonably rapid. The first orders for forty-five ships from British yards and thirty-five from Canada were placed in December 1943 and Swan Hunter delivered the first ship in December 1944, after orders for a further thirty-six had been placed in Canada. Despite her extra power at 5,500hp in a hull 345ft 10in long with a 54ft beam, she was not a lot faster than the Mk2. With twin screws the Mk3 made 13 knots and had a forward draught of

55in; carrying pontoon causeways like other LSTs she could land vehicles over a ramp and had an internal ramp to bring them from the upper deck. The building programme was not completed before the end of the war, however. American references to a 'UK LST Mark 4' probably indicate this ship, as US classes of Mk2 were sometimes described by different mark numbers.

LANDING SHIP, MEDIUM

Fast assault ships
The slow speed of LSTs made their deployment in separate convoys an additional call on escorts, and in 1944 the 203½ft LSM, originally designated LCT Mk7, was built as a ship able to maintain a convoy speed of 12 knots. The single vehicle deck could carry loads of about 150 short tons with (say) five medium Sherman Mk4(A3)s, or six LVTs, when loaded for the beaching draught of 41in. The stores carried in bulk for this draught were limited to 741 tons but on ocean passages her cargo could be as much as 900 tons. A better ship at sea than the LCTs, with her high prow, the LSM (*Fig 23*) had double side-opening doors protecting her ramp. She did not normally carry a causeway, so vehicles were not easily landed on shallow beaches unless a landing point had been prepared (*Pl 45*). After landing her initial cargo, the LSM was used in ferry work; 424 were built, excluding those hulls used for the LSM(Rocket).

LANDING SHIP, VEHICLE

Preloaded trailers and cargo room
In 1942, two large 5,800-ton minelayers were laid down by the Willamette Iron and Steel Corporation of Portland, but were completed as LSVs in 1944. In the same year four 4/5,000-ton net-layers from navy yards were completed as LSVs with space for as many as forty-four DUKWs and 800 troops. The vehicles could be launched through a stern door and ramp. The added cargo spaces, by comparison with an LST, enabled V Amphibious Corps to use fifty 2½-short-ton amphibious Clever-Brook trailers

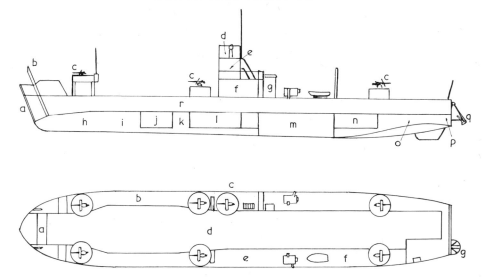

Fig 23 LSM (*Above*) (a) bow doors (b) ramp (c) p and s 20mm
(d) bridge (e) ph (f) charts (g) air intake (h) void (i) ballast (j) troops
(k) magazine (l) mess (m) engines (n) troops (o) fuel (p) steering
(q) kedge (r) vehicle deck (*Below*) Plan (a) ramp (b) officers and
crew (c) extra 20mm gun (d) vehicle well (e) galley (f) stores
(g) anchor grill

carrying rations, fuel and some ammunition preloaded before the
trailers went aboard the LSV *Ozark* for the Iwo Jima landings.
After the initial landing she was used here as an evacuation hospital
ship.

LANDING SHIP, DOCK

Seagoing floating docks
Reference has already been made to the British origins of this
design, developed by the American Bureau of Ships and Gibbs &
Cox of New York. The principle of flooding the LSD cargo
spaces to float off smaller craft was at first thought too risky for
general service personnel of the Royal Navy to attempt; civilian

Plate 46 The LSD HMS *Eastway*, with heavy cranes for loading and repair work abaft her midships stack

floating-dock crews are specially trained. Mr Baker and others at the DNC overcame the many objections with an arrangement of machinery that worked satisfactorily, although the buoyancy of engine room and other machinery space meant that tanks above her waterline as well as those below had to be filled when lowering her. Flooding-down took only $1\frac{1}{2}$ hours and was possible even with some way on; the ship could regain her normal cruising trim in $2\frac{1}{2}$ hours. The 394ft ×44ft cargo deck was flooded to allow amphibians and craft as large as LCTs or LCI(L)s to sail out when the stern doors were opened. The dangers from seas washing around this area, making the half-submerged ship unmanageable, were prevented by lock-gates fitted amidships, but these were taken out after some months.

The first LSDs (*Pl 46*) went into service in 1943; eighteen were built for the American navy and seven ordered for the British navy. In addition to accommodation for landing craft crews and cargo-personnel, the LSD had workshops for metal and woodwork repair of minor craft and could be used to repair LCI(L)s, PT-boats and similar craft. In the dock when flooded, the maximum depth was about eight feet sloping to ten feet aft. Two temporary decks could be installed above the dock-pontoon, and LVTs or DUKWs were loaded on to these by the ship's two 35-ton cranes. The extra decks had a ramp extension to the stern and on LSDs No 13–27 an inboard travelling crane was fitted to position these removable decks.

LANDING SHIPS IN ACTION

Okinawa landings
Okinawa, an island sixty miles long and eighteen miles wide narrowing to a waist only two miles wide at one point (*Fig 24*), lies 350 miles SSW of the Kyusu mainland. One of the largest islands of the Ryuku group, Okinawa was the last offshore defence of Japan. Here the Japanese hoped to hold the amphibious fleets of the Allies and destroy them before they could strike at Japan's homeland. An assault force of 183,000 men in 1,300 vessels assembled during March 1945, and before D-Day, 1 April on Okinawa, a number of operations were mounted against smaller islands in the group. A marine reconnaissance battalion made a night landing on the low reefs of Keise Shima to find them undefended, and on 26 March (D − 5) 77 Army Division began a series of fifteen landings in which they took five Kerama Rheto Islands, defended by only 937 Japanese although bases for 350 suicide boats, which were destroyed. Kerama Rheto then became advance bases after the UDTs had blasted channels for minor craft and the fleet had established shuttle services of tankers and ammunition ships, the latter (including nine LSTs) often loaded with units of fire for particular types of warship so that ships could load ammunition from one or two designated supply vessels.

The bombardment of Okinawa began on D − 5, but the ships, including the British Pacific fleet, could not come in to close range until D − 3, by which time the minefields had been swept. Over 500,000 shells and rockets were fired into the defences, and the Japanese garrison – 70,000 soldiers and 30,000 other troops – was withdrawn from the beach areas. The bombardment was intensified on D-Day after twenty-four 155mm guns were landed (D − 1) on Keise Shima reefs eleven miles south-west of the main landing areas.

213

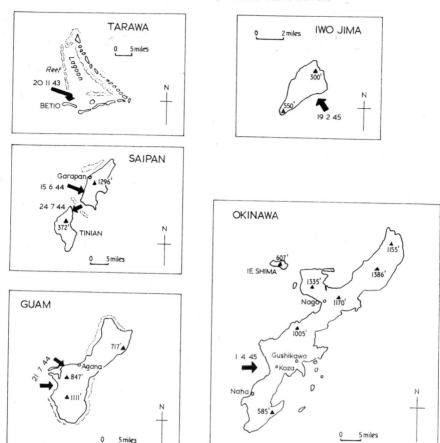

Fig 24   Some Pacific landings

H-Hour was 0830 and eight assault battalions landed on this fine sunny morning against token resistance, with one target beach north of the Bishi and five to the south of this west-coast river. Diversionary landings were made on the south-east coast and repeated on D +1. The main force of LVTs pushed over obstacles and followed the DD tanks, Tare 6 types with medium Shermans on pontoons launched from LSMs. The assault waves, surprised at the lack of resistance, nevertheless exploited their advantage

214

and by 1000 hours had taken the airfield of Kadena, not scheduled for capture until D +3. By 1300 the airstrip on the other flank at Yontan was taken by the marines. Before nightfall, 60,000 men had landed and the beachhead was almost nine miles long and three deep.

The tide had been ebbing since before 1030 but LCMs and LSMs brought in the assault divisions' tanks though the LSMs had difficulty securing a firm beaching where tanks could offload, and as heavy surf and poor weather was forecast for D +1, pressure was put on the LSTs to land the most urgently needed supplies. At night the supply ships usually withdrew and left the ferry craft on the beach, although two LSTs (fitted out before the Iwo Jima landings) acted as mother ships for minor craft and DUKW crews, giving the men the chance of a shower and cooked meals. The offloading of supplies for the build-up began within $5\frac{1}{2}$ hours of the initial landing and continued through D-Day and into the night for LSTs, as the rapid advance of the troops was stretching the supply echelons, many DUKWs and LVTs having – fortunately - much longer journeys to the forward perimeter than was originally expected, though their APAs and AKAs had to move away offshore that night.

The transports were back in the morning and by the evening of D +1 eleven slot berths had been prepared to offload LSTs. By D +2 both airstrips were operational, putting further pressure on ships bringing in supplies, and by D +6 some LVTs and DUKWs were making 40-mile round trips to the perimeter twenty miles inland on the north-east of the beachhead. The drinking water wells, as expected, had been contaminated and four fleet ex-oilers with experts in water purification brought in millions of gallons, not only for troops ashore but also for crews of those major craft which did not have their own desalination plants.

The reefs proved a convenient width in two stretches with hard flat tops about 350yd wide. From these were fixed pontoon piers; twenty-nine LSTs brought in hundreds of pontoons as deck cargo. Sixteen LSTs carried LCT Mk5s or 6s as deck cargo for later ferry work. With preloaded amphibians in LCTs carried by LSDs and the veritable Chinese puzzle – as Admiral Morison describes it in his history – of boxes within vehicles loaded on LSTs, the logistics of this landing took on aspects of high mathematics but stood up to the unexpected stress of rapid advances, the LSTs and other supply craft making 1,000 'secondary' landings by D +10.

On land the opposition began to stiffen on Monday D +7 when XXIV Corps came up against the main Japanese defences near the waist of the island. Through the next two weeks the extent of these defences were probed and found to be well-planned, for the Japanese hoped to hold the Americans on land while their fleets were heavily attacked. But the advance was pushed forward across steep hills and narrow ravines, and on 16 April (D +16) III Amphibious Corps made landings on Ie Shima, a 607ft-high dead volcanic island 3½ miles off Okinawa's west coast, near the waist. In this and other land operations the navy provided supporting fire, the ships assigned from Task Force 54 – thirty-four warships for support work – firing, for example, bombardments on twenty-eight out of the thirty-six days and on twenty-one out of thirty nights suitable for such actions in the period to 17 May, half the ships usually taking part while the other seventeen re-ammunitioned for the next day's shoot.

The fleet was protected by a ring of ten or so radar picket stations on which LSM(R) No 195 was lost and LCS(L) No 25 damaged while among other support ships doing this unpleasant work. The pickets were the first ships met by incoming Kamikaze pilots, a corps which took its name from the divine winds, typhoons that had saved thirteenth-century Japan from the Mongol invaders; their planes had first attacked transports off Leyte in November 1944. As suicide pilots, having no regard for their own lives, men of this corps expected greater success than they were able to achieve, although they nearly forced a withdrawal; the firepower of American ships and craft prevented many planes reaching their targets. LST No 447 and two ammunition ships were sunk by Kamikaze pilots and they probably accounted for most of the other twenty-seven – thirty in all – ships and craft sunk during the campaign, and for many of the 368 damaged. In such battles the

216

reasons for losses cannot always be clearly attributed to one cause, for mines, shore batteries and air bombing may each contribute to a particular ship's loss. One estimate gives over 2,000 Kamikaze pilots killed.

The Japanese launched a seaborne counterattack on 4 May which failed to effect a beachhead they could maintain, and the landing force was destroyed. Later in the month a suicide squad in several planes attempted to land on Yontan airstrip. Only one plane got down on the runway and its squad leapt out hurling grenades and firing automatics; they succeeded in destroying or damaging thirty planes and set fire to 70,000 gallons of fuel, but the installations were quickly repaired and planes continued to fly off in support of ground actions and the Fortress raids on Japan. On 21 May the last ring of defences across the northern part of the island was broken, and on 31 May the second largest town, Shuri, was captured, but the campaign did not end until 2 July.

During the early stages of fighting on Okinawa the mopping-up operations were still uncompleted on Iwo Jima, and in the Philippines they were not to be completed till the war ended. As troops were being supplied in these Pacific theatres, there were also British landings – unopposed – in Rangoon (Burma) on 2 May, and landings by the Australians at Brunei on 10 June and Balik-papan on 1 July, their largest landing in a series of operations to clear the Japanese from Borneo and neighbouring islands. All these campaigns involved many LSTs, LSMs, and support ships with covering fleets of warships backed by fleet trains and other supply ships in shuttle services to Australian, Indian and Hawaiian bases or to the American west coast.

Example outline specifications of landing ships

LST MK2 SPECIFICATION *Hull:* All-welded steel   Length 327ft, beam 50ft 1½in   *Displacement:* 4,080 short tons with full load *Draught:* 37in fwd in beaching trim   *Loads carried:* (see text), 2,100 short tons (1,900 on 542-class) for ocean passages, with 1,750 tons on tank deck and 350 tons on upper deck; for beaching, total designed load 500 tons; ships could also carry 1,060 tons diesel in ballast tanks   *Crew:* Varied with LCVP carried; in 2-davit ships, seven officers, 204 men (increased by 2 +16 in 6-davit ships)   *Assault force accommodation:* Sixteen officers, 147 men (less by extra LCVP crews in 6-davit ships)   *Engines (twin screws):* Two 900hp diesels giving max 10·8 knots   *Range:* 6,000 miles at 9 knots   *Armour:* 15lb STS to gun positions and bridge etc   *Armament:* In US ships, one 3in/50 up to seven 40mm and twelve 20mm authorised; RN ships, one 12lb, six 20mm, four FAM; many LSTs carried smoke generators at the stern.

LSM SPECIFICATION   *Hull:* All-welded steel   Length 203ft 6in, beam 34ft   *Displacement:* 513 short tons light   *Draught:* 41in fwd in beaching trim   *Loads carried:* (see text) maximum 900 tons; 741 tons designed load for beaching   *Crew:* Four officers, forty-eight men   *Engines:* Fairbanks Marine diesel or General Motors Cleveland direct-drive diesels, 1,400hp at 720rpm, two screws giving 12 knots – designed speed 13·3 knots in one reference   *Range:* 3,500 miles at 12(?) knots   *Armour:* 10lb shields to guns and bridge   *Armament:* Six 20mm or two 40mm   The dimensions of LSMs recorded vary slightly, apparently due to minor changes in design.

LSV SPECIFICATIONS   *Hulls:* LSV No 1 USS *Catskill* and No 2 USS *Ozark:* 5,177 short tons displacement unloaded   *Dimensions:* Both ships: length 455ft 6in overall, beam 60ft 2in   *Draught:* 20ft   *Loads carried:* Varied as below but Nos 3 and 4 could take an additional 1,000 troops if no vehicles carried:

	LVT	*DUKW*	*Troops*
Nos 1 and 2	none	44	800
Nos 3 and 4	19	29	800
Nos 5 and 6	21	31	800

Crew: 564 on Nos 1 and 2   *Engines (on these two ships):* Geared turbines giving a total 11,000shp to two props for 18·5 knots

Range: 2,000 miles approx   *Armament:* Two 5in/38 and eight 40mm   LSV Nos 3 and 4 were 4,626 tons (light) and Nos 5 and 6 of 5,041 and 4,900 tons respectively, all with similar dimensions to Nos 1 and 2.

LSD SPECIFICATION   *Hull:* With submersible pontoon deck Length 457ft 9in, beam 72ft   *Displacement:* 7,930 short tons loaded   *Draught:* 15ft 5½in, 30ft 9½in flooded down   *Loads carried:* Included three loaded LCT Mk5 or Mk6, or two LCT Mk3, or fourteen LCM Mk3, each LCT loaded for max draught of 8ft 1in in fwd area of dock   *Alternative loading configuration with portable decks:* Total of ninety-two LVTs or 108 DUKWs (forty-one LVTs or forty-seven DUKWs could be carried in dock area without extra decks)   *Crew:* Seventeen officers, 237 men; in addition, ship's LCVP crews of six officers and thirty men carried on some LSDs   *Engines:* LSD Nos 1–8, steam reciprocating to two shafts; others, geared turbines of 7,000shp (to two props) for 15 knots (Three ships had 9,000shp for 15·5 knots)   *Armour:* Splinter shields to guns and bridge   *Armament:* US ships, one 5in/38, two twin-40mm, two quad-40mm, sixteen 20mm; UK ships, one 3in/50, four 2lb, sixteen 20mm.

12 SALVAGE, REPAIR AND OTHER SPECIAL CRAFT

Stranded craft

An LCA, LCVP and LCM on a beach might be very firmly grounded, needing a nudge from a bulldozer or tractor to get it off. Even LCTs and other major craft might need this help, for the falling tide, an onshore wind or rock outcrop could cause a craft to stick. At Salerno in September 1943, each engineer beach battalion had a team of six bulldozers and twelve men for this and other salvage work. But when a craft had broken-down engines, lost her steering, or was badly holed, she must be either hauled out by the shore party or towed when freed from the beach. If badly holed she also needed supporting by slings between two salvage craft for the trip out to the cargo AKAs detailed to lift her out.

When a surf was running, any minor craft broached-to across a beach usually filled; and of course holes from shot or collision with obstacles also might cause her to fill. Then she needed pumping out, and maybe patching, before being towed off. The APAs at Salerno each launched an LCM Mk3 fitted out for this work. They carried a 500-gallons-per-minute trailer pump, enough hose to reach stranded craft, and were fitted with extra-strong towing cleats for their tow lines, but the commander of 8 Amphibious Force considered that better and more flexible salvage arrangements could be made. He suggested the use of supply ships with LCT and other spares, a scheme that he and other commanders already had under active study with Combined Operations Command.

An LST was a different proposition to refloat, but major landing craft could usually be towed off by companion craft in the flotilla or by tugs. The LST might have to be allowed to dry out completely between tides, but on a reasonable beach she took no harm. At Okinawa and other landings where an LST blocking a berth could seriously slow the unloading programme, tugs were given 3,000lb anchors by which they secured themselves seaward of stranded ships. The tug could then use her powerful winch to heave a stranded ship off. The work of tugs around landing areas was always spiced with good humour, for anyone trying to tow off beached craft is almost inevitably going to get stranded himself from time to time. No doubt somebody has a record figure for tugs towing off tugs – the author's top score is three.

Many different types of craft were used for salvage: LCI(L)s as well as LCMs at Salerno; LCVPs followed in the assault waves in the Pacific, to salvage craft and rescue involuntary swimmers from boats and amphibians that foundered. With the increased use of amphibians, gear had to be landed for damage to be welded, the recovery being much the same as tank and vehicle salvage once ashore.

Fair wear?

Minor craft were designed for beaching, but as the use of pontoon and other jetties increased in ferry work many had to come alongside time and again, suffering unavoidable thumps and bumps ('General, sir; I can only apologise again.') which knocked the unsuspecting passenger off his feet. Worse; the ply sides might spring, and once a craft's frames were broken a difficult repair was needed. For major craft on a beach the accumulation of runnels in the sand where LSTs had been working, the pits left after 'dried out' coasters had floated off on the next tide, and the wreckage of military jetsam along the tide line could put uneven strains on the hulls, props and rudders. At Arromanches, an LCT floating dry dock was used to change bent rudder stocks, replace broken props and do similar repairs, including work on LCT Mk4s with rudders that could be bent sufficiently to seize the stock in even a moderate blow, until guards were fitted.

AUXILIARY REPAIR LANDING SHIPS

Maintenance

The need for service as well as salvage facilities was partly met by work the minor flotilla maintenance staffs carried out aboard LSIs, and for major craft some remarkable running repairs were achieved. At other times the staff on the LCC(FF)s helped. But in the case of major jobs like replacing heavy equipment, work kept the craft out of action too long unless appropriate lifting and other gear was available.

The ARLs were equipped with such lifting gear: a 50-short-ton derrick, and two 10-ton booms from king posts. These modified LST Mk2s had their bows sealed and carried electrical, pipework, sheet-metal and other shops for repair work, including a blacksmith's forge. Their stores included replacement parts for craft and (probably) LSTs. Also carried were ten balsa rafts which could keep damaged minor craft afloat until they were lifted out. The first six ARLs were commissioned in 1943 and in all thirty-nine were built or converted from LSTs-in-building, two of these ships being transferred to the Royal Navy as Landing Ships, Emergency Repair (LSE).

Damage repair

On LSTs and major craft, as on any warship, the crew formed damage control parties who made temporary repairs to keep a ship afloat after bomb or shell hits. In combined operations there was little opportunity to give general ratings or their junior officers much of the specialised training familiar to peacetime damage control parties, though ships and craft carried plugs for shot-holes, and on one major craft a typical set of damage control equipment might be six baulks of timber and a few hundredweight of quick-drying cement. Major damage was made seaproof though not watertight with hammocks, mattresses and any other material that would fill a gaping hole. Most landing ships and craft survived very heavy damage, however, because of the watertight compartments, shut off by doors and hatches with heavy clamps – six to eight turned against wedges sealing the door before going into action. The doors were set a shin-barking foot or so above the deck level, keeping any moderate inrush of water within a compartment until the door could-be closed in an unexpected emergency.

At least one LCT (a Mk4) sailed back to the UK from the Normandy beaches towing her own fore-end. LSTs too survived tremendous punishment, but in their enclosed cargo spaces fire was the biggest hazard, though LST No 448 carrying 300 marines to the Okinawa beaches managed to put out a major fire after twenty-one marines were killed by (probably) a Kamikaze attack. Twelve LST Mk2s were converted to American Auxiliary Repair – Battle Damage Ships. These ARBs provided temporary repairs to major damage in any warship, including LSTs, and worked with the converted minesweepers and other small salvage ships – the ARSs – off landing areas to get damaged ships back to forward bases.

REPAIR AND MAINTENANCE BASES

Local facilities
In European operations, established shipyards were seldom more than a modest towing distance from the assault beaches and landing craft maintenance bases were established in several British and Mediterranean port areas. For the Normandy landings a Combined Operations Repair Organisation (COREP) worked with COTUG, the tug co-ordinating service for Mulberry and other towing operations, in bringing back Allied craft for repair, but in the Pacific few established yards existed. Every use was made of available small-ship slipways although the number of ships, craft and pieces of mechanical equipment to be maintained needed facilities for hundreds of thousands of personnel – service and civilian – to keep the amphibious fleets in operation. Major bases were established in Australia and New Zealand but as the advance moved across the Pacific these became too distant for repair and maintenance work. The US navy CBs therefore built, among

223

their many other construction jobs, a chain of advanced landing craft bases. For every type of construction work they were organised in 'functional units' – a unit might be one man and 100lb of gear; or 1,000 men and 10,000 tons of equipment – able to carry out a particular group of tasks with similar work content. By November 1944 there were some 250 combinations of men and equipment making up different functional units.

Typical of the Pacific landing craft bases was Mobile Amphibious Repair Base No 2's Mios Woendi Island (in the Paidado group), with facilities able to support eighteen LSTs, eighteen LCI(L)s, thirty-six LCTs, sixty LCMs and 240 LCVPs. At Tulgai the CBs built a dry dock out of pontoons, 'six wide and twenty-four long', for repair of LCI(L)s, and it was moved forward as new bases were established at, among other places, Bougainville in the Solomons, Eniwetok in the Marshalls, Saipan and Keyte. At least one facility had a covered slipway for round-the-clock repairs in all weathers and could haul out an LCI(L). Many LCTs and LCI(L)s needing underwater work were taken aboard LSDs.

LANDING CRAFT, EMERGENCY REPAIR AND ARGs

Vehicle maintenance

The Landing Barge, Emergency Repair was among the first amphibious facilities for repair of vehicles in a landing area, its lorries with maintenance crews going ashore to set up repair depots once a beachhead was secured. With the increased number of vehicles, the need for de-waterproofing and the inevitable high frequency of maintenance for vehicles running in salt and sand conditions, greater facilities were needed. The Royal Navy converted thirty LCTs into military workshops for maintenance work in the beach areas, and six were lost during the war. Equipped like garage workshops, these craft were used to maintain the lorries in supply echelons and on occasions the engines of minor ferry craft.

The advent of amphibious tractors, the increasing numbers of supply vehicles, and limited resources ashore in the Pacific suitable

224

for maintenance depots led to the introduction of internal com-
bustion engine repair ships, the ARGs. ARG No 1, USS *Oglala*,
was a converted minelayer of 3,746 tons displacement commissioned in 1943 and able to handle major maintenance and repair
jobs on the many different engines in ships, craft and vehicles.
Fifteen were built by 1945 in various Maritime Commission hulls,
including the EC2-S-C1 Liberty ships, with eight of 4,621 tons
displacement, four of 5,159 tons, one of 4,737 and one of 5,775
tons, the last two being converted submarine tenders.

CASUALTY EVACUATION

Who's missing?
Medics had always gone ashore among the first waves of every landing, and for the raid on Narvik medical orderlies had been trained
as toughly as any other commandos, but with the increased size of
operations, and after the sinking of a British hospital ship moored
well away from a Mediterranean assault, steps were taken to
increase the evacuation facilities for casualties. The first stage of
their journey was by LVT or LCR, perhaps, to the hospital
landing ships and LCTs moored off a beach, where they could
receive some basic care before the longer journey by ambulance
LCVP or LCP(L) to the LSIs' sick bays or to hospital ships.

After Tarawa and other early Pacific operations many casualties
lost touch with their units, causing needless anxiety to relatives
when men were posted as missing. Some were not traced for as
long as six weeks. The resulting home front reactions, particularly
in a democracy, had a direct influence on senior commanders,
and orders were given before Iwo Jima for a much-improved
recording system on casualties' whereabouts. In this landing four
LST(Hospital) were moored 2,000yd off the beach, and as soon as
the beachhead was secured in some depth the full medical facilities
were deployed in support of advanced services. The casualty
stations included the marine division's medical teams with 430
casualty 'beds', an army hospital able to handle 3,160 casualties,
and 8 Field Depot with 1,500 cots.

The supplies of blood plasma, wound dressings and other medical needs in action were flown in, but were of course only a part of the hospital and medical requirements. A great deal of work was in connection with fever casualties despite preventive doses of anti-malaria pills taken by every man in the Far East, and 'anti-everything' injections against major epidemics.

13 BEACH DEFENCES

Off the beach

Neither Allied nor Axis commanders risked assault convoys against superior naval and air forces, though occasionally convoys were caught: 4,000 Germans were lost in their first May 1941 convoy to Crete, and 3,000 Japanese reinforcements for the Solomons died when American planes attacked their convoy of seven transports and eight escort destroyers in the Battle of the Bismarck Sea (1 March 1943). Defending forces at other times proved too weak to do more than delay an assault and relied on their ground defences in the last resort. Properly organised, these could be very effective, though without co-ordination they quickly crumbled; the Japanese losing only 15,000 men when capturing Malaya and the Dutch East Indies with fewer troops than the British and Allied armies which lost 200,000 men (mostly prisoners) during these campaigns.

Coastal batteries in reinforced concrete emplacements with walls up to seven feet thick usually covered inshore minefields. As part of their Atlantic wall the Germans used such positions with four 125mm or 155mm guns (4·9 or 6·1in equivalents) with crews living in the defended area of each emplacement. Most coastal batteries had ranges of 6–12 miles, like the forty-six twin-6in batteries added to UK beach defences in 1940. These guns were intended to engage targets only three miles offshore, however, for without aircraft to spot the fall of shot or sufficient numbers of fully trained crews, firing at extreme range might have wasted the limited supplies of ammunition. Only at Wake Island in 1941 did coastal batteries prevent a landing though they made most minesweeping operations additionally hazardous inshore.

227

As there were many technical difficulties in laying mines inshore at depths around six feet, minesweeping became increasingly a war of technology. The effective German Oyster mine was not used until after 6 June 1944 at Normandy, in case the Allies discovered – as they did when one parachuted on to land later that summer – how they worked. Japanese moored mines were probably in short supply for no fields were found off Leyte Gulf where the Americans expected them that summer. German fields were usually put down offshore by submarine; Japanese minefields around heavily defended islands like Truk, and off Raboul, were bypassed by the Allies as these bases were not attacked. Whether or not mines were laid off the selected landing points, however, the sea areas had to be swept, a precaution amply justified at Salerno where mines delayed the deployment of landing ships although at least one shallow-draught LCT flotilla sailed over a minefield without loss.

The arrival of inshore sweepers was often the defenders' first intimation of the precise beaches chosen for a landing. This knowledge enabled Japanese concentrations to be gathered at Tarawa. Although the Germans had radar warning of approaching invasion fleets, on more than one occasion the sentries' report of sweepers' activity, or their smoke screen, was the first information junior commanders received of imminent action.

Beach emplacements

Apart from the coastal batteries, other guns were in enclosed positions (*Pl 47*) which limited their field of fire but gave overhead protection to guns and crews. Set with a single slit or aperture at one side of the blockhouse, the guns fired diagonally across the beach to enfilade lines of craft and men coming in. The gunners therefore had a greater opportunity of hits than in frontal fire against a line of targets, and the bombarding warships had to fire along reciprocal lines to hit the slit. High-angle anti-aircraft guns, mortars and other weapons with high trajectories had to be in open gunpits, but all guns could be ranged on target areas before the battle. Firing along such fixed lines, the defenders brought a curtain of fire down on the water's edge, especially on deliberately

228

Plate 47   German strong-point emplacement enfilading the beach
and protecting guns' crews

placed gaps in the anti-boat obstacles which funnelled craft into
lanes. Because of poor communication between infantry behind
the beach and mortar positions further inland, Japanese defenders
tended to continue firing on these fixed lines after assault troops
had negotiated the beach obstacles. Nevertheless the majority of
assault casualties in the Pacific, and probably in Europe, came from
mortar fire which easily sank minor craft; a direct hit left only a
blood-red stain on the water where the craft had been.

The Japanese showed an instinctive flair for camouflaging
emplacements and the 7ft-deep communication trenches they
sometimes built between strong points. In the South Pacific they
were helped in this by the terrain (*Pl 48*) and natural materials
like the coconut logs they used for bunkers. Many of these could
withstand the ·50in machine gun fire from American planes. In
Europe it was more difficult to disguise defences, though attackers
could be deceived over the strength of a bunker and the exact
position of its aperture, as many of the support squadron gunners
discovered after the Normandy landings when they inspected

Plate 48 The smoke-shrouded jungle of Mono Island (near Treasury Island) gives defenders cover as LCI(L) No 234 nears the shoreline, 27 October 1943

captured emplacements and realised they were virtually impregnable from the front.

Anti-boat obstacles and shore mines

The British, after considering 'table cloth' nets moored a mile offshore, came up with a 'sea fire' defence (*Pl 49*). At first this was to be a series of perforated pipes laid below the tideline, but experiments proved a beach line more practical, as petrol was fed by gravity through the pipes to flood areas of beach. Once ignited, this burning fuel might have destroyed craft as they beached if the apparatus survived bombardment. Other beach obstacles used by the British were similar to defences elsewhere in the world: stakes with barbed-wire curtains – though wire was used more often on shore; angle-iron 'hedgehogs' of three or four 5ft lengths of about 5in I-section bolted and/or welded to form a spiked obstruction (*Pl 50*); concrete (or coral and concrete in the Pacific) formed into 4ft cubes. At Normandy a line of hedgehogs was set inshore of ramps – single wood or metal spars about twelve feet long supported by a single upright post – making two lines of heavy spikes, each some four feet from the sand and angled at about thirty-five degrees to impale craft. On Gold beach there were 2,500 obstacles in a stretch of $3\frac{1}{4}$ miles, but these inshore defences were not completed right along the coast, though there were sufficient to delay landings and hold craft up to 600yd from defending infantry, as did the 15×12ft gate elements 'C'.

Attached to a selected number of obstacles were mines or shells with impact fuses. The principal shore minefields were laid behind the beaches and in dunes.

In 1940, 200,000 special beach mines, sensitive enough to be set off by a wandering sheep, were laid around the shores of the UK. German Teller and Japanese 'teapot' mines could blast an LVT right over or disable it by damaging the tracks, seriously restricting movement in an uncleared beach area.

Infantry defences and mobile reserves
Early in the war, defence systems were built immediately

Plate 49 United Kingdom beach-fire defences used petrol the senior commanders considered would have to be destroyed in the event of an invasion

Plate 50 German anti-boat mined obstacle prepared for demolition by Royal Navy and Royal Engineer commandos of LCO Clearance Unit

behind likely landing points. A series of mutually supporting strong points, each with all-round defence, barbed wire entanglements and anti-tank dragons' teeth of concrete pyramids, might form a half-mile deep band running several miles along low-lying coasts. Behind such defences mobiles reserves were held inland: fifteen divisions with only 227 tanks in the UK during June 1940, but SS and Panzer divisions as the hammer of the German crust-cushion-hammer defences in Normandy. The crust was infantry without battle transport, the cushion was mobile infantry for counterattacking breaks through the crust, and the hammer was intended to knock the Allies back into the sea. In one version of this defence, 12 SS and 21 Panzer Divisions were expected five miles inland from Gold beach on D +1 and two other divisions of armour were to join them behind the beachhead, but all these forces were held further inland until D +4 when the hammer came down too late.

Japanese tactics changed from beach defence to inland systems where the defenders were less likely to be numbed by bombardment but where attackers became enmeshed in the defence system. Their artillery and ships could not then support them without risk of hitting their own men. This ploy failed in part because it did not exploit a serious weakness of amphibious landings, when assault brigades relied on fire from ships in a more complex operation than using the heavy weapons under their direct control, including mobile artillery.

After the landings

While suicide boats and planes attacked transports off the beach, the crucial battle was fought ashore. In this phase, Allied Sherman and Cromwell tanks broke through the crust at Normandy, though these tanks were vulnerable to the Panther's 75mm and Tiger's 88mm armour-piercing shells. Trapped in a steep-banked lane, one squadron of Cromwells was totally destroyed by a Tiger; the bigger German tanks later proved slower and less reliable than Allied armour, however – serious handicaps in a war of movement, for defenders held most of the advantages *if they could move reinforcements*. Allied strategies, often enacted far from the contested beach, deprived defenders of fuel, while Allied air power and local resistance fighters contributed further to victories for amphibious forces by denying defenders this mobility.

APPENDICES

APPENDIX 1
SUMMARY OF MAJOR LANDINGS AND KEY EVENTS

1937-8   Japanese land invasion of China with landings at Amoy and Bias Bay (nr Hong Kong) in 1938.

1939-40, EUROPE AND AFRICA: *1 September 1939:* Germans invaded Poland, followed by British and French declarations of war. *April 1940:* German troops secretly shipped to Norwegian ports; British countered through Narvik in last Allied major landing without land-based air support. *May 1940:* British evacuated from Norway and 330,000 Allied troops brought out of France through Dunkirk. *September 1940:* Royal Marines Division and small Free French force move to Dakar (West Africa) but only brief French landing. *October 1940:* Germans deferred invasion of UK.

1941, EUROPE AND AFRICA   *May:* successful British and Free Norwegian raid by 650 troops on Lofoten Is. (northern Norway); Germans took Crete after island saturated with paratroops and despite 4,000 men lost in one assault convoy. *Summer:* British commando raids in Mediterranean, including Litani River (Syria) landings, with heavy losses. *December:* Vaagsö Is. raid by 556 commandos convinced Hitler that future invasion likely through Norway.

1941, FAR EAST AND PACIFIC   *7 December:* Japanese destroy US fleet at Pearl Harbour, Hawaii; Japanese landings in Thailand, Malaya and the Philippines (defended by 102,000 Americans); on 22 December in heavy weather 43,110 men of Japanese Seventy-sixth Army land on 20-mile front in Lingayen Gulf, Luzon Is. (northern Philippines), many craft capsized.

1942, EUROPE AND AFRICA   *March:* Royal Navy destroyer exploded against lock gates of St Nazaire (France). *May:* 2,000 British took

Madagascar to deny Japanese possible base off East Africa. *August:* Canadian raid in force against French Channel port of Dieppe established at heavy cost methods of tackling beach defences. *November:* Allied invasion of Morocco and Algeria showed difficulties in marshalling large numbers of craft even against little or no resistance.

1942, FAR EAST AND PACIFIC *January:* Japanese landed in Celebes and New Britain, taking Rabaul (capital of Australian New Guinea Territories) in four days. Twenty-one Japanese battalions attacked Singapore on 8 February and the garrison surrendered on 15 February; Royal Navy and Dutch ships defeated in Battle of Java Sea on 27 February. *March:* Japanese from Philippines and South Vietnam in ninety-seven ships with escorts made initial Java landings on 1 March; on 8 March several New Guinea landings took place including those at Lae; on 28 March Sumatra conquest completed by Japanese Guards Division from Singapore. *7–9 May:* At Battle of the Coral Sea, 300 miles south of Guadalcanal, US carrier fleet tactically defeated but Japanese convoys for Port Moresby (New Guinea), intended landing withdrawn; various Solomon Is. occupied by Japanese, including Tulgai, the chief town of the Solomons, and locations in the Nggela group north of Guadalcanal; American forts in Manila Bay surrendered on 5 May as last US resistance in the Philippines but Japanese were reaching outer areas of their conquests.

Battle of Midway, 1,000 miles WNW of Hawaii, broke Japanese air supremacy when Americans fired or sank four largest Japanese aircraft carriers between 3–7 June. Japanese continued offensive probes from northern New Guinea, south down the Kokoda Trail, and landed in the far north on the Aleutian islands of Attu and Kiska. Japanese now moved into the defensive phase of their war.

August: first US counterstroke on 7 August in landings at Tulgai and on Guadalcanal's north shore; fighting in heavy jungle severely restricted troop movements, a factor the American commanders grasped more quickly than the Japanese High Command although the Japanese did not finally withdraw until February 1943.

1943, EUROPE AND AFRICA *June:* First British daylight launching of minor craft after heavy sea and air bombardment to capture Greek island of Pantelleria. *July:* Allies invasion of Sicily proved seaborne forces could be brought through rough weather to land on time, though seasickness was a major factor in reducing ability to fight on landing. *September:* Allies crossed Messina Strait to Italy; a number of successful outflanking raids made by commandos in the toe of Italy; Allies landed

APPENDIX I

at Salerno where only their superior air and naval fire support enabled the initial beachhead to be held in the first few days.

1943, FAR EAST AND PACIFIC *Summer:* American landings in New Guinea, to support Australian land forces, faced more natural than defence hazards: all but one craft swamped when landing 800 men at Nassau Bay; 60,000 Japanese in major bases on Shortlands and Bougainville Is. some 100 miles from Munda Point, New Georgia, where major airfield behind coastal swamps and reefs was taken by Americans in an overland attack after a series of landings elsewhere on the island. *September:* Australians landed under air attack at Lae on 4 September, and on 22 September near the Song River on the same New Guinea northern coast to take Finchhafen. *October:* Japanese seaborne counter-attack defeated at Finchhafen on 17 September; New Zealand Brigade seized Treasury Is. (south-west of Bougainville) on 27 September. *November:* American landings in New Britain including those at Arawe and in the jungles of Cape Gloucester, but Rabaul base on north of the island not attacked as 180,000 Japanese bypassed in south Pacific; the US landing at Tarawa was fiercely opposed (20 November).

1944, EUROPE *January:* Allies landed at Anzio in what proved a deceptively easy initial assault which became a battle lasting until the summer. *June:* Allied invasion of Europe launched on 6 June at Normandy for probably the last sustained supply of major armies through the restricted confines of prefabricated ports; Mediterranean landings on Elba fiercely resisted and hampered by poor co-ordination between various elements of Allied landing forces. *August:* Allied landing in south of France, sometimes called the Champagne landings from the welcome given to troops. *November:* landings in Schelde Estuary on Walcheren, a heavily fortified and flooded island over which British commandos fought in the last seaborne major landing of the war in Europe.

1944, FAR EAST AND PACIFIC *February:* Americans recaptured Marshall Is. including Eniwetok on 18 February as launching base for Marianas campaign. *March:* Americans began recovery of Admiralty Is. (north of New Britain); 20 March, 80,000 Americans landed in swamps of Hollandia (northern New Guinea) when a single enemy bomb exploded an ammo dump on one beach destroying equivalent of eleven LST-loads of stores etc. *May:* Americans land on Biak Is., off north-west New Guinea, to take three airfields despite some Japanese holding out here until mid-August. *Summer:* Marianas recaptured by Americans in battles for Saipan, Tinian and Guam; on 30 July in New Guinea landing they took Mar six weeks before originally expected to make landings on the island's north-west coast. *September:* 70,000 US troops landed unopposed on Morotai Is. north-west of New Guinea; 45,000 US troops began recovery of Palau Is. to provide air bases for liberation of the Philippines. *October:* 200,000-strong US Sixth Army landed at Leyte in Philippines where Japanese expected major battle, reinforcing their garrison of 22,000 from the 360,000 men on other islands. *December:* American landings on Mindoro (west central Philippines) opposed only by suicide planes.

1945, EUROPE   Germany surrendered on 8 May.

1945, FAR EAST AND PACIFIC   *January:* British advanced southward along Burma coast; American landings in Philippines on north-west Luzon where 80,000 Japanese concentrated their defences in a southern redoubt. *February:* Americans found Japanese defences in Iwo Jima caves and 400 blockhouses etc more formidable than expected, these being the most heavily fortified beach defences in the Pacific. *March:* First heavy incendiary raids on Japanese cities. *Mid-April:* By this date over forty landings by Americans in the Philippines; Okinawa assault (1 April) was the largest American landing in the Pacific; troops came ashore to token resistance but defence stiffened inland. *May:* Leyte finally cleared of Japanese; British landed unopposed at Rangoon (capital of Burma); last pockets of resistance cleared on Iwo Jima. *June:* 29,000 Australians landed in Brunei Bay (Labuan Is. off north-west Borneo) unopposed in initial landings. *July:* largest Australian landing at Balikpapen (east Borneo) on 1 July with 663 Australian casualties and over 2,000 Japanese killed. *August:* Atomic bombs dropped on Hiroshima on 6 August and Nagasaki on 9 August; Japanese surrendered on 14 August.

APPENDIX 2
TYPICAL LANDING CRAFT POWER UNITS

PETROL ENGINES

FORD V8 SCRIPPS MARINE CONVERSION 65bhp at 3,300rpm with two banks (each of four cylinders) arranged to form a vee. In typical LCA installation: cruising speed at 2,800rpm; slow running 700rpm; astern (reverse) 1,500rpm; consumption on one test: 5·21 Imp galls per hour at 2,800rpm, but varied probably between 4½–5¼ galls per hour depending on sea conditions; oil pressure 30lb/sq in; circulating cooling water temp (typical) 140°F with sea temp 50°F. Manufacturer: Ford Motor Company.

CHRYSLER 6-CYLINDER (IN LINE) Crown engine, 60bhp at 3,200rpm (by 1946, developed 115bhp at 3,200rpm); 250·6 cu in piston displacement. Manufacturer: 1974 Chrysler Marine Products Division, Detroit.

CHRYSLER 8-CYLINDER (IN LINE) Royal engine, 115bhp at 3,200rpm (by 1946, developed 141bhp at 3,200rpm). Manufacturer: 1974 Chrysler Marine Products Division, Detroit.

KERMATH SEA WOLF 8-CYLINDER (IN LINE) 225bhp from total piston displacement of 678cu in; 5in bore, 5¾in stroke. Manufacturer: Kermath Manufacturing Co, Detroit.

Other petrol engines included Hall Scott 250bhp and the supercharged 750bhp; 1974 makers, White Engines Inc, Canton, Ohio; US Palmer, 150bhp; Thornycroft and Parson conversions of Ford V8.

DIESELS

PAXMAN-RICARDO 12-CYLINDER TPM 500bhp at 1,375rpm (later modifications gave between 400 and 1,000bhp); idling speed 700–50rpm; cylinders in two banks of six arranged to form 60° vee with two blocks of three in each bank; compression ratio 17:1; fuel: Admiralty gas oil (diesel) or type closest; consumption: ·42lb per brake-horsepower/hour; weights: bare engine 61cwt, gearbox – an SLM reverse/reduction box – 23½cwt including cooler. Manufacturer: 1974 Ruston Paxman Diesels Ltd, Colchester, UK.

GRAY 2-CYCLE DIESELS   The following range all had common components with a basic 4¼in bore cylinder of 71cu in and 5in stroke. (Over 50,000 Gray engines were supplied to US navy in World War II, many using interchangeable parts.) Fuel injectors were located in same position as petrol engine sparking plugs to allow high-pressure injection of finely atomised fuel, obviating the need for a precombustion chamber; scavenging air was blown under pressure to clear cylinder heads; compression ratio, 16:1. Landing craft engines in this group included the 4-cylinder 100bhp, 6-cylinder 165bhp and 8-cylinder 225bhp. Manufacturers: Gray Marine Motor Company; diesels based on General Motors truck engines.

Other diesel engines included the Kermath 100hp; the Superior 150bhp (manufactured by the National Supply Co, United States); the Buda 6-DHMR of 105hp (Buda Co, Harvey, Illinois); the Model 6051 converted lorry engine typically used in sets for LCS(L) Mk3 (manufacturers General Motors).

APPENDIX 3

PRINCIPAL ALLIED ASSAULT VESSELS AND
AMPHIBIANS: ABBREVIATIONS

Before 1942, British practice was to place the descriptive element of a title before LC for Landing Craft, eg ALC (Assault Landing Craft), MLC (Mechanised Landing Craft), though these early craft were redesignated LCA, LCM, etc. In minor craft titles a subgroup's descriptive suffix was not always shown in brackets as (Large), (Small), etc though these are included in the following list, as are basic designs where these differed essentially from their sub-groups.

AA	Type of Landing Barge, Vehicle
AGC	Amphibious Force Command Ship (originally Auxiliary Ship General Service, Combined Operations Communications HQ)
AKA	Auxiliary Ship Cargo Attack
ALC	*see LCA*
AMc(U)	Auxiliary Coastal Minesweeper (Underwater Locator)
APc	Auxiliary Coastal Transport (Small)
APA	Auxiliary Personnel Attack
APD	High Speed Transport (Destroyer) (originally Auxiliary Personnel Destroyer)
APY	*see LCI(L)*
ARB	Auxiliary Repair, Battle Damage
ARG	Auxiliary Repair, Internal combustion engine
ARL	Auxiliary Repair Landingcraft, Ship
BB	Type of Landing Barge, Vehicle
BPC	Original designation (Bombardment Patrol Craft, possibly) for LCF No 1
CC	Type of Landing Barge, Vehicle
DD-tank	Duplex-drive (amphibian) tank
DUKW	Amphibious truck

FDT	Fighter Direction Tender
HSC	see LCS types
LBE	Landing Barge, Emergency Repair
LBF	Landing Barge, Flak
LBG	see LBF
LBK	Landing Barge, Kitchen
LBO	Landing Barge, Oiler
LBS	see LBF
LBW	Landing Barge, Water
LBV	Landing Barge, Vehicle
LCA	Landing Craft, Assault
LCA(FT)	Landing Craft, Assault(Flame Thrower)
LCA(HR)	Landing Craft, Assault(Hedgerow)
LCA(OC)	Landing Craft, Assault(Obstacle Clearing)
LCC	Landing Craft, Control
LCE	Landing Craft, Emergency Repair
LCF	Landing Craft, Flak
LC(FF)	Landing Craft (Flotilla Flagship)
LCG(L)	Landing Craft, Gun(Large)
LCG(M)	Landing Craft, Gun(Medium)
LCH	Landing Craft, Headquarters (sometimes used for Landing Craft, Hospital)
LCI(D)	Landing Craft, Infantry(Demolition)
LCI(G)	Landing Craft, Infantry(Gun) or (Gunboat)
LCI(M)	Landing Craft, Infantry(Mortar)
LCI(L)	Landing Craft, Infantry(Large)
LCI(R)	Landing Craft, Infantry(Rocket)
LCI(S)	Landing Craft, Infantry(Small)
LCM	Landing Craft, Mechanised
LCM(G)	Landing Craft, Mechanised(Gunboat)
LCM(R)	Landing Craft, Mechanised(Rocket)
LCN	Landing Craft, Navigation
LCP	Landing Craft, Personnel
LCP(L)	Landing Craft, Personnel(Large)
LCP(M)	Landing Craft, Personnel(Medium)
LCP(N)	Landing Craft, Personnel(Nested)
LCP(S)	Landing Craft, Personnel(Small)
LCP(Sy)	Landing Craft, Personnel(Survey)
LCP(R)	Landing Craft, Personnel(Ramped)
LCP(U)	Landing Craft, Personnel(Utility)
LCR(L)	Landing Craft, Rubber(Large)
LCR(S)	Landing Craft, Rubber(Small)

LCS(L)	Landing Craft, Support(Large)
LCS(M)	Landing Craft, Support(Medium)
LCS(R)	Landing Craft, Support(Rocket)
LCS(S)	Landing Craft, Support(Small)
LCT	Landing Craft, Tank
LCT(A)	Landing Craft, Tank(Armoured)
LCT(H)	Landing Craft, Tank(Hospital)
LCT(R)	Landing Craft, Tank(Rocket)
LCV	Landing Craft, Vehicle
LCVP	Landing Craft, Vehicle Personnel
LCW	Landing Craft, Air Propelled
LSB	Landing Ship, Bombardment: later LSM(R)
LSC	Landing Ship, Carrier (Derrick-Hoisting)
LSC	*see LCS(M) and (S)*
LSD	Landing Ship, Dock
LSE	Landing Ship, Emergency Repair
LSF	Landing Ship, Fighter Direction
LSG	Landing Ship, Gantry
LSH	Landing Ship, Headquarters
LSHQ	Landing Ship, Headquarters
LSI(H)	Landing Ship, Infantry(Hand-Hoisting)
LSI(L)	Landing Ship, Infantry(Large)
LSI(M)	Landing Ship, Infantry(Medium)
LSI(S)	Landing Ship, Infantry(Small)
LSM	Landing Ship, Medium
LSM(R)	Landing Ship, Medium(Rocket)
LSP	Landing Ship, Personnel
LSS	Landing Ship, Sternchute
LST	Landing Ship, Tank
LST(H)	Landing Ship, Tank(Hospital) (also known as LST(Evacuation))
LSV	Landing Ship, Vehicle
LVT	Landing Vehicle, Tracked
LVT(A)	Landing Vehicle, Tracked(Armoured)
MLC	*see LCM*
MLC	Motor Landing Craft (forerunner of LCM-type)
SB	Scout Boat (unofficial abbreviation)
TL	*see LCM*
TLC	*see LCT*
TR	*see LCV*
PGM	Motor Gunboat
R-craft	*see LCP*

VLC	*see LCV*
WL	*see LCM*
YR	*see LCV*
Z-craft	Z-lighter

BIBLIOGRAPHY

HISTORIES

C. Bateson, *The War with Japan: a Concise History* (Cresset Press, 1968)
Building the Navy's Bases in World War II (Vols 1 and 2, United States Navy Departments of Yards and Docks, 1947)
History of the Second World War series and allied books (HMSO) including B. Collier, *The Defence of the United Kingdom* (1957), L. F. Ellis, *Victory in the West* (1962), M. M. Postan, *British War Production* (1952), S. W. Roskill, *The War at Sea* (Vol 1 1954, Vol 2 1956, Vol 3 1961)
Historical Review of Landing Operations by Japanese Forces (United States Army Far East Military History Section, 1952)
Samuel E. Morison, *History of United States Naval Operations in World War II* (Vols 1–15, Little Brown & Co, Boston, 1949–51; Oxford University Press, 1954 et seq)
C. P. Stacey, *The Canadian Army 1939–45* (Ministry of Defence, Ottawa, 1948)
Telford Taylor, *The Breaking Wave* (Weidenfeld & Nicolson, 1967)
The 2nd Army History, an official diary in the care of the Imperial War Museum, London
The History of the Marines in World War 2 series (United States Marine Corps Historical Branch) including *Assault on Peleliu* (1950), *Battle for Tarawa* (1947), *Campaign for the Marianas* (1946), *Iwo Jima: Amphibious Epic* (1954), *Marines in the Central Solomons* (1952), *Okinawa: Victory in the Pacific* (1955), *Recapture of Guam* (1954), *The Guadalcanal Campaign* (1949), *The Marshalls: Increasing Tempo* (1954)
The United States Army in World War 2 series (United States Army Office of History), particularly Karl C. Dod, *The Corps of Engineers: the War against Japan* (1966)
A. J. Watts and B. G. Gordon, *The Imperial Japanese Navy* (Macdonald, 1971)

BIBLIOGRAPHY

MEMOIRS AND BIOGRAPHIES

P. Bull, *To Sea in a Sieve* (Peter Davies, 1956)
E. T. Higgins, *Webbed Foot Warrior* (Banner Books, USA)
L. E. H. Maund, *Assault from the Sea* (Methuen, 1949)

PROCEEDINGS AND PAPERS

Proceedings (various) of the United States Naval Institution
The Royal Institution of Naval Architects' transactions: *Ships of the Invasion Fleet* and *Notes on Development of Landing Craft* (papers given by R. Baker, 24 September 1946 and 27 March 1947)

ARTICLES AND REFERENCES

Allied Craft and Ships (United States Division of Naval Intelligence publication ONI 226)
Amphibious Operations August to December 1943 (United States Fleet publication)
Firepower and Amphibious Assault (*United States Marine Corps Gazette* Vol 36)
Headquarters Invasion Ship 'Hampshire' (*The Trident* Vol 8)
Jane's Fighting Ships 1946 (Jane's)
LST: Kingpin of Invasion Fleet, The Mass Produced "Landing Craft Infantry" at Todd Managed Shipyard (articles in *Marine Engr & Shipping Review*, now *Marine Engineering/Log*, February 1945 and June 1944)
LSI HMAS *Westralia* ship's newspaper
Observers' Fighting Vehicle Directory: World War II (Vandervee)
Story of 5th Assault Regiment RE (*Royal Engineers Journal* Vol 40)
United States Navy Bureau of Ordnance in World War 2 (United States Navy Department Bureau of Ordnance)
With the 2nd Army in NW Europe (*RASC Review* Vol 1 No 1)

ACKNOWLEDGEMENTS

The author would like to thank the many friends whose reminiscences over the years prompted the writing of this book, and the individuals and organisations whose help made the undertaking possible: the Dravo Corporation, Pittsburgh; the Historical Branch, United States Marine Corps; the Historical Division, United States Corps of Engineers; the Imperial War Museum, London; *Marine Engineering/Log* magazine, New York; Mr S. L. Morison, late of the United States Naval Historical Centre; the Motor Vehicle Manufacturers' Association of the United States; the National Archives and Records Service, Washington; the National Maritime Museum, London; Mrs Jean R. Nielsen, for typing and secretarial work; Mr A. M. Preston, naval historian; Mr J. E. Rock, for preparing the Figures; the Royal Institution of Naval Architects.

Grateful acknowledgement is made to the following for permission to reproduce photographs: Historical Department, Royal Marines (*plate 8*), the Imperial War Museum (*plates 1, 3, 5, 6, 9, 11, 12, 18, 19, 21–35, 38, 40, 41, 43, 44, 46, 47, 49, 50*), Dr Dieter Jung (*plates 15–17*), Keystone Press Agency (*plate 20*), the Ministry of Defence (*plate 39*), the National Archives and Records Service, Washington (*plates 2, 4, 7, 14, 42, 45, 48*), the Royal Corps of Transport (*plate 13*), the United States Marine Corps (*plates 10, 36, 37*).

Figure 2 is based on documents kindly provided by the Historical Branch, United States Marine Corps.

247

INDEX

Alternative abbreviations are not indexed separately for Allied ships and craft in Appendix 3. Illustration numbers are indexed in italics and outline specification page numbers in bold type.